Language, Literacy, and Inquiry

Anthology of Readings

BEDFORD/ST. MARTIN'S
Boston ◆ New York

Manufactured in the United States of America.

3 4 5   10 09 08

For information, write: Bedford/St. Martin's, 75 Arlington Street, Boston, MA 02116   (617-399-4000)

ISBN-10: 0-312-46369-3
ISBN-13: 978-0-312-46369-4

Acknowledgments
Acknowledgments and copyrights are continued at the back of the book on pages 280-284, which constitutes an extension of the copyright page.

Sherman Alexie, "This Is What It Means to Say Phoenix, Arizona" from *The Lone Ranger and Tonto Fistfight in Heaven.* Copyright © 1993 by Sherman Alexie. Used by permission of Grove/Atlantic Inc.

Lorraine Ali, "Do I Look Like Public Enemy Number One?" Copyright © 1999 Condé Nast Publications. All rights reserved. Originally printed in *Mademoiselle.* Reprinted by permission of Condé Nast. "Same Old Song: Controversy over pop music is as old as Elvis, but now we're in a cultural arms race." From *Newsweek,* October 9, 2000, p. 68. Copyright 2000 Newsweek, Inc. All rights reserved. Reprinted by permission of Newsweek, Inc.

Contents

Fiction ● ○

Poetry ● ○

Nonfiction

●

○

CATHERINE G. LATTERELL
Identity: Examining the Everyday

IDENTITY AND WALLETS

On August 24, 2003, the *Corpus Christi Caller-Times* newspaper reported the following story. Recently, Casimiro Naranjo III opened his mail to discover that someone had sent him the wallet he lost 46 years earlier when he was a 19-year-old Marine stationed in Okinawa, Japan. Construction workers who were renovating a building on the U.S. base discovered his wallet in a ventilation duct and used the identification cards inside to send it back to him. Everything inside the frayed but still intact brown leather wallet holds special meaning to Naranjo. Among other items, the wallet contained black and white photos of his sister (then 12) and brother (then 17), a pawn shop receipt for his high school class ring (never seen again), a ration card, a military ID card, and a small religious medal that his mother had given him before he left for boot camp. This small token was particularly meaningful to him now, Naranjo explained, because his mother had recently passed away. The only item in the wallet that Naranjo did not remember was a small photo of a young woman. He could not recall who she was or why he had her picture. "How convenient for him to have forgotten," joked his wife.

What do the contents of a wallet reveal about a person's identity? Imagine how your life would be thrown into disorder if you lost your wallet. How would such a loss affect your ability to function normally — at least until you could replace the lost items? In many ways, our wallets and purses represent our identity to the world. For instance, like Naranjo, most of us carry several forms of identification in a wallet or purse: pool or gym memberships, driver's licenses, library cards, ATM cards, video store cards, club membership cards, school IDs, coffee club cards, discount cards, and credit cards. Even wallet-sized photos identify our families and friends.

1

This is the nature of identification, yet most people do not connect their identification to their sense of identity. After all, what do all of these pocket-sized pieces of plastic and paper really say about us? They identify us to others like bank tellers, librarians, and sales clerks so that we can make transactions. They help to label us to others. However, for Naranjo, each item in his recovered wallet helps construct a portrait of his 19-year-old self. Each item has a story to tell about his identity at that time.

What stories could someone piece together about you based solely on an examination of your wallet and its contents? For this initial assignment, write a one-page profile about yourself using only your wallet or purse and its contents to represent your life. Your profile should answer the following questions.

- Taken separately or together, how do the contents of your wallet construct an image of your identity?
- What assumptions might someone make about your personality, values, or identity based on what you carry in your wallet?

Add a final paragraph that answers this question:

- If all they had to go on is your wallet, what would people miss or be unable to know about you?

Questions about identity can be deeply philosophical, and the act of answering them can require us to think about our beliefs, values, and life goals. Asking "What makes us who we are?" is partly a question about individual beliefs and actions and partly a question about how the people, places, and things in our lives help make us who we are.

If identity provides us with the means of answering the question "Who am I?" it might appear to be a question about personality, but this is only part of the story. Identity is different from personality. Personality describes specific qualities individuals have, such as inherent shyness or sociability, but identity requires some active engagement and choice. For example, we choose to *identify with* a particular identity or group; we choose our friends and we choose how to dress every morning. These kinds of choices lead others to make conclusions about who we are. However, there are some things about ourselves that we cannot choose. For instance, we do not choose our ethnicity or where we were born.

Assumption 1: Identity Is What We're Born With

For many people, answering questions about identity begins by listing details that can be found on our birth certificates—name, sex, ethnicity, and family origins. People wishing to research their family histories locate the birth certificates of known family members because these documents provide essential information about the identities of ancestors. As the experts from the PBS television series *Ancestors* explain, birth certificates record a range of vital facts about identity.

They almost always include:	*They may also include:*
name of child	maiden name of mother
sex of child	ages of parents at time of birth
race of child	birthplaces of parents
date of birth	occupations of parents
place of birth	family address
names of parents	child's order in family
	name of attending physician or midwife
	exact time of birth
	physical description of child

The importance of birth certificates might suggest that identity is basically fixed and stable from the time of birth. Consider sex and ethnicity, two labels applied at birth that are at the heart of how many people think about identity. Both are generally understood as clear-cut categories from which identity is established. They can act as compass points that ground us as we go through life, giving us a sense of stability, of knowing who we are. But are they so clear cut? Firoozeh Dumas, in her essay "The 'F Word' " (p. 75), explores the connections between language, ethnic and national identities, and the fluidity of personal identity. Perhaps what birth certificates provide, along with family histories, are markers of identity.

However, the assumption that identity consists merely of what we are "born with" can underemphasize the influences or impact of larger social forces that also affect identity. Consider gender identity, for example. Although it is true in one sense that sex is established at birth, it is important to note that developmental psychologists have concluded that a person's understanding of what it means to be male or female develops through social interaction over time. During preschool years, children begin to discover what gender identity means. They carefully observe who's a boy, who's a girl, how they dress, what they do, and how they are treated. In fact, children's understanding and expectations about gender are largely influenced by what they see and experience. Gender identity is not fixed at birth; rather it is a process that evolves over time.

Similarly, the meaning of ethnic identity and nationality is something worked out within larger social and cultural settings. One illustration is the story of Barack Obama, U.S. senator for Illinois, as told in his memoir, *Dreams from My Father: A Story of Race and Inheritance* (1997). Born in 1961 to a white American mother and a black Kenyan father, Obama was raised in Hawaii by his mother and her parents. His father left the family to attend Harvard University and eventually returned to Kenya, where he worked as a government economist. His mother's second husband was Indonesian, and Obama spent several years of his childhood in Jakarta before returning to the United States to live with his grandparents and follow in his father's footsteps to Harvard,

<table>
<tr><td colspan="9" align="center">**CERTIFIED COPY OF BIRTH REGISTER**</td><td>BRC</td></tr>
</table>

CERTIFIED COPY OF BIRTH REGISTER									BRC

State of Minnesota, County of ___Benton___

Recorded in Book ___F___ Page ___289___ Line ___239___ Birth No. _____ Place of Birth (City or Township) _St. George Twp._

FULL NAME OF CHILD	Sex	Single Twins Triplets	No. in Order of Birth	No. of Child of this Mother	Legiti-mate	DATE OF BIRTH			
						Month	Day	Year	Hour
Joseph James Latteral	M	D	--	7	yes	Nov.	2	1932	10:45PM

FATHER

NAME		Fathers Date of Birth	Birthplace	OCCUPATION
James Latteral		34 yrs of age	Minn.	Farmer

MOTHER

FULL MAIDEN NAME		Mothers Date of Birth	Birthplace	OCCUPATION
Grace Barthelemy		33 yrs of age	Minn.	Housewife

ATTENDING PHYSICIAN, MIDWIFE, PARENT OR OTHER INFORMANT

NAME		ADDRESS	Date of Report
J.F. Schatz		---------------	11-4-32

REGISTRAR

NAME		ADDRESS	Date of Filing
Lester B. Lewis		Foley, MN	11-25-32

STATE OF MINNESOTA)
)ss.
County of ___Benton___)

I, _____ Alice C. Engelmeyer _____ County Recorder in and for said County and State, do hereby certify that the forgoing is a full and complete transcript of the entries appearing on record in the Register of Births now remaining in my said office relating to the Birth of said ___Joseph James Latteral___ ___ and the whole thereof.

WITNESS my hand and the seal of said office hereto affixed at Foley , Minnesota, this

___13th___ day of ___May___ A.D. 19 __98__.

By _____ *Alice C. Engelmeyer* _____ County Recorder

_____ Deputy

This birth certificate identifies Joseph James Latterell, whose last name is misspelled, as the "legitimate" seventh child of James Latterell ("Farmer") and Grace Barthelemy ("Housewife"). What assumptions are built into this document?

where he earned a law degree. Obama's story suggests that a person's sense of identity is not just the sum of the facts of his or her birth. In his opening remarks at the 2004 Democratic National Convention, Obama said that his parents gave him "an African name, Barack, or 'blessed,' believing that in a tolerant America your name is no barrier to success." He continued, "I stand here today, grateful for the diversity of my heritage, aware that my parents' dreams live on in my two precious daughters. I stand here knowing my story is part of the larger American story." Obama identifies himself in terms of his African heritage and his family, and then goes beyond the facts of his birth by identifying himself within the larger context of American culture.

In reality, the facts of our birth are merely starting points for understanding identity. Larger social and cultural forces also play important roles in shaping our sense of identity—including our ideas about gender and race. As America becomes increasingly multiethnic, Thornton asks, "Is race really something we can choose, or is it chosen for us?" His essay opens space for examining the dynamic tension between how we see ourselves and how others see us.

As the readings in this chapter illustrate, personal identity cannot be separated from the social contexts we live in. This chapter encourages you to examine how some taken-for-granted aspects of identity, such as gender, ethnicity, and even able-bodiedness, are shaped or influenced by larger cultural forces.

What questions can you ask to uncover the benefits and limitations of the assumption that identity is what we're born with?

- To what extent is our sense of identity predetermined by the facts of our birth?
- To what extent is our sense of identity a negotiation of social and cultural forces?
- In what ways does the concept that identity is what we're born with help us investigate identity? How does this concept of identity hinder or constrain us?

Assumption 2: Identity Is Shaped by Culture

From this perspective, cultural attitudes and assumptions largely define identity and allow us to label or identify others. People do not live in a vacuum, after all. Instead, we pick up the influences of our surroundings. The student identi-kit picture, shown on page 6, helps illustrate this perspective. To create a self-portrait, this student combined cultural objects that are meaningful to his sense of identity. What this identi-kit picture demonstrates is the extent to which personal identity is connected to our social relationships (our friends, family, and community), to the material objects we choose, and to the various cultural contexts of our lives.

According to this viewpoint, identity is shaped through *acculturation*. Acculturation is the process by which we absorb the practices, attitudes, and beliefs of particular social groups. Culture connects us by providing a shared set of customs, values, ideas, and beliefs. In this chapter, you will examine how the *cultural markers of identity* that we choose—such as the types of cars we drive, the clothes we wear, and the music we listen to—can affect our sense of identity. These markers allow us to label ourselves and others as belonging to a particular social group or as having certain shared interests or values.

Consider, for example, what it means to label someone as "normal." What, after all, is normal? Is normal defined by how you look? How easy your name is to pronounce? Where you shop for clothes? Is it normal to have a pierced tongue and a couple of tattoos? Is normal desirable? Clearly, the label "normal" is loaded with a range of cultural assumptions. Attempting to define "normal" reveals that identity shifts with us as we move in different social settings or contexts. What is viewed as normal on a college campus may not be seen the same way in the workplace or in a social setting. By naming and describing some characteristics that we associate with the term "normal," we can uncover the common assumptions behind the ways that we group ourselves and others.

The concept of "normal" also helps illustrate that our daily lives are saturated with cultural messages about what is valued over what is not. In her essay "Masks," Lucy Grealy addresses the question, "What does it mean to live

This identi-kit was created in response to an assignment that asked students to construct a hyperconscious image of one aspect of their identity. For this student, sports and fitness are important factors in how he sees himself. The baseball, glove, and football also illustrate his connection to communities of teammates. The barbells, weight bench, and superhero costume — a humorous touch — show that this student connects his identity to popular notions of masculinity and strength. Courtesy of Tom Matisak

outside of the social norm?" Grealy, whose face was disfigured by cancer when she was a child, writes of her experience as an adolescent: "I wanted nothing to do with the world of love; I thought wanting love was a weakness to overcome. And besides, I thought to myself, the world of love wanted nothing to do with me." It may be nice to think that our culture accepts everybody for who they are, but, as Grealy's story reminds us, the social and cultural forces that help shape our sense of identity are not neutral. Instead, they operate like a powerful lens through which we make judgments about ourselves and others.

What questions can you ask to uncover the benefits and limitations of the assumption that identity is shaped by culture?

- What count as cultural markers of identity? How do they help others to identify who you are? How accurately do they convey who you are? How do you identify yourself through them?
- How do shared sets of customs, values, attitudes, and beliefs work together to form the cultural contexts of your life? How do they affect your everyday life?
- What are the consequences—both positive and negative—of recognizing that identity is a process of acculturation? In other words, how does your absorption of the culture around you shape who you are and how you live?

Assumption 3: Identity Is Shaped by Personal Choices

Another common assumption about identity is that it is shaped by our personal choices or decisions. According to this viewpoint, to understand identity we must examine the choices we make in our daily lives—choices about our social relationships and anything else we care about. Rather than seeing all matters of identity as determined by larger cultural forces that are beyond our control, this viewpoint recognizes that individuals participate in and make decisions about their identities.

Certainly this assumption is based in truth. After all, we are not simply dupes of Madison Avenue's marketing machines, blindly accepting the trends, fashions, and cultural attitudes that they sell. Rather, we make choices. Consider, for example, the personal choice described by Kathy Wilson in "Dude Looks Like a Lady" (p. 72). For Wilson, her "barely there" hair is inextricably connected to her identity: "I am a black woman whose bald head makes me invisible to some, boyish to others, and beautiful to me." Her short hair boldly signifies to others not only her sense of self, but also her sense of what is beautiful, both of which seem to be at odds with the mostly white, mainstream cultural attitudes she finds herself up against. Wilson's essay supports the idea that personal decisions can be crucial to one's sense of identity, and that personal choices can outweigh the importance of cultural influences and the expectations of others.

What's more, the identity that we convey to others changes according to different social contexts. That is, our individual identities are in constant flux. Recall this chapter's initial assignment, "Identity and Wallets," which includes a list of identification cards. The cards illustrate the idea that identity, unlike identification cards, is not fixed or permanent. While ID cards include a photo and a series of facts (where we live, height, weight, an identification number), the "facts" of our identities are not so fixed. They change and evolve. This is what it means to call identity an open text. ID cards show proof of the ever-evolving nature of identity. The photos in these cards never seem up-to-date, and many

"When I grow up, I want to . . ."

| be a lawyer. | be a counselor. | be a United States Marine. |
| Alexander Ugori, 10 | Serina K. Grousby, 10 | Shjawn Quinn, 11 |

When you were 10, what did you want to be when you grew up, and why? Fifth graders at the Peabody School in Cambridge, Massachusetts, were asked this question. When asked why he wants to be a lawyer, Alexander Ugori, 10, responded, "Because I like arguing. And my mom says I'm good at arguing." Shjawn Quinn, 11, said he is inspired by his dad, a former marine, and by what Shjawn believes the military has to offer: "I like that you can serve your country and you can get free houses . . . and I'd like to get to shoot a rifle and a two-barrel shotgun." Photos courtesy of Jim Walker

of us carry pictures of family and friends that are also out-of-date. Pull out one of these old pictures or IDs and look for details that reveal a now-discarded or changed aspect of your identity.

Another example that illustrates the idea that identity is an open text are the photos and responses of a group of fifth graders who were asked, "What do you want to be when you grow up?" (see the photos above). How would you have responded to this question when you were 10 years old? Do you still have the same life and career goals, or have they changed? After all, you are not exactly the same person you were when you were ten.

This third assumption suggests that despite the larger cultural contexts in which we live, we shape our identities through the choices we make. According to this view, identity is not fixed, but shifts over time and in different situations.

What questions can you ask to uncover the benefits and limitations of the assumption that identity is a personal choice?

- How does your sense of personal choice help you define your sense of identity?
- How does believing that everything is a matter of personal choice constrain or limit your ability to investigate identity? That is, what does it leave out?

JOAN T. MIMS AND ELIZABETH M. NOLLEN
The Message of the Media

We are a visual culture. We see thousands of visual images every day, yet we pay attention to only a few of them. Vision is our primary way of receiving information from the world around us. There is so much to see that we filter out what we don't need or what doesn't grab our immediate attention. Movie posters try to convince us to see a summertime blockbuster, magazine ads try to lure us into buying a particular product, artists and photographers try to get us to feel a certain emotion, while billboards demand our attention no matter where we turn. All visual media compete to send us their messages. The choices we make and the things we buy, even how we perceive and value ourselves, are all affected by the images that are presented to us. American popular culture relies heavily on visual representation; even music is represented visually through the use of music videos. Learning to "read" these images and discovering what responses they are intended to provoke in us is an important part of understanding our culture.

Let's picture an imaginary advertisement. The woman is beautiful and graceful. The man appears wealthy and sophisticated. The white sand beach is wide and private; the sparkling blue water is cool and clear; tropical sunshine bathes the scene. The car in the foreground is a gold-colored luxury convertible. But why aren't the car's tires getting mired in the sand? Why aren't the woman's white shoulders sunburning? In reality, these might be issues you or I would have to think about, but this ad has nothing to do with reality. This is advertising—that shadow world that separates us from our money by luring us into popular mythology.

What mythology? Here's how it goes: Unpopular? Popularity is as easy as changing the brand of jeans you wear. Unsuccessful? You must drive the wrong kind of car. Unattractive? Just wear a new shade of lipstick. Misunderstood? It's not your personality; it's your poor cellular service.

We are in general a well-educated society. Why, then, are we so easily misled? Why do we buy the myths that advertising sells? We buy—and buy and buy and buy—because we desperately want the myths of advertising to be true.

For some time now, our culture has been as visual as we are verbal. We absorb images faster than our brains can process data, but the images remain imprinted in our minds. All those images influence our thoughts and the decisions we make in ways we may never have considered. From the time that we begin to learn to read, we are encouraged to recognize the power of words—to interact with a text, to weigh it for prejudice, to appreciate it with discernment. But images are as powerful as words, and they communicate ideas and impressions that we, as thinking individuals, should *question,* just as we question what we are told or what we read. How can the same skills we use to read be applied to "reading" visual images like billboards, photographs, political cartoons, drawings, paintings, and images on television, movie, and computer screens?

ASKING THE RIGHT QUESTIONS

Effectively deconstructing media images depends on taking those images apart and asking the right questions.

1. What do I see when I look at the image?

    How is color used?
    What is the significance of the layout?
    What are the relative sizes of the objects that compose the image?
2. What is the role of text (any language that accompanies the image)?
3. Where did I first see this image?
4. Who is the target audience?
5. What is the purpose of this image?
6. What is its message?

The easiest questions help solve the mystery of the more difficult ones, so let's think about the obvious. What is really there to be seen when you look at the photo, the ad, or the cartoon strip?

TAKING THE IMAGE APART

Color

Although the images you see in this textbook are reproduced in black and white, most of the media representations around you make careful use of color. When you encounter an image, is your eye drawn to a certain spot on a page by the strength of a color, by the contrast of colors, or by the absence of color? How is color being used to catch your eye and hold your focus on a certain part of the visual?

Layout

Closely related to the use of color is the layout of objects on a page. What relationships are established by how close or how far apart objects or people are placed? What is your eye drawn to first because of its position? Sometimes the focal point will be right in the center of the ad or photo and therefore obvious to the viewer. At other times, the object the composer of the image most wants you to appreciate, the one that is central to the image's message, may be easily overlooked. Because English is read from top to bottom and left to right, we tend to look first to the upper left-hand corner of a page. That spot is often used to locate the composer's focal point. At other times the eye may come to rest at the bottom right-hand corner of a page.

Size

The relative size of the people and objects in an image may also help the designer communicate his or her message. A viewer's eye may be drawn to the largest object first, but that may not be where the message lies. To help you see how relative size of objects can communicate a strong message, look at the photograph titled "To Have and To Hold" (p. 14).

Text

Deciding whether a visual image should be accompanied by text or written language is another significant consideration for the photographer, artist, or ad designer. Sometimes the image may be so powerful on its own that text would be an irritating distraction. Think about the photograph of the Marines raising the flag on Iwo Jima during World War II or the shot of the three firefighters raising the flag at Ground Zero in New York City after 9/11. These images speak for themselves. When text is included, other factors have to be examined. How much text is there? Where is it located? How big is the type size? Is more than one font used? Does the text actually deliver the message? Does it enhance the message? Is part of the text a familiar slogan associated with the product like Burger King's "Have it your way"? Is a well-known and easily recognized logo or symbol like the Nike Swoosh part of the text? All of these considerations hinge on the importance of the text to the overall message of the visual image.

Location

To properly evaluate a visual image, the discerning viewer must know where the image appeared. Did you see this image on a billboard? On the side of a bus? In the pages of a magazine? Images in *Smithsonian* magazine will have a different purpose than those in *Maxim*. The location of a visual will help you determine the intended target audience.

Target Audience

For whom is this image intended? What are the characteristics of this target audience of viewers? What is the age range? What is their socioeconomic status? What work do they do? Where and how do they live? All this information must be taken into account by the photographer, artist, or designer if the image is to convey its intended message. For example, an ad for baby formula would most likely not hit its target audience if it were placed in *Rolling Stone,* and an ad for a jeweled navel ring in *House Beautiful* probably would not find a receptive audience.

Purpose

Every image has a purpose. If the image is an advertisement on a billboard, on a Web site, or in a magazine, the most obvious question to ask is "What is this ad for?" In today's ads, the answer isn't always readily apparent. The actual object being sold may be a tiny speck on the page or even completely absent. In the imaginary ad described earlier, the product might be the woman's alluring sundress, the man's starched khakis and sports shirt, or the convertible. Or maybe it's an ad for an exotic vacation spot. If the image is a photograph, its purpose may be to commemorate a special moment, object, or person or to illustrate an event or feeling. If the image is a cartoon, its purpose may be to entertain or to make a political or social statement through humor.

Message

"What is the purpose of this image?" may be the most obvious question to ask, but it isn't the most important one. The most important question is "What is the message of this image?" That's a very different question. This question challenges the viewer to probe beyond the obvious visual effects — color, shading, size of objects, text or lack thereof, relative placement of objects — to ferret out the message. This message always seeks to evoke a response from the viewer: Wear this, drink this, click here, think this way, feel this emotion, affirm this value. Using all the information you have assembled by answering the earlier questions, answer this one.

Now you are prepared to deconstruct or "read" the visual images that form such a large part of our popular culture.

READING VISUAL IMAGES

Let's practice with two different types of images: a photograph and a cartoon strip.

Look at the image on the next page and consider some questions. What do you see in this photograph by Jean-Christian Bourcart? What event is being captured? What do the sizes and positions of the two figures indicate about their relationship? How many modern couples would find this pose an appealing one to place in their wedding albums?

To Have and To Hold

How is color used?   You are seeing this photograph in black and white, but it's easy for your mind to fill in the color here—green grass and greener trees. Even in color, however, the two principal figures would be largely black and white. The white dress of the bride and the black formal wear on the groom let us know right away what event we are viewing. Here the lack of bright color works to emphasize the serious moment being captured on film.

What is the significance of the layout?   Think about the layout and composition of this photograph. Why did Bourcart place the couple outdoors? Perhaps he used a natural setting to reinforce the notion that a wedding is a "natural" cultural ritual. Practically speaking, this shot would have been difficult to frame indoors; the relative depth perception of the two figures is what makes the composition unique.

What is the relative size of the objects that compose the image?   In this particular photo, relative size is the most important feature. Things are not equal. The groom is front and center, dominant, in control. The tiny, fragile doll bride held in his hand resembles the decorative figurine often found atop a wedding cake.

What is the role of text?   No text accompanied the original photograph. The original title in French was "Le Plus Beau Jour De La Vie," which means "the most beautiful day of one's life."

What was the original location of the image?   This photograph appeared in *Doubletake* magazine. Certainly the source is appropriate, since, after the first casual glance, the viewer's eye locks onto the two figures in their unusual pose.

Who is the target audience?   The target audience might include future brides and bridegrooms, anyone interested in photography, or an even wider group of people who are intrigued by the unusual ways that the eye conveys messages about the world and the culture around us.

What is the purpose of this image?   At first glance, this photograph may have been taken to capture an unusual image. Perhaps its intent is to preserve, in a whimsical way, one significant day in the life of a couple. Many families have albums full of wedding photos. But perhaps this photographer had something more serious in mind.

What is the message?   What is the photographer really trying to accomplish? Certainly he has chosen an off-balance approach to arrest our attention. But more is being said. Perhaps Bourcart wishes to tell us what he believes marriage offers young couples. Does he wish to make a statement about male-female relationships? On a day that seems perfect, is there an indication that life won't be "happily ever after" for this bride and groom?

Next let's work on deconstructing a very different type of visual representation, a comic strip (p. 16).

What do you see when you look at this image?   With a comic strip, the viewer's eyes must travel left to right across the panels, focusing on a number of frames, each of which may offer a visual, text, or both. Often the strip's creator relies on a steady group of repeat readers who over time have learned to appreciate the personalities of the strip's characters and the subtle messages they deliver from the writer.

How is color used? Although most strips appear in black and white in daily newspapers, many appear in color on Sundays, giving readers a chance to learn more about the characters and the strip's designer. This *Mallard Fillmore* strip appeared in a Sunday newspaper with minimal but effective colorization. Against a light blue background, the duck is green with a yellow bill, and the soda can is a lighter shade of green. We know it's a Sprite can because Mallard says so. The human finger is peach-colored.

What is the significance of the layout? To some extent, the layout of a cartoon strip is prescribed: It is a series of panels. But the artist still has a great deal of flexibility with layout within the various panels. The most interesting feature in this layout is the shifting view we have of Mallard the duck. At first we see his face, but he turns to the side when addressed by the finger, and by the middle of the strip he has his back to us. We viewers are made to feel outside the conversation, as though we are merely eavesdropping. By the last two panels, Mallard has turned his face to the readers, making us a part of the scam he's pulling.

What is the relative size of objects that compose the image? It's certainly no accident that the clearly recognizable "invisible finger of marketing" is as large as Mallard's head in every panel except the final one, when Mallard takes control of the situation. From time to time, as consumers we may feel "under the thumb" of advertising; this comic strip offers a graphic rendering of that concept.

What is the role of text? As in many comic strips, the text here is crucial to the message. Generally, comic strips rely much more on text than ads or photographs do. The first significant language issue arises in the title of this strip. Mallard Fillmore's name is a play on the name of an American president, Millard Fillmore, whose term of office reflected his own rather lackluster personality. A mallard is actually one type of duck. We'll pursue the rest of the text when we examine the message of the strip.

What was the original location of this image? This comic strip is syndicated and appears regularly in many newspapers across the country.

Who is the target audience? The target audience of this comic strip is not children. Although the duck might catch their eye, the level of sophistication of the humor clearly places this strip beyond their understanding. And certainly a degree of sophistication is required to grasp the irony here. The reader needs to know something about popular culture: What's a Sprite? Nikes? Lugz? What's hip-hop? What's an icon? Knowing that the U.S. government at times pays farmers not to grow certain crops such as soybeans in order not to flood the market and drive prices down explains the fifth panel. Bruce Tinsley, the strip's writer, is not expecting everyone to agree with his opinion, but his target audience is every consumer who is subject to advertising's wiles.

What is the purpose of this image? Because this is a cartoon strip, we expect it to be entertaining or humorous. To determine if that is its only purpose, let's think about the message.

What is the message? So what is Tinsley trying to say? Here is an ordinary duck, who might as well be you the reader, attempting to drink a popular beverage with a powerful marketing firm behind it. According to the finger of advertising, the entire ad campaign designed to elevate Sprite to a new level of "cool" or popularity could be devastated if Sprite were to be associated with this quite ordinary duck. The duck, however, represents the consumer, and he's not as dumb as he looks. He asks to be paid not to harm Sprite's fledgling coolness: He wants to be paid not to drink it. But he plans to take the cash, succumb to the lure of advertising—and buy Nikes or Lugz. What a cycle! What a message! Manufacturers pay advertisers to manufacture an image for a product, and that image alone—not the product—often fuels our wants and loosens our wallets.

WRITING ABOUT AN IMAGE

Using these same questions we have been asking, let's see what one student has to say about decoding a third kind of media, an advertisement.

MONUMENTAL TASTE: USING PATRIOTISM TO
MARKET DIET COKE

Robert E. Arthur

What do I see as I flip through a magazine and come across this advertisement? Mount Tastemore, South Dacola, a revamped version of Mount Rushmore, where the fathers of our nation's history—Washington, Jefferson, Roosevelt, and Lincoln—are all smiling back at me, seeming to be very pleased with the beverage they are holding. There are people lined up at the bottom, many dressed in our nation's colors of red, white, and blue, staring up and pointing excitedly at the iconic landmark. One man, dressed in a blue sweatshirt, is holding a can of the ever-wonderful diet Coke in one hand and pointing eagerly skyward with the other. I focus on the four presidents smiling out at me, all of whom seem to be offering me their diet Cokes. I see the advertisers' way of promoting the cola by revising one of our nation's most recognizable and sacred landmarks. My eyes then drift upward towards the title, "Monumental Taste," which provides a further explanation of the advertisement by its play on words. After being subconsciously persuaded by the ad's graphics, my attention shifts to the text underneath the visual, which reinforces the ad's message, "Mt. Tastemore, South Dacola—the most refreshing tourist attraction in America," and the play on words of the diet Coke logo, "Just for the monumental taste of it!" Finally, my eyes move to the order form for the Special Offer mentioned at the bottom of the page and the legalese that accompanies it. I've been hooked, and this is exactly what the advertisers want.

The advertisement's color scheme not only attracts the eye of the consumer, but also furthers the patriotic theme in the ad. The red in the soda cans, the clear blue sky above the presidents' heads, and the large white letters spelling out "Monumental Taste" above the landmark add to this red, white, and blue theme. Also, the adoring spectators lined up at the bottom, many sporting our nation's colors, seem entranced by the remarkable landmark. These colors were wisely chosen by the advertisement's designers. In the U.S. flag, white stands for purity while red signifies valor and hardiness (and coincidentally is used in many restaurants because it is an appetite stimulant). Finally, blue represents justice, perseverance, and vigilance. Why not showcase these meaningful patriotic colors when trying to sell "all-American" products like diet Coke? After all, few consumers who see this ad will remember that the U.S. government took possession of Mount Rushmore and the surrounding Black Hills region from the Sioux Indians in 1877, only three years after gold was discovered there. However, that isn't what the advertisers want the potential buyer to reflect on here.

While the colors of an advertisement are often responsible for its initial impact on the reader, the text provided with the visual plays a key role in the message to the consumer. The text, especially the title, "Monumental Taste," provides a better explanation of the ad, using an adjective with both literal and figurative meanings to get the point across in a humorous way. Viewers of all ages can easily recognize the double meaning of the phrase and also pick up on the opinion that not only is this soda's taste remarkable, it's good enough for Honest Abe and his peers, too. Of all of the inhabitants of Mount Taste-more, Lincoln is the only one holding a caffeine-<u>free</u> diet Coke, which is most likely a play on his monumental role in the freeing of thousands of African slaves. The can he is holding is also the only one boasting red, white, and blue lettering, thus furthering the patriotic theme throughout the advertisement. The ad's slogan, "Mt. Tastemore, South Dacola — the most refreshing tourist attraction in America," is another way humor is injected into the text of the advertisement, making it more appealing to those of us who enjoy tastefully humorous things.

In reality, the head of Washington stands as high as a five-story building (about 60 feet). This head would thus be fitting for a person about 465 feet tall. In the advertisement, both the title and the soda cans are much larger in scale than Mt. Tastemore itself. This sizing persuades the reader to focus her attention on these areas first. The twelve people staring up at the presidents are dwarfed by them but are still clearly visible. The text at the bottom of the visual is smaller than that in the title or on the diet Coke cans, but important parts of it are much bigger than that and thus more significant. For example, "Mt. Taste-more, South Dacola — the most refreshing tourist attraction in America," "diet Coke duffel," and "Just for the <u>monumental</u> taste of it!" are significantly larger than the surrounding text.

The purpose of creating such an advertisement is obvious — to persuade people to drink diet Coke. But by offering the duffel bag as an added incentive, the people who see the ad will not only buy diet Coke but will become living billboards for the product as they carry their diet Coke duffels around with them on their "tasteful" travels. These duffel bags, emblazoned with the huge red letters spelling out the product's name, are an excellent example of effective co-branding.

Advertisements don't need to say, "Buy this product, or you won't be cool." We do that for them. What if the paparazzi catch a celebrity strolling down Rodeo Drive with one of these "haute couture" duffel bags casually thrown over her shoulder? Presto! Fans will rush to order their own duffels, thus becoming walking billboards for the product just as the advertisers in-tended. For good measure, these consumers will be further influenced by the subliminal message delivered by the small "d" in the brand's name. They will believe that whoever drinks diet Coke will not only be cool, but thin-ner, too. So these proud duffel bag-toting Americans are not only patriotic but cool and thin as well. Soon, as more and more people proudly sport their diet Coke duffels while sipping their diet Cokes, advertisers will enlarge the promotional campaign to extol the soda's fabulous taste to consumers around the globe. Isn't it cool to look and buy "American" even if you don't live here? After all, if this "refreshing" and "monumental" drink is good enough for America's most beloved leaders, it should be good enough for those millions of global consumers who wish to "get a taste of" our popular culture.

JOAN T. MIMS AND ELIZABETH M. NOLLEN
Advertising Yesterday and Today

The Hathaway Man, pictured here in a print advertisement from the 1960s, was a debonair icon of men's fashion, reminiscent of a leading man from the Golden Age of Hollywood. Sporting an eye patch, holding fencing equipment, and wearing the "Rolls Royce" of shirts, this gentleman is as self-assured as James Bond.

Five ways to identify a Hathaway shirt—at a glance

IT'S AS EASY to recognize a Hathaway shirt as a Rolls Royce—if you know these subtle signs:

1. Notice how generously the shirt is cut. More cloth than you get in a mass-produced shirt. Ergo, more comfortable.

2. Look at the *buttons*. They are unusually large. And the *stitches*—unusually small.

More than 30,000 stitches in one shirt.

3. Now look at our *cuffs*. They have *square corners*. This applies to our French cuffs *and* to the kind you button.

4. Where the front tail joins the back tail, you always find our hallmark—the letter **H** discreetly embroidered in scarlet.

5. The men who wear HATHAWAY shirts are individualists, so they seldom wear *white* shirts.

The shirt illustrated above is a fine Karnac cotton from Egypt, woven for Hathaway in Waterville. The rectangular checks are copied from a rare French original. Retails at $8.95. Write C. F. Hathaway, Waterville, Maine. In New York, call MUrray Hill 9-4157.

The Hathaway Man

In this ad for Skechers sneakers, we move from the Hathaway Man's eye patch and fencing equipment to music icon Christina Aguilera's fishnet stockings and boy toys. Displacing Britney Spears as the "Skechers girl," Aguilera, raised in New York and Philadelphia by parents of Irish and Ecuadorian descent, gives a new edge and a new global appeal to the advertising campaign for this popular brand of shoes.

What changes in our culture explain the differences between the Hathaway ad and the Skechers ad? Consider changes in gender roles, the boom in young consumers, and the effect of the music industry on advertising. What selling strategies do these advertisements use? Consider the use of text, celebrity endorsement, cobranding, sex appeal, and target audience. Do these two ads represent a way of fitting in or a way of standing out?

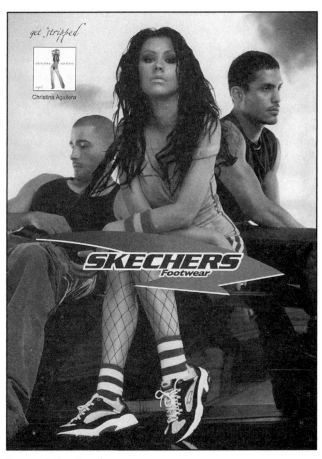

Sex and the Sneaker

JOHN FOLLIS
Mad Ave.

I remember a day, early in my career, when I was young and naive and on staff at a large agency. On this particular day management had gathered the troops to screen the agency reel for one of those "Aren't-We-Great" morale-boosting meetings. As the lights dimmed, the hushed crowd gazed at beautifully shot images of puppies and children and Kraft marshmallows seductively blended with seamless editing and incredibly composed music. The lights came back up and, after a rousing hand, the erudite CEO,[1] pipe in hand, took the stage and opened the floor for questions.

After listening to him answer inquiries like, "Gee, how'd you get that puppy to lick the little girl's face," I decided to take advantage of this unexpected opportunity to "Ask the Cheese." Eventually, The Cheese nods in my direction and I spit it out:

"Do you have any reservations about advertising a product like marshmallows—which is almost 100 percent sugar with zero nutritional value—and targeting mothers and young children?"

As if a party guest had just knocked over the host's best crystal vase, a sudden uncomfortable silence filled the room. A few heads turned to see which of their coworkers was so bold, or stupid, to put the agency CEO on the spot in front of his entire staff. The CEO calmly paused, took a few slow puffs on his pipe, and with carefully measured words, responded:

"It is my belief that it's the government's role to decide which products should or shouldn't be advertised. And as long as the product is legal, it's the agency's responsibility to do the best job possible to advertise its clients' products." I suddenly had visions of the corporate Gestapo[2] quickly escorting me out of the room and beating me senseless.

As the days passed, I never second-guessed the legitimacy of my question. I just began to second-guess the timing of it. I also began to wonder how much it affected my termination several months later.

I can't imagine how anyone could be part of a campaign like Joe Camel, even if they smoke. It utterly amazes me that anyone can say with a straight face that a campaign featuring a cartoon camel is not directed at kids.

Obviously, some people just see it as a job they're paid (very well, no doubt) to do. Maybe it's no different than being a criminal lawyer:

---

[1] **CEO:** Chief executive officer, the highest officer in a business or corporation.
[2] **ESL Gestapo:** Nazi Germany's secret police.

Judge: We have 14 witnesses that claim they saw your client shoot the woman. His fingerprints are on the gun and we have it on videotape. How does your client plead?
Defense attorney: Not guilty.

A copywriter buddy of mine is one of the most talented writers in the business. The guy's amazing. After moving around a bit he settled into a high-level, well-paying job at a huge agency. He's got a couple of young kids and a nice home in a fancy neighborhood. I called him the other day just to catch up. When I asked about his job, I sensed a slight tone of resignation. He told me he's working on a battery account which features a fictitious family called "The Puttermans."

The Puttermans can only be described as a plastic-coated, alien-looking, TV family-from-hell, with giant batteries fused to their spines. The spots consist of bad sitcom-like shenanigans.[3] By the time you read this The Puttermans will probably have been put to rest with the other ill-fated ad characters.

It doesn't seem so long ago that my writer buddy and I sat around talking about the advertising hacks who sell out for the money to do the dreck we both hated. Now, with a family and mortgage, my friend has new priorities. Before our chat concluded, he shared what seemed like an attempt at vindication. The five-year-olds at his daughter's birthday party wanted his autograph when they heard he was the guy who did the Putterman commercials.

During my career I've had to work on some challenging assignments (infant anal thermometers comes to mind) but never anything that I've really had a problem with—like Spam[4] or Barney.[5] I have, however, been involved with a few products that seemed a bit, shall we say, questionable.

I had to struggle to keep a straight face when a marketing consultant started going into a little too much detail about a high-tech toilet seat called the "Santi-Seat."

Apparently, I'm not alone. I've heard similar tales of woe from other agency owners. In one such case, the agency was approached by a company called Burial at Sea. Apparently, if your dearly departed was so inclined, a burial at sea could be arranged. When the company was asked how they used their boats when business was slow, we were told, "porno movies."

For every advertisable product on the market there's a hidden army of trade salespeople. Everyday, these people pack their suitcases with pencil erasers or GI Joe Battle Action accessories or whatever it is they're selling and take off on the road to places like Wilmington and Boise and Greenville trying to

---

[3]*shenanigans:* Tricky or mischievous behavior.
[4]**ESL Spam:** A processed, canned meat product.
[5]**ESL Barney:** A large, friendly purple dinosaur that stars in a children's television program.

make quota to keep their jobs so they can do the same thing for another year. In the Great Sales War these men and women are the infantry, the front-line grunts. Compared to them, ad people are the air force, the glamorous flyboys who get the credit. The ad agency, equipped with the latest high-tech weaponry, goes in for the kill with a blitzkrieg[6] campaign. But even if it's a stupid product, most ad people don't have to devote too big a part of their lifetime trying to sell it.

One of my clients was an umbrella company. They made good quality umbrellas — they didn't break with the first gust of wind. The guy I dealt with was the sales director. Nice guy. Smart guy. But basically, the guy was an umbrella salesman. He'd travel around the country with a bag full of umbrellas: the standard, the mini, the micro-mini, the full-size, the golf, the automatic, the semi-automatic, the designer line, the cane-style, the water-resistant.

This guy spent about 80 percent of his waking hours dealing with umbrellas. Don't get me wrong. Umbrellas are certainly an important and necessary part of society. I just wouldn't want to devote my life to selling them.

Thirteen years after the "Marshmallow Incident," I find myself having lunch with the very man to whom I addressed my provocative question. When I bring up the incident he confesses to a lack of recollection. Prefacing it with how young and naive I was, I recall the scene.

"Hmmm . . . so what did I answer?" he asks curiously.

"You said that it's the government's role to determine which products should or shouldn't be advertised and that as long as a product is legal it's the agency's responsibility to do the very best job possible to advertise its clients' products."

With hardly a pause the ex-CEO speaks in a soft but certain manner, "I think my answer would be different today."

He goes on to say how we all must be willing to accept more social responsibility for the decisions we make in business. I feel vindicated.

A year later, I notice a blurb in the trades about my converted CEO pal. He has just passed away.

In the agency business there's always pressure. The creatives feel it to get great work produced. The account people feel it to keep their clients happy and spending their money. The president feels it to be winning new business. The chairman feels it to be making a profit and keeping his Board happy. And the Board feels it to keep its stockholders happy. If you work in an agency, there's the additional pressure of never-ending deadlines, demanding bosses, and corporate politics. And if the agency loses a client, which happens all the time, you could be out of a job.

---

[6]*blitzkrieg:* German for lightning war, an attack waged with great speed and force.

When people are subjected to that kind of pressure they can do some strange things. I once knew an art director who physically attacked an account exec with a metal T-square just for being asked to make the logo bigger.

There's a saying, "It's only advertising." It's true. It's not like finding a cure for AIDS. However, if you're serious about the business, and most are, it can feel like mortal combat. I've worked with many whose philosophies are Survival of the Fittest, and The End Justifies the Means.

Somewhere there was some kind of survey done about which careers the public respected most. I'm not sure which ranked the highest, but I know "Advertising Executive" ranked somewhere at the bottom. I think it was between "Lawyer" and "Used Car Salesman." I guess the American public figures that being saved from ring-around-the-collar isn't like being saved from cancer or nuclear war.

How soon they forget about those cute little Dancing Raisins. And Clara Peller and her "Where's the beef?" Don't tell me that didn't have some socially redeeming value. Even President Bush used that line. And does anyone actually watch the Super Bowl for the game?

But I have to admit, it does seem a bit weird when some woman working on a cure for AIDS is in some lab cubicle somewhere making 25K while the guy who came up with "It's Bubblicious!" is sitting in some corner office making a half mil.

Hey, welcome to Mad Ave.

JERRY BIHLE

Shirley and Son

JENNIFER POZNER
Triumph of the Shill

Here's how you make an Absolut Hunk martini: Add four parts famous-brand vanilla vodka, one part simple syrup, one part fresh lime juice, a splash of pineapple juice, and one giant heaping of product placement.

Last year, on *Sex and the City,* PR diva Samantha landed her aspiring-actor lover a starring role in an ad campaign for a well-known liquor company. Samantha and her friends salaciously sipped Absolut Hunk martinis as the campaign took off, and a beefcake shot of the boy toy stripped down, oiled up, and wearing nothing but a strategically placed vodka bottle was plastered on billboards and bus shelters all over the show's New York setting. Just as Steven Spielberg used real-life firm 3 Ring Circus to craft futuristic commercials for Lexus, Reebok, and other sponsors for use in *Minority Report,* according to *Newsday, Sex and the City's* producers approached Absolut—not the other way around—and ceded the creative process to the vodka peddler's ad shop, TBWA/Chiat/Day.

The resulting publicity was all too typical of the merging of news, entertainment, and public relations in today's media market. Headlines such as the *Arizona Republic's* "'City' Slickers; Bid Adieu to Carrie & Co. with Your Own Sippin' Party" helped the Absolut Hunk martini travel from the boob tube to the bar scene, while the *Washington Post, Newsday,* and other outlets printed the recipe so readers could make the cocktail at home. And without spending one red cent for prime-time spots or print spreads, Absolut managed the ultimate score: During Katie Couric's interview with Absolut Hunk actor Jason Lewis, NBC's *Today* mimicked *Sex and the City* and digitally inserted the hottie's ad in Times Square as if it were an actual, real-life billboard.

Corporate sponsors have long lorded their lucre over television networks, using their purchasing power to promote programs they consider worthy and threatening to withhold ad buys to squelch content they deem controversial (or geared toward the nonwhite, low-income, or aging demographics undesirable to them). But product placement exacerbates advertisers' already-active influence over what we watch, see, and hear in sitcoms, dramas, and reality TV—not to mention radio, film, video games, and even broadcast journalism. With the arrival of brand integration, advertisers no longer have to rely on veiled financial blackmail—or even commercial breaks—to get their messages through. Instead, marketers are weaving their products and services directly into the plots of popular TV shows, where not even the most careful TiVo jockey can fast-forward through them.

It's not just that sets and characters are subtly dressed with recognizable brands, as in years past. This sort of scenic plug certainly still exists, more blatantly than ever: Close-ups of Sydney Bristow's Nokia cell phone are common on ABC's *Alias*, while over on Fox, Kiefer Sutherland's *24* character drives a manly Ford Expedition; shots of sponsors' goods are ubiquitous on almost all reality shows, from *The Bachelor's* fridge full of Pepsi to the picture phones used by aspiring singers on *American Idol* and lovelorn losers on *Joe Millionaire*.

But product placement also makes its way into dialogue, as when the romantic lead of the WB's short-lived 2000 series *Young Americans,* whose production was funded by Coca-Cola, interrupted a tender moment to ask the object of his puppy love, "Will you pass me a Coke?" The ever-popular makeover genre gives *Queer Eye for the Straight Guy's* Fab Five the perfect platform to pose, praise, and primp with Neutrogena sunless tanner, Norelco nose-hair trimmers, Redken pomade, and a wide range of other name-brand beauty, fashion, and interior-design products, all of which are aggressively promoted in "shopping guides" on Bravo's website. (Apparently, all this shilling is motivating men to the malls: As reported in several newspapers, a survey by PR firm Jericho Communications, unaffiliated with the show, found that "men were five times more likely than women to go shopping" on a Wednesday after a new *Queer Eye* episode aired, and respondents said they'd be most likely to purchase products endorsed by Carson Kressley, *QE's* fashion expert, than any other celebrity.)

Daytime TV, meanwhile, resembles nothing so much as the Home Shopping Network. Viewers can wake up to Katie Couric telling NBC audiences where they can buy must-have fall fashions; then listen to Ellen DeGeneres read promotional copy for cruises, home spa treatments, and other gifts she bestows on her talk-show audience; and spend the afternoon watching Oprah chow down on Costco's chicken pot pies and gush over Isaac Mizrahi's clothing line for Target. And, most dangerously, celebrities are being stealthily hired to tout branded drugs and risky medical procedures on the talk-TV circuit— as when Carnie Wilson hyped gastric-bypass surgery on *Good Morning America* without disclosing that she was paid for her endorsement.

The last several years have seen brand integration rise to brazen new levels. Entire episodes of popular programs are being crafted for companies that aren't satisfied with simple set dressing or one-off dialogue plugs. A January 2000 episode of *Friends* revolved around Rachel's desire to sneak mass-produced pseudo-antiques past roommate Phoebe, who objected to chain furniture franchises sucking individuality from people's homes. By the close of the half hour, Pottery Barn's name was plugged (and praised) more than a dozen times, and Phoebe was so smitten with their tables, lamps, linens, and tchotchkes that she just had to buy more.

Even those producers who refuse to sell their sets or scripts to corporate sponsors can find, over time, that resistance is futile. The ad industry is fighting back against TiVo and other ad-skip technology by altering preexisting content in ways that could threaten the visual and editorial integrity of programming. Products that didn't originally exist, such as a soda can in a cop's hand or a logo on a high-schooler's t-shirt, can be digitally inserted into TV reruns. A rep from Princeton Video Imaging, the tech gurus behind "virtual advertising," told the *Detroit News,* "Our technology allows you to insert Coke in one episode, then Pepsi [the next time it shows], then Dr. Pepper in the third. It gives the seller the chance to monetize that real estate over and over again."

Even more disturbing than marketers plundering our programming for "monetizing opportunities" is the newest trend: content created for the sole purpose of pushing products. On the premiere of ABC's *Extreme Makeover: Home Edition,* a group of designers were given a week to remodel the house of a suburban, middle-class family whose rosy-cheeked little daughter survived leukemia. Cameras captured the family cavorting at a name-brand vacation resort while the team, led by *Trading Spaces* toolmaster Ty Pennington, renovated their home with Craftsman tools, stocked their kitchen with Kenmore appliances, and filled their living room with electronics from Toshiba, Panasonic, and Sony—all of which were available for purchase from a Sears-sponsored, link-filled "As Featured On" section of ABC.com (which viewers were prompted to visit at the end of the program). The sentimental climax came when the young cancer survivor gasped with glee at the life-size dollhouse Pennington had built for her. The happiness on that brave little girl's face, Pennington mused, is what this was all about.

Well . . . not quite. *EM: Home* is about what most reality TV series are about: manufacturing poor excuses for entertainment around sponsors' goods. According to the *New York Times, EM: Home* was the most lucrative branded-entertainment deal ABC has ever inked, with Sears paying more than $1 million for narrative integration in each of the six episodes, as well as purchasing commercials during each hour.

Brand integration is largely responsible for the reality-TV genre as we know it today, and not vice versa. Widely acknowledged as the instigator of both the current reality craze and the ubiquity of product placement, *Survivor* was only greenlighted after executive producer Mark Burnett explained to CBS that instead of the network paying actors, advertisers would pay the network for a starring role. In the words of *Advertising Age,* Burnett "envision[ed] *Survivor* as a commercial vehicle as much as a TV drama." The adventure theme is simply a pretext for contestants to interact with brands such as Doritos, Mountain Dew, Bud Light, and Saturn, to the tune of more than $3.7 million each for the initial series and $12 million for the second installment, with the price tag rising exponentially each season. That may seem pricey, but as the head of sales for CBS told *Advertising Age,* it was "one of the best bargains in TV history." In addition to months of prime-time exposure to viewers who can't tune out product plugs without losing track of the action, advertisers use *Survivor* imagery in their marketing campaigns and get added exposure from countless clips played on news and infotainment programs.

This phenomenon was even more unabashed on NBC's *The Restaurant,* an "unscripted drama" that followed celebrity chef Rocco DiSpirito as he harangued waitstaff, trained line cooks, and schmoozed customers in a carefully edited quest to launch a Manhattan eatery over six prime-time hours in the summer of 2003. (The show will return this summer.) The series was crafted by Burnett, conceived by Ben Silverman (the self-described "media synergist" responsible for ABC's product-laced *Who Wants to Be a Millionaire?*), and produced by Silverman's production company, Reveille, and Magna Global Entertainment, a branded-entertainment development wing of media giant Interpublic that is "dedicated to the creation of original television programming that is funded by and serves the needs of Interpublic's clients." In this case, according to the *New York Post,* Magna clients Coors, American Express, and Mitsubishi paid between $4 and $6 million in development and advertising for story-driving presence in *The Restaurant.* NBC didn't have to pay a dime for the series—all the networks had to do was save half the commercial time during the show's run for the sponsors, and reap cross-promotional benefits from AmEx ads starring DiSpirito.

No wonder the main item on *The Restaurant's* menu was a hot, steaming plate of product placement. Logo-studded opening credits featured an AmEx "Open" sign on the door, along with customers charging meals to their AmEx cards. DiSpirito talked shop in his Mitsubishi Endeavor, invited the bouncy Coors Twins to the restaurant's opening, and issued stilted commands to his employees—some reportedly dubbed in by producers—such as "Don't come back without Coors for all these people." ("I will forever be trained to hold a Coors Light bottle by the neck with the label facing outwards," Albert Davis, the restaurant's espresso maker, told the *Baltimore Sun*.)

Despite the heavy-handed dialogue and conspicuously brand-conscious camera work, *Restaurant* insiders spun the shilling as seamless. Silverman told the *Hollywood Reporter* that product placement was "organic to the concept," "fit in naturally," and "even lent credibility to the environment." But like most product placement proponents, their enthusiasm was disingenuous: In one interview, Burnett defended the series' creative purity ("The whole show was unscripted. Every story line was organic and raw," he told *Newsday*); in the next, he admitted to the *Hollywood Reporter* that brand integration is "a very good business move" because it offers "a great opportunity for sponsors to have more control" over content. Burnett told *Daily Variety* that his "future is dramatic television like this," because these shows are "the next evolution of storytelling." Magna's Robert Riesenberg sang the same tune in the *St. Louis Post-Dispatch:* "The kind of organic product integration found in *The Restaurant* represents a bold new era in television."

This bold new era may soon define scripted programming as well. That's the theory behind a sit-com pilot—produced for close to a million bucks by Viacom, Sony Entertainment, and Anonymous Content—which would star Plato, the puffy purple creature from Sony Walkman commercials, as he tries to fit in at college. If any network picks up the series, it will probably be due to the show's appealingly discounted licensing fee, made possible by Sony's investment. Still, executive producer Lenny Bekerman insists that there is "no mandate" to put Sony gadgets in the show. "It's not a 22-minute commercial," he told NPR's *Marketplace.* "It's a stand-alone television series." But if an alien from an electronics ad gets his own series, how can it possibly be anything but a sitcom-length commercial? Official mandate or no, if produced, *Plato* will exist primarily to sell the Sony-product lifestyle to young adults, as Bekerman explained: "We're not going to see [Sony electronics] because they're blatant or they're product placement; we're going to see them because . . . every college student would wear a Walkman or have a stereo in their room or have a laptop."

If these trends continue unabated, entertainment crafted around commercial messages will replace traditional narrative. Eric Yaverbaum, president of Jericho, the firm that conducted the *Queer Eye* shopping survey, can't wait. "Sitcoms are not blatant ads, which makes them much better sales vehicles. Look at a Target or a Wal-Mart—why don't they have their own show? I don't know if it will take another decade for it to happen, but it will happen," he said in a phone interview. The line between commerce and content has degraded to such a degree that by 2002, BMW had launched a DirecTV channel on which all programs feature BMW automobiles.

In their March 2003 *Monthly Review* essay "The Commercial Tidal Wave," Robert W. McChesney and John Bellamy Foster note that because 80 percent of U.S. ad spending is funneled through the eight largest conglomerates that own advertising agencies, the clout of companies like Interpublic—which brought us *The Restaurant*—has grown, "which gives them considerable ability to name their tune with corporate media firms more than willing to play ball." Among many examples McChesney and Foster point to is a series of top-level meetings held in 2000 by USA Network, in which major advertisers were invited to "tell the network what type of programming content they wanted." When networks manufacture content to meet advertisers' needs and advertisers give content to networks for free, it's a win–win for marketers and big media— but viewers are losing big. "We're trying to create marketing platforms through television for our clients," Riesenberg told the *Philadelphia Daily News.* "It's not at all about making better television. We don't profess to be able to do it better. It's really about finding that right fit, and then integrating them into that fit."

The biggest of all the myths promoted by reality TV is that these programs exist simply because the public demands them, as "proven" by ratings. It's not nearly that simple: Behind *Survivor*'s long-term, landscape-shifting impact was the relentless promotion of the series by CBS's parent company, Viacom. To generate buzz, more than 100 affiliate radio stations ran segments, including dozens of drive-time interviews with Burnett (which folks could listen to while driving past Viacom-owned billboards for the show), while 16 of CBS's TV stations and Viacom's MTV and VH1 covered *Survivor* as if its ins and outs were news. Eventually, *Entertainment Tonight* and a slew of other infotainment programs jumped on the bandwagon, interviewing booted contestants (after they had appeared on CBS's *Early Show*, of course), a practice that has become de rigueur for broadcast tabloids and respected news outlets alike.

The PR blitzkrieg made it appear as though there were overwhelming yet spontaneous popular interest in the show; all the biggest reality series have achieved their spectacular popularity by replicating *Survivor*'s strategy of multi-platform media attention, product integration, and public relations. That's the dirty little secret behind the corporate media contention that they are bombarding us with ad-rich, quality-poor reality shows simply because that's supposedly what the public wants.

This cross-promotional strategy extends not only to the shows themselves but to their stars. Take, for example, Eden's Crush, a 2001 marketing scheme–turned–WB show–turned–girl group created to test the power of the AOL Time Warner empire. The show was *Popstars*, and girls at home were encouraged to identify with the hundreds of contestants competing to become Spice Girls clones. Though the show also pushed Salon Selectives hair-care products, on this *American Idol* precursor the wanna-be pop stars themselves were the ultimate product placement. "You can't buy that kind of advertising," producer David Foster told the *St. Petersburg Times*, not acknowledging that the entire series was one long ad. Warner Music Group chairman Roger Ames saw it slightly differently, calling the WB tie-in "a huge running start" for future record sales and a "dream come true," because "even if you could buy all the advertising in the world, there's the difference between advertising and editorial, and this is editorial." The value of the media time given to the yet-unformed group was estimated to be at least $20 million. Because of the built-in fan base sure to result from so many hours of "editorial" exposure on network TV, Warner's London/Sire Records inked a recording contract before the band had a name — or even singers. Not until the songs were written, the show placed in the prime-time lineup, and the pre- and post-production planned were the artists plugged in, like an afterthought. Once selected, Eden's Crush appeared on WB affiliate news stations in New York and Chicago, guest-starred on the WB's *Sabrina, the Teenage Witch*, were featured on the Warner Brothers–syndicated infotainment show *Extra*, and conducted an AOL live chat. The group's first single sold more than 200,000 copies right out of the gate.

By the time this format was rehashed with *American Idol*, the infotainment circuit, primed by several seasons of reality hype, was hungry for any information Fox would give. Outtakes ran on every channel, seemingly at every hour, for months — especially on Fox itself — with clips, contestant interviews, and *Idol* gossip as a daily mainstay. Hundreds of kids were humiliated, insta-celebrity was bestowed upon several nominally talented contestants, millions of home viewers subscribed to AT&T wireless to vote for their favorite singer, and eventual winner Kelly Clarkson appeared everywhere. All that cross-promotion guaranteed both ratings gold for Fox and an astonishing debut for Clarkson's single, which broke the Beatles' record for fastest-ever rise to number one on the *Billboard* charts. "I was like, How did that happen?" Clarkson exclaimed, a bit dazed, on an *Idol* reunion show.

Gee, I wonder.

Watching *American Idol* is like sitting through an endless, commercialized hall of mirrors—it's a real-life version of the over-the-top product placement in *Josie and the Pussycats*. Fox has reaped millions by making *Idol* wanna-bes literally do backflips over corporate logos, gulp Coke, shampoo with Herbal Essences, and drive Ford Focuses in mini-commercials disguised as music videos. The contestants who succeed are as much commodities as the products they hawk: Clarkson's humble, aw-shucks personality helped her win the *Idol* title, but by the time she promoted her single "Miss Independent" during the show's second season, the producers attempted to remake her hair, makeup, and persona in Christina Aguilera's sexed-up image. "Image" was the euphemism mean-spirited judge Simon Cowell used every time he told Kimberly Locke, an African-American contestant who made it to third place during *Idol*'s second season, that her great voice couldn't compensate for her too-big body and "weird" (read: black) hair. (Cowell didn't stop haranguing Locke until she relaxed her hair.)

If current trends continue, this tyranny of image—and the way it seeks to strip away what little diversity exists in mass media—will only worsen. Media insiders say the future of scripted television is an immediate, interactive model in which viewers will be able to instantly purchase products they see on their favorite shows. For six months in 2002, *Days of Our Lives* and *Passions* fans who admired, say, the nightie some soap vixen wore while she seduced her evil twin's fiancé could score one of their very own by tuning into ShopNBC's "Soap Style," a pilot arrangement in which items featured on the soaps were sold on NBC's shopping channel and website, helped along by guest appearances from soap stars. Jericho's Yaverbaum told *Bitch* he predicts "a scrolling ticker at the bottom of every show. It'll be like this: You like the bed Frasier's sleeping in? Buy it at x furniture store." His advice to marketers: "It's obvious. Television has this captive audience—people think these people are *real,* they want to be like them. Let them know directly that these characters are wearing your fashions and you'll sell like crazy the next day. Cut the network in on your sales and everybody will make a whole lot of money."

Brilliant from a business standpoint, this model has serious implications for programming. One-look-fits-all casting will worsen, as will the homogeneity and vapidity of storylines. Considering how steadfastly fashion advertisers cling to young anorexics as the female ideal, average-size and older actresses will find it even harder to score roles once shows are designed to sell clothes off characters' backs. Let's say Pottery Barn creates a family drama that revolves around a set full of their furniture: What are the chances that abortion or racial profiling would be discussed by characters whose main function is to showcase a trendy couch? Dozens of years and mergers ago, before commercialism so thoroughly permeated every aspect of media content, television occasionally gave difficult social issues the dramatic treatment they deserved. But a ground-breaking miniseries like *Roots* wouldn't happen in the TV future Yaverbaum imagines, since advertisers aren't interested in the horror of slave owners branding human beings—they're only interested in positive branding opportunities.

Potentially quality content is already being pushed out of the way to make room for programming built around embedded ads. By February 2003, Fox had devoted 41 percent and ABC a third of its sweeps offerings to reality shows. Scripted shows other than established franchises like *Law & Order* and *CSI* are finding it increasingly difficult to survive. Sally Field's 2002 series *The Court,* about a female Supreme Court justice, was yanked after only three episodes; the laugh track–less *Andy Richter Controls the Universe* was canned before it was ever allowed to develop an audience. The same fate befell last fall's detective drama *Karen Cisco,* which many critics felt had promise; it was replaced by *Extreme Makeover, EM: Home, The Bachelorette,* and *Celebrity Mole.* Discussing the greed that governs such programming decisions, *Bernie Mac* producer Larry Wilmore told *Entertainment Weekly* that despite his show winning an Emmy and a slate of other awards in its first season, Fox has regularly pre-empted *Mac* in favor of ratings draws like *Joe Millionaire.* "Now, this is an award-winning, groundbreaking show. Let alone, when was the last time a black show has been in that position?" Wilmore asked. "They don't care. . . . They'll pull us for whatever reality show brings that 30 share." And even when a reality series is likely to be a ratings flop (anyone remember *Are You Hot?*), the comparatively small investment involved means that networks still consider such fodder less risky than nurturing expensive scripted fare.

As advertisers seek broader, deeper, and more direct control over media content than they had even in the early days of television (when soap operas actually sold soap to housewives), defenders of brand integration claim their opponents are misguided Chicken Littles, fearing falling sky where no danger exists. According to Madison Avenue execs and network reps, we needn't worry our pretty little heads about the ads that populate our programs because TV is simply returning to its golden age. Since branded entertainment wasn't so bad in the '50s, they ask, what real harm could it possibly pose today?

Though seductive, this argument is not just factually specious but historically unsophisticated. For example, tobacco advertising contributed to widespread health problems among the TV-watching and moviegoing population during those "simpler days" when the Marlboro Man was a trusted friend. The real difference between then and now is one of scope: Advertiser-controlled content is more threatening today than at any prior point because of the sheer breadth and inescapable power of our modern mediated landscape. Yesteryear's housewives could turn off "their stories" if they were annoyed by silly soap jingles. Today, it's nearly impossible to tune out the commercials woven into hundreds of TV shows, blockbuster films, music and talk-radio programs; thousands of mass-market magazines and newspaper stories; and millions of Internet sites. Media consolidation compounds the problem, as corporate media owners increasingly consider artistic vision and cultural relevance extraneous to their pursuit of astronomical profits.

Yet among the most disturbing aspects of brand integration is the ho-hum response it too often fetches. Why should we care about product placement degrading content, we wonder, when TV has become so bland, risk-free, and hackneyed that a show like *According to Jim* is an ABC mainstay? It's an understandable reaction to media that have so consistently frustrated, alienated, and disappointed us. But if we care at all about independent thought and cultural diversity, we must demand that programming improve, not accept its commercial erosion with a sigh.

Advertisers are banking on our apathy in their slow quest to condition us to become the very shopping-obsessed drones parodied in *Josie and the Pussycats.* As one product-placement expert told the *Boston Globe,* viewers will grow accustomed to hypercommercialism before, during, and after TV shows because "it's a matter of time. . . . What may seem intrusive today will likely be normal five years from now." This is deeply disturbing, and not only in terms of its negative effects on entertainment. Advertising is profoundly manipulative at its core. Its imagery strives to deprive us of realistic ideas about love, beauty, health, money, work, childhood, and more in an attempt to convince us that only products can bring us true joy; numerous studies show that the more ads we view, the worse we feel about ourselves. How much worse will this psychological exploitation become when woven directly into our narratives?

The stronger a foothold advertisers gain over entertainment—whether they peddle their influence through old-school ad buys or new-school product placement—the more power they have to define our collective values, and the more poisonous media images of women are becoming. Nothing demonstrates this more blatantly than the piggish reality genre: *Joe Millionaire*'s entire premise is that women are evil gold diggers who deserve to be lied to and humiliated for our enjoyment; on *America's Next Top Model,* nearly nude teen girls are berated by judges for sounding too smart when they speak and being "plus size" at 5'10" and 135 pounds.

Mike Darnell, Fox's reality guru and the brains behind *Joe Millionaire* and its progenitor, *Who Wants to Marry a Multi-Millionaire,* once told *Entertainment Weekly* that his dream project would be a beauty pageant featuring female prisoners: "You give them a chance to get a makeover, and it's a 40-share special." I can see it now: Corporations using prison labor could present themselves as socially responsible businesses rehabilitating incarcerated women via telemarketing and product assembly skills. Connie Convict, an unkempt, underfed inmate who spends her day booking American Airlines reservations and bagging Starbucks espresso beans, could emerge as a beauty queen, with a little help from some benevolent cosmetics line: "Maybe she found it behind bars . . . maybe it's Maybelline!"

Unless we get serious about product placement—collectively, and quickly—we shouldn't be shocked if "Miss San Quentin" sashays her way to prime time.

JAY CHIAT
Illusions Are Forever

I know what you're thinking: That's rich, asking an adman to define truth. Advertising people aren't known either for their wisdom or their morals, so it's hard to see why an adman is the right person for this assignment. Well, it's just common sense—like asking an alcoholic about sobriety, or a sinner about piety. Who is likely to be more obsessively attentive to a subject than the transgressor?

Everyone thinks that advertising is full of lies, but it's not what you think. The facts presented in advertising are almost always accurate, not because advertising people are sticklers but because their ads are very closely regulated. If you make a false claim in a commercial on network television, the FTC will catch it. Someone always blows the whistle.

The real lie in advertising—some would call it the "art" of advertising—is harder to detect. What's false in advertising lies in the presentation of situations, values, beliefs, and cultural norms that form a backdrop for the selling message.

Advertising—including movies, TV, and music videos—presents to us a world that is not our world but rather a collection of images and ideas created for the purpose of selling. These images paint a picture of the ideal family life, the perfect home. What a beautiful woman is, and is not. A prescription for being a good parent and a good citizen.

The power of these messages lies in their unrelenting pervasiveness, the twenty-four-hour-a-day drumbeat that leaves no room for an alternative view. We've become acculturated to the way advertisers and other media-makers look at things, so much so that we have trouble seeing things in our own natural way. Advertising robs us of the most intimate moments in our lives because it substitutes an advertiser's idea of what ought to be—What should a romantic moment be like?

You know the De Beers diamond advertising campaign? A clever strategy, persuading insecure young men that two months' salary is the appropriate sum to pay for an engagement ring. The arbitrary algorithm is preposterous, of course, but imagine the fiancée who receives a ring costing only half a month's salary? The advertising-induced insult is grounds for calling off the engagement, I imagine. That's marketing telling the fiancée what to feel and what's real.

Unmediated is a great word: It means "without media," without the in-between layer that makes direct experience almost impossible. Media interferes with our capacity to experience naturally, spontaneously, and genuinely, and thereby spoils our capacity for some important kinds of personal "truth."

Although media opens our horizons infinitely, it costs us. We have very little direct personal knowledge of anything in the world that is not filtered by media.

Truth seems to be in a particular state of crisis now. When what we watch is patently fictional, like most movies and commercials, it's worrisome enough. But it's absolutely pernicious when it's packaged as reality. Nothing represents a bigger threat to truth than reality-based television, in both its lowbrow and highbrow versions—from *Survivor* to A&E's *Biography.* The lies are sometimes intentional, sometimes errors, often innocent, but in all cases they are the "truth" of a media-maker who claims to be representing reality.

The Internet is also a culprit, obscuring the author, the figure behind the curtain, even more completely. Chat rooms, which sponsor intimate conversation, also allow the participants to misrepresent themselves in every way possible. The creation of authoritative-looking Web sites is within the grasp of any reasonably talented twelve-year-old, creating the appearance of professionalism and expertise where no expert is present. And any mischief-maker can write a totally plausible-looking, totally fake stock analyst's report and post it on the Internet. When the traditional signals of authority are so misleading, how can we know what's for real?

But I believe technology, for all its weaknesses, will be our savior. The Internet is our only hope for true democratization, a truly populist publishing form, a mass communication tool completely accessible to individuals. The Internet puts CNN on the same plane with the freelance journalist and the lady down the street with a conspiracy theory, allowing cultural and ideological pluralism that never previously existed.

This is good for the cause of truth, because it underscores what is otherwise often forgotten—truth's instability. Truth is not absolute: It is presented, represented, and represented by the individuals who have the floor, whether they're powerful or powerless. The more we hear from powerless ones, the less we are in the grasp of powerful ones—and the less we believe that "truth" is inviolable, given, and closed to interpretation. We also come closer to seeking our own truth.

That's the choice we're given every day. We can accept the very compelling, very seductive version of "truth" offered to us daily by media-makers, or we can tune out its influence for a shot at finding our own individual, confusing, messy version of it. After all, isn't personal truth the ultimate truth?

JOHN LEO
The Selling of Rebellion

Most TV viewers turn off their brains when the commercials come on. But they're worth paying attention to. Some of the worst cultural propaganda is jammed into those sixty-second and thirty-second spots.

Consider the recent ad for the Isuzu Rodeo. A grotesque giant in a business suit stomps into a beautiful field, startling a deer and jamming skyscrapers, factories, and signs into the ground. (I get it: Nature is good; civilization and business are bad.) One of the giant's signs says "Obey," but the narrator says, "The world has boundaries. Ignore them." Trying to trample the Rodeo, the hapless giant trips over his own fence. The Isuzu zips past him toppling a huge sign that says "Rules."

Presumably we are meant to react to this ad with a wink and a nudge, because the message is unusually flat-footed and self-satirical. After all, Isuzus are not manufactured in serene fields by adorable lower mammals. The maddened giant makes them in his factories. He also hires hip ad writers and stuffs them in his skyscrapers, forcing them to write drivel all day, when they really should be working on novels and frolicking with deer.

But the central message here is very serious and strongly antisocial: We should all rebel against authority, social order, propriety, and rules of any kind. "Obey" and "Rules" are bad. Breaking rules, with or without your Isuzu, is good. Auto makers have been pushing this idea in various ways since "The Dodge Rebellion" of the mid-1960s. Isuzu has worked the theme especially hard, including a TV ad showing a bald and repressive grade-school teacher barking at kids to "stay within the lines" while coloring pictures, because "the lines are our friends."

A great many advertisers now routinely appeal to the so-called postmodern sensibility, which is heavy on irony (wink, nudge) and attuned to the message that rules, boundaries, standards, and authorities are either gone or should be gone. Foster Grant sunglasses has used the "no limits" refrain. So have Prince Matchabelli perfume ("Life without limits"), Showtime TV (its "No Limits" campaign) and AT&T's Olympics ads in 1996 ("Imagine a world without limits"). No Limits is an outdoor-adventure company, and No Limit is the name of a successful rap record label. Even the U.S. Army used the theme in a TV recruitment ad. "When I'm in this uniform I know no limits," says a soldier—a scary thought if you remember Lt. William Calley in Vietnam or the Serbian Army today.

Among the ads that have used "no boundaries" almost as a mantra are Ralph Lauren's Safari cologne, Johnnie Walker scotch ("It's not trespassing when you cross your own boundaries"), Merrill Lynch ("Know no boundaries"), and the movie *The English Patient* ("In love, there are no boundaries").

Some "no boundaries" ads are legitimate—the Internet and financial markets, after all, aim at crossing or erasing old boundaries. The antisocial message is clearer in most of the "no rules" and "antirules" ads, starting with Burger King's "Sometimes, you gotta break the rules." These include Outback steakhouses ("No rules. Just right"), Don Q rum ("Break all the rules"), the theatrical troupe De La Guarda ("No rules"), Neiman Marcus ("No rules here"), Columbia House Music Club ("We broke the rules"), Comedy Central ("See comedy that breaks rules"), Red Kamel cigarettes ("This baby don't play by the rules"), and even Woolite (wool used to be associated with decorum, but now "All the rules have changed," an ad says under a photo of a young woman groping or being groped by two guys). "No rules" also turns up as the name of a book and a CD and a tag line for an NFL video game ("No refs, no rules, no mercy"). The message is everywhere—"the rules are for breaking," says a Spice Girls lyric.

What is this all about? Why is the ad industry working so hard to use rule-breaking as a way of selling cars, steaks, and Woolite? In his book *The Conquest of Cool,* Thomas Frank points to the Sixties counterculture. He says it has become "a more or less permanent part of the American scene, a symbolic and musical language for the endless cycles of rebellion and transgression that make up so much of our mass culture . . . rebellion is both the high- and mass-cultural motif of the age; order is its great bogeyman."

The pollster-analysts at Yankelovich Partners Inc. have a different view. In their book *Rocking the Ages: The Yankelovich Report on Generational Marketing,* J. Walker Smith and Ann Clurman say rule-breaking is simply a hallmark of the baby boom generation: "Boomers always have broken the rules. . . . The drugs, sex, and rock 'n roll of the '60s and '70s only foreshadowed the really radical rule-breaking to come in the consumer marketplace of the '80s and '90s."

This may pass—Smith says the post-boomers of Generation X are much more likely to embrace traditional standards than boomers were at the same age. On the other hand, maybe it won't. Pop culture is dominated by in-your-face transgression now and the damage is severe. The peculiar thing is that so much of the rule-breaking propaganda is largely funded by businessmen who say they hate it, but can't resist promoting it in ads as a way of pushing their products. Isuzu, please come to your senses.

READ MERCER SCHUCHARDT
Swoosh!

The early followers of Christ created a symbol to represent their beliefs and communicate with one another in times of persecution. The well-known Ichthus, or "Christian fish," consisted of two curved lines that transected each other to form the abstract outline of fish and tail. The word for *fish* also happened to be a Greek acronym wherein:

- Iota = Iesous = Jesus
- Chi = Christos = Christ
- Theta = Theos = God
- Upsilon = Huios = Son
- Sigma = Soter = Savior

Combining symbol and word, the fish provided believers with an integrated media package that could be easily explained and understood. When the threat of being fed to the lions forced Christians to be less explicit, they dropped the text. Without the acronym to define the symbol's significance, the fish could mean anything or nothing, an obvious advantage in a culture hostile to certain beliefs. But to Christians the textless symbol still signified silent rebellion against the ruling authorities. Within three centuries, the faith signified by the fish had transformed Rome into a Christian empire.

Today, in an electronically accelerated culture, a symbol can change the face of society in about one-sixteenth that time. Enter the Nike Swoosh, the most ubiquitous icon in the country, and one that many other corporations have sought to emulate. In a world where technology, entertainment, and design are converging, the story of the Swoosh is by far the most fascinating case study of a systematic, integrated, and insanely successful formula for icon-driven marketing.

The simple version of the story is that a young Oregon design student named Caroline Davidson got $35 in 1971 to create a logo for then-professor (now Nike CEO) Phil Knight's idea of importing and selling improved Japanese running shoes. Nike's innovative product line, combined with aggressive marketing and brand positioning, eventually created an unbreakable mental link between the Swoosh image and the company's name. As Nike put it, there was so much equity in the brand that they knew it wouldn't hurt to drop the word *Nike* and go with the Swoosh alone. Nike went to the textless format for U.S. advertising in March 1996 and expanded it globally later that year. While the Nike name and symbol appear together in ads today, the textless campaign set a new standard. In the modern global market, the truly successful icon must be able to stand by itself, evoking all the manufactured associations that form a corporation's public identity.

In the past, it would have been unthinkable to create an ad campaign stripped of the company's name. Given what was at stake — Nike's advertising budget totals more than $100 million per year — what made them think they could pull it off?

First, consider the strength of the Swoosh as an icon. The Swoosh is a simple shape that reproduces well at any size, in any color, and on almost any surface — three critical elements for a corporate logo that will be reproduced at sizes from a quarter of an inch to 500 feet. It most frequently appears in one of three arresting colors: black, red, or white. A textless icon, it nevertheless "reads" left to right, like most languages. Now consider the sound of the word *Swoosh*. According to various Nike ads, it's the last sound you hear before coming in second place, the sound of a basketball hitting nothing but net. It's also the onomatopoeic analogue of the icon's visual stroke. Reading it left to right, the symbol itself actually seems to say "swoosh" as you look at it.

However it may read, the Swoosh transcends language, making it the perfect corporate icon for the postliterate global village.

With the invention of the printing press, according to Italian semiotician Umberto Eco, the alphabet triumphed over the icon. But in an overstimulated electronic culture, the chief problem is what advertisers call "clutter" or "chatter" — too many words, too much redundancy, too many competing messages. Add the rise of illiteracy and an increasingly multicultural world and you have a real communications problem. A hyperlinked global economy requires a single global communications medium, and it's simply easier to teach everyone a few common symbols than to teach the majority of non-English speakers a new language.

The unfortunate result is that language is being replaced by icons. From the rock star formerly known as Prince to e-mail "smileys" to the NAFTA-induced symbolic laundry labels, the names and words we use to describe the world are being replaced by a set of universal hieroglyphs. Leading the charge, as one would expect, are the organizations that stand to make the most money in a less text-dependent world: multinational corporations. With the decline of words, they now can fill in the blank of the consumer's associative mind with whatever images they deem appropriate.

After watching Nike do it, several companies have decided to go textless themselves, including Mercedes-Benz, whose icon is easily confused with the peace sign (an association that can only help). According to one of their print ads, "right behind every powerful icon lies a powerful idea," which is precisely the definition of a global communications medium for an accelerated culture. Pepsi's new textless symbol does not need any verbal justification because it so clearly imitates the yin-yang symbol. In fact, a close look reveals it to be almost identical to the Korean national flag, which is itself a stylized yin-yang symbol in red, white, and blue.

Never underestimate the power of symbols. Textless corporate symbols operate at a level beneath the radar of rational language, and the power they wield can be corrupting. Advertising that relies on propaganda methods can grab you and take you somewhere whether you want to go or not; and as history tells us, it matters where you're going.

Language is the mediator between our minds and the world, and the thing that defines us as rational creatures. By going textless, Nike and other corporations have succeeded in performing partial lobotomies on our brains, conveying their messages without engaging our rational minds. Like Pavlov's bell, the Swoosh has become a stimulus that elicits a conditioned response. The problem is not that we buy Nike shoes, but that we've been led to do so by the same methods used to train Pavlov's dogs. It's ironic, of course, that this reflex is triggered by a stylized check mark—the standard reward for academic achievement and ultimate symbol for the rational, linguistically agile mind.

If sport is the religion of the modern age, then Nike has successfully become the official church. It is a church whose icon is a window between this world and the other, between your existing self (you overweight slob) and your Nike self (you god of fitness), where salvation lies in achieving the athletic Nietzschean ideal: no fear, no mercy, no second place. Like the Christian fish, the Swoosh is a true religious icon in that it both symbolizes the believer's reality and actually participates in it. After all, you do have to wear something to attain this special salvation, so why not something emblazoned with the Swoosh?

DAMIEN CAVE

The Tyranny of "Abercrappie"

Abercrappie" is what my youngest brother called Abercrombie & Fitch after Ryan, our fifteen-year-old sibling, begged for the worn-looking, overpriced clothes du jour.

Shirts, pants, sweaters, socks — Ryan wanted Abercrombie everything and he stumped for the stuff like a wide-eyed activist. In the kitchen, tossing punches at Josh and me, he used the word "quality." When I walked away, he chased me with a speech about owning "just a few things that you love to wear." He even suggested that I pick up some Abercrombie — "It might help you get a girlfriend," he offered with very little tact.

Christmas was only a few days away and the smart-alecky banter — "I want X" vs. "So what, you can't have it" — rang typical, as much a part of our family's holiday tradition as egg nog. But a specific brand request: That was new.

I remembered longing for Air Jordans,[1] Champion sweatshirts, even Ralph Lauren Polo shirts. But my parents shamed me into either buying them myself or squeezing them out of relatives. On occasion, Mom or Dad gave in, but they always had a choice. Never, strong as my longing was, had one designer inspired the single-branded passion I heard in Ryan's voice. Somehow, Abercrombie was different: more manipulative and more coveted than both its past and present rivals.

That drug-like draw angered me. After watching packs of pimply teenage boys in Massachusetts malls ogle the boobs and brands of the opposite sex, I couldn't help but want Ryan to swim against the current in this sea of conformity.

I swore I would never buy him the Abercrombie clothing I saw his peers wearing like a uniform. In fact, I decided I would play with his repulsive desire by putting a "Just kidding!" note inside an Abercrombie gift-certificate envelope.

First, though, I tried to fight back with words.

"Why would you want to be a billboard?" I asked. "They're not paying you to advertise their name."

Ryan went for finely tuned sarcasm. "But it's just so cool," he said, trying to irk me in the short term while offering the kind of self-deprecation that just might convince me to give him what he wanted later on.

---

[1] **ESL Air Jordans:** Expensive sneakers named for famous basketball player Michael Jordan.

By that time, my question was largely rhetorical. I already knew the real reason he was lusting after these clothes. Only two months earlier, Ryan had begun fusing himself to Nicole, a blond A student who won our family's favor by staunching Ryan's class-clown tendencies.

But while she kept his bragging to a minimum, Nicole also amplified Ryan's navel-,chest- and shoulder-gazing. When I picked her up on Christmas night, she wore a yellow Abercrombie T-shirt, and as I drove the magnetic couple back to our family's house, A&F earned at least as much air time as the latest gossip about teachers and other high school trysts. Nicole, like many women present and past, had become the arbiter of her man's taste. And in her court, Abercrombie was king.

"I think it's all she wears," said my mother that same afternoon, chuckling. She had already decided that Nicole passed muster, so her criticism remained light. Still, as a frugal New Hampshire native who stocks her shelves with generic foods and her closets with closeouts, my mom became easily incensed when discussing Abercrombie's prices.

"Seventy dollars for pants! It's outrageous."

What's more, as a mother who objects to premarital sex with a puritanical fervor, she also objected to the company's marketing campaign. Essentially, it sexualizes America's love of the aristocratic golden boy and girl—the blond, WASPish,[2] Ivy League[3] party animals most recently represented by Jude Law and Gwyneth Paltrow in *The Talented Mr. Ripley.*

Ads for Ralph Lauren, Tommy Hilfiger and Nautica have played on similar themes for years, but Abercrombie's models look younger, more collegiate. And Abercrombie plays closer to the frat-boy mentality, plastering naked male chests in most of its 205 store windows, while selling 300-page, quarterly catalogs that cost $6 and include interviews with porn stars and articles about drinking.

Indeed, women appear in the ads as well, but the boys rule. When they're not baring their asses to clamber naked aboard a dock or lying prostrate in the grass, the models huddle, flex and pose in store foregrounds like ten-foot trophies, a fact that most teens couldn't help but notice and want to copy in their own lives.

My mother didn't much care about whether the bare butts were male or female. She objected to what she perceived as the encouragement of sex. In so doing, she was in cahoots with[4] Illinois Lt. Gov. Corinne Wood, who called for a consumer boycott of Abercrombie because of the sexually explicit nature of its holiday "Naughty or Nice" catalog.

But as I tried to decide what to buy Ryan and my two other adolescent siblings for Christmas, the sex didn't bother me. The brand's dominance did.

---

[2]***ESL WASPish:*** Characteristic of a White Anglo-Saxon Protestant.
[3]***ESL Ivy League:*** A group of prestigious universities located in the eastern United States.
[4]***ESL in cahoots with:*** Cooperating with.

That dominance, in my opinion, has less to do with skin than with the company's fusion of two settings: the city of hip-hop lore, and the college of the frat-inspired free-for-all. The former can be seen in the company's baggy, urban-inspired designs; clean-cut models on grassy fields embody the latter.

Sex is a mythical part of these settings, but parents often fail to realize that these places—and thus Abercrombie—symbolize more than the longing to get naked. Ultimately, they represent freedom, excitement—a wide array of adventures that remain off-limits to the teenage children of today's SUV-driving parents.

The Reynoldsburg, Ohio, company has posted twenty-nine consecutive quarters of record sales and earnings, making it one of the world's best-performing retail brands. Surveyed teenagers repeatedly rank it near the top in terms of "coolness." To see that success only in terms of sex implies that teenagers are nothing more than their hormones, and that they are the company's only customers.

Neither implication is correct. I know adults who wear Abercrombie clothing, if only the shirts that carry the company name on the inside label. And as for sex: Yes, many teenagers' bodies insist that the subject come up, and often. But hormones affect more than sexual desire. As adults, in our own lives, we know this. But when we eye our sons and brothers, amnesia[5] strikes.

Somehow we have forgotten—probably because of our fears—that the hormone-inspired energy of youth leads most often to neither sex nor violence. The brandishing of bare chests by teenage boys and their incessant raunchy[6] chatter represent a healthy desire to learn, to push against adult boundaries, to discover the art of living. It's the same force that can be heard on the first Beck[7] album, completed before he was old enough to vote.

Even though Abercrombie taps into this pent-up energy with controversial content, the images don't matter. The company is "cool" not because of the sex or the beer, but because these subjects signify a much wider idea, namely the freedom to live as the kid—not the parent—sees fit.

Opining on Abercrombie's appeal, however, didn't much change my decision to boycott the store. I still wanted Ryan to be above it all. But after putting my note in the gift certificate envelope, my smugness stung me. I already had bought books and movie passes. I feared the trick certificate placed me at risk of becoming the pedantic big brother.

So I gave in. On Christmas Eve, I bought Ryan a fleece jacket, marked down from $49.99 to $29.99. I justified it by remarking that the name "Abercrombie" only appeared on the inside tag and on the zipper. Ryan had

---

[5]*amnesia:* A loss of memory.

[6]*ESL raunchy:* Sexually explicit or obscene.

[7]*ESL Beck:* Beck Hansen, a songwriter and performer who blends folk, electronic, punk rock, and rap influences.

been getting good grades, so I figured he deserved it. I figured my love should trump my politics. I figured his tastes mattered more than mine.

Much to my surprise, my parents did the same thing. On Christmas morning, Ryan opened not just my Abercrombie box, but several others. We had resisted the call of the $70 pants, but ultimately we had given in. We had conformed, accepting Ryan's argument for "quality" and "clothes worth loving." And we all knew it. Mom, Dad and I glanced at Ryan as he stripped to try on each jersey, then stared guiltily back at each other.

"I can't believe it," Dad said.

"The little twit got what he wanted," I added. "And Abercrappie won. They got us."

Then and now, I continue to fight back. I explain to Ryan how he's been made a pawn, a cookie-cutter version of youth. I'm hoping that he'll learn to dress and live for himself, not his peers or his girlfriends. I'm hoping he'll rebel against Abercrombie and his peers.

If and when he does, we'll still have other battles to fight. Joshua, my thirteen-year-old brother, coiner of the term "Abercrappie," didn't get any of the company's clothing for Christmas. But when he opened the surf sweatshirt I got him, his first question was: "Where did you get it?" And as he watched Ryan open box after box from Abercrombie, Josh's eyes opened wide with yearning. Later, he dropped hints that maybe Abercrombie wasn't so bad.

Ultimately, I'm not surprised. When Hannibal Lecter[8] asked, "What do we covet?" he couldn't have been more right in answering, "We covet what we see."

My only wish is that suburban, teenaged style looked less like a dress code. I wish Abercrombie had stiffer competition; that kids would demand more from their merchants. But most of all, I wish Ryan, Nicole and so many other teenagers would act as smart and savvy as I know they are.

Until then, I'll buy them what they want—then try and convince them to hate it.

---

[8]***ESL Hannibal Lecter:*** Cannibalistic serial killer of Thomas Harris's novels *Red Dragon, The Silence of the Lambs,* and *Hannibal* and their film versions.

EMILY WHITE

High School's Secret Life

Calhoun High is located on the outskirts of Seattle, Washington. A school with a population consisting of mostly working-class white kids, it's located near the freeway. From the Calhoun parking lot, you can hear the traffic, constant as breathing. In 1999, Seattle is a booming new-rich economy, and Calhoun has recently erected a new school building: shiny and modern, with wheelchair ramps and automatic doors, a computer lab with state-of-the-art equipment. The building is so new it seems to have no ghosts. Walls are made of materials such that the moment graffiti is written, it can be washed away.

I spend a series of mornings loitering in the Calhoun cafeteria, observing the tribes of this particular high school. The smell of heat-lamp food, the overhead fluorescent lights, the lunch ladies in their hair nets—all of it brings up my own past in the Washington High cafeteria, where I looked around furtively, trying to find my two friends. Sitting on the sidelines now, I can still feel the adolescent loneliness in my guts.

The cafeteria is high school's proving ground. It's one of the most unavoidable and important thresholds, the place where you find out if you have friends or if you don't. The cafeteria is the place where forms of human sacrifice occur, the merciless rituals of cruelty on which the kids thrive.

Although Calhoun's new building was supposed to be big enough for all of the kids, it seems that more and more of them keep coming out of the woodwork. Because of overcrowding, lunch happens in three shifts: ten-thirty, eleven-fifteen, and noon. Kids who've drawn first lunch often don't seem very hungry—they're wiping the sleep from their eyes and panicking about forgotten homework. They drink coffee, hunched over like harried executives. All the special ed kids are assigned to first lunch. During second lunch, the pace picks up, but the luckiest kids have third lunch, the "fun" lunch.

Each group of kids moves in and out quickly, and in the brief interludes of emptiness, custodians move through with giant brooms. Every time they migrate, the kids leave items behind: backpacks, notebooks, jackets, eyeglasses.

If the cafeteria is the place where kids experience the most prolonged moments of relative freedom, it's also the place where they experience an unobstructed nearness. In these free moments, violence can erupt, and Calhoun has employed an armed cafeteria monitor, a nice guy in a golf shirt with a gun tucked discreetly into his belt.

As the school's ground zero, the cafeteria's tension derives from the way the kids are both in and out of school. It's a decentered environment, a place where they can make independent choices: sit where they want to sit, whisper to their friends whom they are separated from in class.

Cafeteria life at Calhoun is a game of chance: devastation comes when a kid draws the wrong lunch. One girl tells me about how she used to feel like she had friends, but then all her friends were assigned to third lunch and she was stuck in second by herself. The second-lunch destiny changed her idea of herself as a girl with friends. Now she sees her crowd only after school, and there are many stories she never hears, many plans she is left out of. She tries not to be bitter when she talks to me, but she's clearly troubled that there's no way to cross over into the third-lunch realm now, a realm as distant as the Emerald City.

This girl hovers somewhere on the edge of a tribe; she's not a complete outcast but she isn't popular either. She's arty and bohemian, she possesses a complex prettiness that boys will probably notice later. Although she is clearly in a bind, stuck without her friends, her loneliness is relatively manageable and escapable. Other kids operate on a deeper level of loneliness: an obese girl valiantly ignores the snickers of the boys across the aisle from her as she eats during first lunch; a boy at second lunch has some strange muscle condition that causes him to swat the air, as if he's surrounded by insects.

No matter whether it's first, second, or third lunch, the popular kids always cluster around the same geographical area of the cafeteria: in the front, near the windows. The popular kids sit so close together sometimes they can barely move, smashed into one or two long tables, often remaining on the benches out of sheer will and masterful balance. This is what it means to be part of a crowd: to always have people jammed next to you on the cafeteria bench.

At Calhoun, virtually all the popular kids are physically well proportioned; one girl I interview will later describe them as "the kind of kids who get their way because they have perfect hair, perfect teeth, et cetera." Their conformity is remarkable: in haircuts, necklaces, the way they slouch, the way they use their voices. They all imitate one another because the imitation speaks of their power. In this context, conformity is not a cop-out but a way of broadcasting the fact that you aren't a weirdo, that you are speaking in the signs of the chosen ones.

The popular kids at Calhoun dress overwhelmingly in the ubiquitous trendy brand Abercrombie & Fitch. They sport the logo on T-shirts, pants, bags, baseball hats. Calhoun is a school that emphasizes athletics, and Abercrombie & Fitch is a clothing line advertised by soccer-playing boys with perfect tanned bodies and sleek girl models with Grace Kelly class. The mystique of the brand is very East Coast, Kennedy clan, Martha's Vineyard, prep school. In other words, it has nothing to do with the working-class history of Calhoun, where most kids end up going to a local college and never grow up to drink Bloody Marys on Sundays in the Hamptons.

Between the extremes of the popular kids and the loners, there's a vast middle region. The tribes within this region are numerous. A group of overgrown Girl Scouts called the "natural helpers" are neither popular nor outcast; they are girls who are always busy doing charity work, committing an extreme number of good deeds. There are theater kids, who sit near the back of the cavernous space, immersed in the news of the next play, good at acting confident, always an edge of an act about them, always making entrances and exits. There are the computer geniuses, at Calhoun all of them unwashed, disheveled boys; they never seem to look in mirrors or out the window at the natural world. The screens of their computers take their eyes away from everything. A boy carefully pops open his laptop as he devours the cafeteria's fluorescent orange nachos, careful not to drip on his keyboard.

One of the most notable groups in the Calhoun cafeteria appears during third lunch: a gang of boys, huge but not athletic, class clowns, druggies, and rock and rollers. They possess a screaming, ballistic life drive and although they seem to differ in matters of style, their formidable restlessness—their energy of trouble—holds them together. From the moment they enter the cafeteria, the man with the gun hovers around them. Even when I am sitting on the opposite end of the room, I can hear them going wild. Even in my position as an invisible extra to the drama, trying to disappear into the background, I am a little afraid of them, of where their energy might settle, of what might happen if it settles in the wrong place.

This particular week has been designated Multicultural Week. It's a time when kids are encouraged to look up from their lunches and recognize the larger world. Posters advertise, *Celebrate Diversity!* The multiculturalism club is putting on an around-the-world potluck. One day a lone, red-faced girl dances a Scottish jig in the cafeteria, celebrating her heritage, jumping around diligently to a scratchy tape of bagpipes. The spectacle of the girl displaying herself before everyone silences the tribes and lowers the volume of each conversation. For a moment, as she begins her strange dance, there's only a flabbergasted stillness.

Some days messengers travel from tribe to tribe, proving that webs can be formed even if they are fragile and fleeting. One day I watch the natural helpers moving from table to table, collecting money for the "penny wars." The idea is that if everyone contributes a penny, all the pennies will be given to the local homeless shelter. In the name of the penny wars, these girls reach out to the other kids in the cafeteria with a slightly condescending smile; with their jars held out, they cross the boundaries of the tribes. It is interesting to watch the rush of this moment, when boundaries are crossed and the lonely kids are being addressed, even if it's only a plea for pennies. The computer geeks look up at the natural helpers as if they are angels. The rowdy boys, the fat girl, the boy swatting the air, the arty girls, the pale orchestra kids, the boy with a T-shirt that says *Porn Star*—they all are amazed that these natural helpers suddenly stand in front of them. "Give a penny for the penny wars!" the helpers say, beaming like saints.

LUCY GREALY
Masks

Having missed most of fourth grade and all but a week or so of fifth grade, I finally started to reappear at school sometime in sixth grade during my periodic "vacations" from chemotherapy. I'd mysteriously show up for a week or two weeks or sometimes even three or four, then disappear again for a couple of months.

Most of the sixth-grade class consisted of children I'd grown up with. They were, for the most part, genuinely curious about what had happened to me. They treated me respectfully, if somewhat distantly, though there was a clique of boys who always called me names: "Hey, girl, take off that monster mask — oops, she's not wearing a mask!" This was the height of hilarity in sixth grade, and the boys, for they were always and only boys, practically fell to the ground, besotted with their own wit. Much to their bewilderment and to the shock of my teachers, I retorted by calling out to them, "You stupid dildos."

Derek used to say that word all the time, and I thought it a wonderful insult, though I didn't have a clue as to what a dildo was. After being reprimanded enough times for wielding this powerful insult, I finally asked my brother what it meant: an artificial penis, he informed me. I gave up using the word. I'd known children in the hospital with artificial limbs, and I'd known children with urinary tract problems.

The school year progressed slowly. I felt as if I had been in the sixth grade for years, yet it was only October. Halloween was approaching. Coming from Ireland, we had never thought of it as a big holiday, though Sarah and I usually went out trick-or-treating. For the last couple of years I had been too sick to go out, but this year Halloween fell on a day when I felt quite fine. My mother was the one who came up with the Eskimo idea. I put on a winter coat, made a fish out of paper, which I hung on the end of a stick, and wrapped my face up in a scarf. My hair was growing, and I loved the way the top of the hood rubbed against it. By this time my hat had become part of me; I took it off only at home. Sometimes kids would make fun of me, run past me, knock my hat off, and call me Baldy. I hated this, but I assumed that one day my hair would grow in, and on that day the teasing would end.

We walked around the neighborhood with our pillowcase sacks, running into the other groups of kids and comparing notes: the house three doors down gave whole candy bars, while the house next to that gave only cheap mints. I felt wonderful. It was only as the night wore on and the moon came out and the older kids, the big kids, went on their rounds that I began to realize why I felt so good. No one could see me clearly. No one could see my face.

For the end of October it was a very warm night and I was sweating in my parka, but I didn't care. I felt such freedom: I waltzed up to people effortlessly and boldly, I asked questions and made comments the rest of my troupe were afraid to make. I didn't understand their fear. I hadn't realized just how meek I'd become, how self-conscious I was about my face until now that it was obscured. My sister and her friends never had to worry about their appearance, or so it seemed to me, so why didn't they always feel as bold and as happy as I felt that night?

Our sacks filled up, and eventually it was time to go home. We gleefully poured out our candy on the floor and traded off: because chewing had become difficult, I gave Sarah everything that was too hard for me, while she unselfishly gave me everything soft. I took off my Eskimo parka and went down to my room without my hat. Normally I didn't feel that I had to wear my hat around my family, and I never wore it when I was alone in my room. Yet once I was alone with all my candy, still hot from running around on that unseasonably warm night, I felt compelled to put my hat back on. I didn't know what was wrong. I ate sugar until I was ready to burst, trying hard to ignore everything except what was directly in front of me, what I could touch and taste, the chocolate melting brown beneath my fingernails, the candy so sweet it made my throat hurt.

The following spring, on one of the first warm days, I was playing with an old friend, Teresa, in her neat and ordered back yard when she asked, completely out of the blue, if I was dying. She looked at me casually, as if she'd just asked what I was doing later that day. "The other kids say that you're slowly dying, that you're 'wasting away.' " I looked at her in shock. Dying? Why on earth would anyone think I was dying? "No," I replied, in the tone of voice I'd have used if she'd asked me whether I was the pope, "I'm not dying."

When I got home I planned to ask my mother why Teresa would say such a thing. But just as I was coming through the front door, she was entering from the garage, her arms laden with shopping bags. She took a bright red shirt out of a bag and held it up against my chest. It smelled new and a price tag scratched my neck.

"Turtlenecks are very hard to find in short sleeves, so I bought you several."

I was still a tomboy at heart and cared little about what I wore, just so long as it wasn't a dress. But turtlenecks—why on earth would I want to wear turtlenecks in the spring? I didn't ask this out loud, but my mother must have known what I was thinking. She looked me straight in the eye: "If you wear something that comes up around your neck, it makes the scar less visible."

Genuinely bewildered, I took the bright-colored pile of shirts down to my room. Wouldn't I look even more stupid wearing a turtleneck in the summer? Would they really hide my "scar"? I hadn't taken a good long, objective look at myself since the wig fitting, but that seemed so long ago, almost two years. I remembered feeling upset by it, but I conveniently didn't remember what I'd seen in that mirror, and I hadn't allowed myself a close scrutiny since.

I donned my short-sleeved turtlenecks and finished out the few short months of elementary school. I played with my friend Jan at her wonderful home with its several acres of meadow and, most magnificent of all, a small lake. There was a rowboat we weren't allowed to take out by ourselves, but we did anyway. Rowing it to the far shore, a mere eighth of a mile away, we'd "land" and pretend we'd just discovered a new country. With notebooks in hand, we logged our discoveries, overturning stones and giving false Latin names to the newts and various pieces of slime we found under them.

Jan had as complex a relationship to her stuffed and plastic animals as I had to mine, and when I slept over we'd compare our intricate worlds. Sometimes, though not too frequently, Jan wanted to talk about boys, and I'd sit on my sleeping bag with my knees tucked up under my nightgown, listening patiently. I never had much to offer, though I had just developed my very first crush. It was on Omar Sharif.

Late one night I'd stayed up and watched *Dr. Zhivago* on television with my father. Curled up beside him, with my head against his big stomach, I listened to my father's heart, his breathing, and attentively watched the images of a remote world, a world as beautiful as it was deadly and cold. I thought I would have managed very well there, imagined that I would have remained true to my passions had I lived through the Russian Revolution. I, too, would have trudged across all that tundra, letting the ice sheet over me and crackle on my eyebrows. For weeks I pictured the ruined estate where Zhivago wrote his sonnets, aware that the true splendor of the house was inextricably bound to the fact that it was ruined. I didn't understand why this should be so, and I didn't understand why imagining this scene gave me such a deep sense of fulfillment, nor why this fulfillment was mingled with such a sad sense of longing, nor why this longing only added to the beauty of everything else.

Elementary-school graduation day approached. I remembered being in second grade and looking out on a group of sixth-graders preparing for graduation. It had seemed like an unimaginable length of time before I'd get there. But now I was out there mingling in the courtyard, remembering the day when I laid my head down on the desk and announced to the teacher, "I'll never make it." I could even see the classroom window I had gazed out of. So much had happened in four years. I felt so old, and I felt proud of being so old. During the ceremony I was shocked when the vice-principal started speaking about *me*, about how I should receive special attention for my "bravery." I could feel the heat rising in me as he spoke, my face turning red. Here I was, the center of attention, receiving the praise and appreciation I'd been fantasizing about for so many years, and all I could feel was intense, searing embarrassment. I was called up onto the platform. I know everyone was applauding, but I felt it more than heard it. In a daze I accepted the gift Mr. Schultz was presenting me with, a copy of *The Prophet*. I could barely thank him.

Later, alone in my room, I opened the book at random. The verse I read was about love, about how to accept the love of another with dignity. I shut the book after only a page. I wanted nothing to do with the world of love; I thought wanting love was a weakness to be overcome. And besides, I thought to myself, the world of love wanted nothing to do with me.

The summer passed, and junior high school loomed. Jan, Teresa, and Sarah were all very excited at the prospect of being "grown-ups," of attending different classes, of having their own locker. Their excitement was contagious, and the night before the first day of school, I proudly marked my assorted notebooks for my different subjects and secretly scuffed my new shoes to make them look old.

Everyone must have been nervous, but I was sure I was the only one who felt true apprehension. I found myself sidling through the halls I'd been looking forward to, trying to pretend that I didn't notice the other kids, almost all of them strangers from adjoining towns, staring at me. Having seen plenty of teen movies with their promise of intrigue and drama, I had been looking forward to going to the lunchroom. As it happened, I sat down next to a table full of boys.

They pointed openly and laughed, calling out loudly enough for me to hear, "*What* on earth is *that?*" "*That* is the ugliest girl I have *ever* seen." I knew in my heart that their comments had nothing to do with me, that it was all about them appearing tough and cool to their friends. But these boys were older than the ones in grade school, and for the very first time I realized they were passing judgment on my suitability, or lack of it, as a girlfriend. "I bet David wants to go kiss her, don't you, David?" "Yeah, right, then I'll go kiss your mother's asshole." "How'll you know which is which?"

My initial tactic was to pretend I didn't hear them, but this only seemed to spur them on. In the hallways, where I suffered similar attacks of teasing from random attackers, I simply looked down at the floor and walked more quickly, but in the lunchroom I was a sitting duck. The same group took to seeking me out and purposely sitting near me day after day, even when I tried to camouflage myself by sitting in the middle of a group. They grew bolder, and I could hear them plotting to send someone to sit across the table from me. I'd look up from my food and there would be a boy slouching awkwardly in a red plastic chair, innocently asking me my name. Then he'd ask me how I got to be so ugly. At this the group would burst into laughter, and my inquisitor would saunter back, victorious.

After two weeks I broke down and went to my guidance counselor to complain. I thought he would offer to reprimand them, but instead he asked if I'd like to come and eat in the privacy of his office. Surprised, I said yes, and that's what I did for the rest of the year whenever I was attending school. Every day I'd wait for him, the other guidance counselors, and the secretaries to go on their own lunch break. Then I'd walk through the empty outer office and sit down in his private office, closing the door behind me. As I ate the food in my brown paper bag, which crinkled loudly in the silence, I'd look at the drawings his own young children had made. They were taped to the wall near his desk, simplistic drawings in which the sky was a blue line near the top and the grass a green line near the bottom and people were as big as houses. I felt safe and secure in that office, but I also felt lonely, and for the very first time I definitively identified the source of my unhappiness as being ugly. A few weeks later I left school to reenter chemotherapy, and for the very first time I was almost glad to go back to it.

My inner life became ever more macabre. Vietnam was still within recent memory, and pictures of the horrors of Cambodia loomed on every TV screen and in every newspaper. I told myself again and again how good I had it in comparison, what a wonder it was to have food and clothes and a home and no one torturing me. I told myself what fools those boys at school were, what stupid, unaware lives they led. How could they assume their own lives were so important? Didn't they know they could lose everything at any moment, that you couldn't take anything good or worthwhile for granted, because pain and cruelty could and would arrive sooner or later? I bombed and starved and persecuted my own suffering right out of existence.

I had the capacity of imagination to momentarily escape my own pain, and I had the elegance of imagination to teach myself something true regarding the world around me, but I didn't yet have the clarity of imagination to grant myself the complicated and necessary right to suffer. I treated despair in terms of hierarchy: If there was a more important pain in the world, it meant my own was negated. I thought I simply had to accept the fact that I was ugly, and that to feel despair about it was simply wrong.

Halloween came round again, and even though I was feeling a bit woozy from an injection I'd had a few days before, I begged my mother to let me go out. I put on a plastic witch mask and went out with Teresa. I walked down the streets suddenly bold and free: No one could see my face. I peered through the oval eye slits and did not see one person staring back at me, ready to make fun of my face. I breathed in the condensing, plastic-tainted air behind the mask and thought that I was breathing in normalcy, that this freedom and ease were what the world consisted of, that other people felt it all the time. How could they not? How could they not feel the joy of walking down the street without the threat of being made fun of? Assuming this was how other people felt all the time, I again named my own face as the thing that kept me apart, as the tangible element of what was wrong with my life and with me.

At home, when I took the mask off, I felt both sad and relieved. Sad because I had felt like a pauper walking for a few brief hours in the clothes of a prince and because I had liked it so much. Relieved because I felt no connection with that kind of happiness: I didn't deserve it and thus I shouldn't want it. It was easier to slip back into my depression and blame my face for everything. . . .

I viewed other people both critically and sympathetically. Why couldn't they just stop complaining so much, just let go and see how good they actually had it? Everyone seemed to be waiting for something to happen that would allow them to move forward, waiting for some shadowy future moment to begin their lives in earnest. Everybody, from my mother to the characters I read about in books (who were as actual and important as real people to me), was always looking at someone else's life and envying it, wishing to occupy it. I wanted them to stop, to see how much they had already, how they had their health and their strength. I imagined how my life would be if I had half their fortune. Then I would catch myself, guilty of exactly the thing I was accusing others of. As clear-headed as I was, sometimes I felt that the only reason for this clarity was to see how hypocritically I lived my own life.

Once, during a week of intensive chemotherapy toward the end of the two and a half years, I was sent to another ward, as 10 was already full when I checked in. My roommate was a girl who'd been run over by an iceboat; the blades had cut her intestines in two, and she'd had to have them sewn back together. She got a lot of attention, lots of calls from concerned relatives and school friends, and I was both a little jealous of her and a little contemptuous because she was taking her accident a bit too seriously for my taste. After all, she'd lived, hadn't she? She'd had one operation and they might do another one the next week, but after that it would be all over, so what was the big fuss about?

MICHELLE LEE
The Fashion Victim's Ten Commandments

We Fashion Victims hold certain truths to be self-evident. Without so much as a raised eyebrow, we allow a set of ridiculous, yet compelling, rules to govern our wardrobes, our purchases, our desires, even our own sense of self-worth. It's these unquestioned tenets that have helped bring us to the sorry state we find ourselves in today.

1. Thou Shalt Pay More to Appear Poor

It takes a great deal of time and money to look as though you put no effort into dressing. Since a garment today rarely remains a popular item in our wardrobes beyond a few months, we require it to be worn out before we buy it. Fabrics are prewashed and grayed out to appear less new. Designers sew on decorative patches, slash gaping holes into the knees of jeans, and fray the hems. Dresses and shirts are prewrinkled. Jeans are stonewashed, sandblasted, acid-washed, and lightened, they're iron-creased and bleached to "whisker" at the upper-thigh as if they were passed down to you by your mother, who inherited them from her father, who had worn them in the wheat fields a century ago. Designers add "character" to clothes by messing them up, like Helmut Lang's famous $270 paint-spattered jeans. Jeans, blasted and stained dust-brown, by CK, Levi's, and Dolce & Gabbana, cost up to $200. In fact, Calvin Klein's "dirty" jeans sold for $20 more than a pair of his basic, unblemished ones. In 2001, Commes des Garçons produced a peasant dress, priced at a very unpeasantlike $495, described by discount shopping website Bluefly.com as "given a chic tattered look."

Fashion may be bent on newness, but we apparently can't stand it when something looks *too* new (who can bear the blinding whiteness of new sneakers?). The industry has taken to calling the shabby, imperfect look "distressed"—a word that carries a connotation of pain and suffering. This fashion agony doesn't come cheap, from Jean-Paul Gaultier's distressed leather pants for $1,560 and two-piece distressed leather jacket and bustier for $2,740 to Versace's distressed ball gowns and midpriced shoe maker Aldo's distressed leather pumps for $70.

2. Thou Shalt Covet Useless Utility

To the Fashion Victim, there's nothing wrong with clothes that serve no purpose other than looking cool. But if a garment can create the illusion that it's functional as well, it's all the better. A part of us knows that fashion is frivolous, so we attempt to justify our participation in it by making our clothes seem useful. We're grasping at straws to rationalize making some of our unnecessary purchases. Shirts come with hoods whose sole purpose is to hang behind one's neck. The polar fleece vest was pitched as functional in a climbing-the-Alps sort of way, but if you really wanted something to keep you warm, wouldn't you give it sleeves? Cargo pants, with their multitude of pockets, seemed infinitely useful . . . imagine all the odds and ends you could carry. Countless designers, including Calvin Klein, Gucci, and Versace, interpreted the military style for the runway, and mall retailers followed suit with their versions, like Abercrombie's Paratroops and American Eagle's Cargo Trek Pant. Ralph Lauren even produced an army-green cargo bikini with pockets at the hip (for toting beach grenades?). The fashion world's idealized image of the utilitarian future appears to involve lots of zippers, buckles, Velcro, pull closures, straps, and strings — no matter if they actually serve a purpose or not.

3. THOU SHALT OWN MINUTELY DIFFERING VARIATIONS OF THE SAME THING

Fashion Victims own duplicates of items that are just different enough to not be *exactly* the same. The average American owns seven pairs of blue jeans. Certainly, each pair could be cut and colored differently, but are those seven pairs really that different? Rosa, a twenty-six-year-old office manager in Chicago, owns more than fifteen pairs of navy-blue jeans that she's amassed over the last two years, picking up one or two pairs a month. "Some are regular-waisted, some are boot-cut, others are tapered, one has red stitching on the sides and on the pockets, some are button-fly, some are a bit darker," she explains. "Even though they all look the same, they each have their special style." All that variety means she doesn't wear each pair very often. "I have a few clothes that I have in my closet that I've only worn once or twice," she says. "But it's hard to part with them because I always feel like, 'Maybe I'll wear it *one* more time.'" Fashion Victims all share in this mind-set, and as a result, we could have two walk-in closets stuffed to the gills and still never feel like we have enough. So we continue to buy.

4. THOU SHALT BELIEVE SUBMISSIVELY IN THE FASHION LABEL'S REACH

Today when you buy a designer's clothes, you're also buying a lifestyle. Ralph Lauren (a.k.a. Ralph Lifschitz from the Bronx) knew this when he created Polo, a brand meant to evoke the image of the affluent, holiday-in-Hyannisport set. As a result, our favorite clothing brands can sell us practically anything else—hand cream, lipstick, perfume, nail polish, dishes, pillows, candles, duvets, music. You can not only wear Ralph Lauren, Calvin Klein, Banana Republic, Eddie Bauer, Donna Karan, Liz Claiborne, Nautica, and Versace, but you can dress your bedroom in them, too. Love how Club Monaco clothes look? Buy the retailer's line of cosmetics. Hooked on Victoria's Secret bras? Well, they must have good skin-care products if they make good bras, right? Like Armani suits? Buy their line of gourmet chocolates. Just as automakers like Jaguar, Vespa, and Harley-Davidson have their own branded clothing lines, retailers and designers have left their mark on the automotive world with special-edition cars like the Eddie Bauer Ford Explorer and Expedition, the Coach-edition Lexus, the Subaru Outback LL Bean edition, the Joseph Abboud Special Edition Buick Regal, and the Louis Vuitton edition of Chrysler's PT Cruiser.

5. THOU SHALT REQUIRE VALIDATION OF THINE OWN STYLISHNESS

The art of dress is quite frequently built on the opinions of others. We may like to think that how we dress is an extension of how we see ourselves, but more commonly, it's an expression of how we want *others* to see us. "We dress to communicate our social identities to others," says Kim Johnson, PhD, a professor at the University of Minnesota who teaches courses on the social psychology of clothing. "Dress informs others of how willing you are to participate in fashion and at what levels you're playing." In our appearance-centered society, one of the most common ways we butter up strangers and acquaintances is to compliment them on their clothes. We shower people with praise for their sense of style and expect to receive praise in return, like the sometimes sincere "You look great," which never fails to elicit the awkward yet gushing "You do *too.*"

6. THOU SHALT DRESS VICARIOUSLY THROUGH THY CHILDREN AND PETS

It's not enough for Fashion Victims to dress themselves in designer clothes; they often feel it necessary to share their impeccable taste with others. Someone once told me, "You give what you want to receive." People choose items for others that reflect their own taste, rather than the recipient's. We Fashion Victims live by this. We dress our kids (and others' children when we buy gifts) in mini-me lines like Moschino kids, GapKids, babyGap, Old Navy Kids,

Diesel Kids, Ralph Lauren kids, Prada kids, and Guess? Kids. Small sizes don't mean small prices. A baby leather jacket costs $200 at Polo. A jean jacket from Diesel Kids costs $109—more than a grown-up size at many stores. Then there's the $125 tulle dress for girls by Christian Dior, the $175 sweater by Missoni Kids, the pink knit pant set by Baby Dior, $93 trousers by Young Versace, and $68 bootleg jeans by Diesel. Before Dolce & Gabbana's kiddy line, D&G Junior, ran into some trouble in 2000 when its licensee Nilva went belly up, it carried several categories of clothing like "Denim Rock Star," "Lord Rapper," and "Logomania." There were gold denim jackets, tiny shearling coats, and a red leather racing-team jacket for $599. With most kids' clothes, there's not even the possibility of an outfit becoming a long-lasting part of a wardrobe because they outgrow things so quickly, so laying out exorbitant amounts of cash is truly like throwing money into a bottomless pit.

7. THOU SHALT FEIGN ATHLETICISM

Most of our lives are wholly un-rugged, so we attempt to reinsert that missing ruggedness through our wardrobes. Labels like the North Face and Patagonia, which create functional garb for the mountaineering über-athlete, have become fashionable brands to traipse around town in. Timberland boots are as ideal for digging through CDs at the Virgin Megastore as they are for hiking through backwoods Montana. Columbia Sportswear recently produced a parka that detects when the wearer's skin temperature has dropped and releases stored body heat, which will no doubt become a must-have item for those climbing the Himalayas—or picking up an iced latte at Starbucks *(brrrr)*.

Those of us who aren't triathletes or marathoners still enjoy examining the sole of a sneaker and seeing very scientific-looking springs, air pockets, gel, and pumps. Employees at the Nike Sport Research Laboratory hold PhD's or master's degrees in human biomechanics and bioengineering. In March 2002, Adidas introduced ClimaCool sneakers, designed to keep feet cool with a "360-degree ventilation system." Athletic shoe makers spend millions of dollars on research to develop supersneakers that add more bounce, absorb shock, improve traction, and cushion arches. And when the Fashion Victim buys these supersneakers, he is delighted over his purchase and can't wait to wear them when he meets his buddies for a drink, no doubt at the local sports bar.

8. THOU SHALT BE A WALKING BILLBOARD

In a way, wearing a logo is like wearing gang colors. Just as the Bloods and Crips brandish red and blue bandannas, the Fashion Victim wears the designer logo as a proud badge of membership. It's an act that's tribal at its core.

"It's like schoolchildren all nagging for the coolest trainers [sneakers, for you non-Anglophiles]," says Vella. "If you're seen to be wearing the right thing, you're in."

A brand name can add immediate "worth" to two identical products. "Branding is unfortunately the cornerstone of many fashion labels today—not the design, the innovation, the cut, or any other skill honed by the designer. And what the brand stands for is everything," says Debi Hall, fashion-branding strategist for JY&A Consulting in London. "As the Japanese say, name is the first thing—without a name, a garment in today's highly capitalistic, value-added culture is worth very little. Take the vintage phenomenon: Even if a secondhand YSL dress is without a label, because it once had a name, it is still worth something. If, however, it is simply a secondhand dress with a name nobody has heard of, then it will go for pennies."

Still, not every Fashion Victim is so taken with the visible logo. Some fashion-conscious folk have been known to consider a visible label such a deal-breaker that they'll take the time to remove it. A few years back, hipsters in London started a trend by tearing the *N* off their New Balance sneakers. And according to *New York* magazine, the late Carolyn Bessette Kennedy once had employees cut the labels out of skiwear she had bought. Emily Cinader Woods, cofounder and chairman of J. Crew, says that unlike her friend Michael Jeffries—CEO of Abercrombie & Fitch, a company notorious for slapping its name conspicuously on everything—she's always been adamant about no logos. "There are so many brands that you might love an item or the color but the logo keeps you from buying it," she says. On the other hand, when you're around people who are familiar with various brands—as is typical for the Fashion Victim—it's possible to be a walking billboard without ever displaying the brand name on your body. I once wore a sleeveless J. Crew top to the office, and two co-workers that day remarked in passing, "I like that—J. Crew?" The brand's familiar look and prevalence in their mail-order catalogs had made the clothes recognizable enough that they didn't need an obvious swoosh, polo player, or little green alligator sewn across the chest. I had been a moving J. Crew billboard all day without the presence of any visible logos.

9. THOU SHALT CARE ABOUT PARIS HILTON'S GAULTIER MICRO-MINI

The socialite's role in the fashion game is to look stunning at events in couture gowns, and casually upper class when attending a summer soiree in the Hamptons. A gossipworthy socialite should be trailed by at least one rumor of out-of-control partying, like making out with someone other than her date or accidentally letting her Galliano gown slip down and flashing her fellow partygoers. Her job is to *be* the answer to the question: "Who actually wears those clothes?" These are the women who can afford the Fendi furs and Gucci pantsuits, but like celebrities, they are also the frequent recipients of loans and freebies from designers—residing below the A-List celebrity, but above B-List TV actresses and pop stars in the fashion hierarchy. In magazines, they seem somehow superhuman. Mostly whippet-thin (perfect for fitting into the sample size), the pretty and privileged attend trunk shows, where they're wined, dined, and shown exquisite new designs. Their job description also includes sitting front row at catwalk shows. Of course, these women are expected to do something in return: They are obliged to wear (and showcase) the designer's clothes.

The fashion system is built on want. Looking at socialites' clothes in *Vogue* is like drooling over the estates in *Architectural Digest* or flipping through the *DuPont Registry* to catch a glimpse of the Bentleys and Aston Martins you'll never be able to afford. We live vicariously through the socialite—who has deep enough pockets to buy designer threads of a caliber most of us will never even see in person. Perplexing as our interest may be, the Fashion Victim eats up every morsel, but not without a tinge of jealousy, of course. "I *love* looking at those rich bitches," says Rita, a 49–year-old website editor in Stamford, Connecticut. "But what kills me is that a lot of them don't really have great taste—they just have great resources. If they had to put together a wardrobe like the rest of us mere mortals—from the Gap, Banana Republic, etc. —I doubt they'd be so fabulous. But you do get good fashion ideas from looking and it's nice to daydream."

10. THOU SHALT WANT WITHOUT SEEING

Curiously, selling clothes today does not always require actually *showing* the clothes. "Sex sells, sells, and keeps selling," says Marc Berger, fashion director of *GQ.* "A sexy woman in an ad will always grab the attention of a man. It's a great marketing ploy." The no-show advertising technique is frequently justified with "We're selling an image." Ads are another example of fashion's hypnotic power over us. All a company needs to do is get our attention—whether or not we love the clothes is insignificant. In recent years, Abercrombie & Fitch's controversial magalog, the *A&F Quarterly,* has raised eyebrows with its photos of tanned all-American dudes and dudettes, often with zero body fat and zero clothing—a buff naked guy holding a film reel in front of his privates, a couple wearing nothing but body paint, a group of disrobed guys flashing their smiles (and nearly everything else) by the pool. The image: cool, horny coeds. In 1999, a Sisley campaign shot by Terry Richardson simply showed the faces of two female models in a half-sexy, half-goofy liplock. Two years later, an ad for the retailer featured a self-portrait of the moustached Richardson wearing a snake around his neck and nothing else. The image: sexy,

ELLEN FEIN AND SHERRIE SCHNEIDER
Don't Talk to a Man First

Never? Not even "Let's have coffee" or "Do you come here often?" Right, not even these seemingly harmless openers. Otherwise, how will you know if he spotted you first, was smitten by you and had to have you, or is just being polite?

We know what you're thinking. We know how extreme such a rule must sound, not to mention snobbish, silly, and painful; but taken in the context of *The Rules,* it makes perfect sense. After all, the premise of *The Rules* is that we never make anything happen, that we trust in the natural order of things— namely, that man pursues woman.

By talking to a man first, we interfere with whatever was supposed to happen or not happen, perhaps causing a conversation or a date to occur that was never meant to be and inevitably getting hurt in the process. Eventually, he'll talk to the girl he really wants and drop you.

Yet, we manage to rationalize this behavior by telling ourselves, "He's shy" or "I'm just being friendly." Are men really shy? We might as well tackle this question right now. Perhaps a therapist would say so, but we believe that most men are not shy, just not *really, really* interested if they don't approach you. It's hard to accept that, we know. It's also hard waiting for the right one—the one who talks to you first, calls, and basically does most of the work in the beginning of the relationship because he must have you.

It's easy to rationalize women's aggressive behavior in this day and age. Unlike years ago when women met men at dances and "coming out" parties and simply waited for one to pick them out of the crowd and start a conversation, today many women are accountants, doctors, lawyers, dentists, and in management positions. They work with men, for men, and men work for them. Men are their patients and their clients. How can a woman not talk to a man first?

The Rules answer is to treat men you are interested in like any other client or patient or coworker, as hard as that may be. Let's face it, when a woman meets a man she really likes, a lightbulb goes on in her head and she sometimes, without realizing it, relaxes, laughs, and spends more time with him than is necessary. She may suggest lunch to discuss something that could be discussed over the phone because she is hoping to ignite some romance. This is a common ploy. Some of the smartest women try to make things happen under the guise of business. They think they are too educated or talented to be passive, play games, or do *The Rules.* They feel their diplomas and paychecks entitle them to do more in life than wait for the phone to ring. These women, we assure you, always end up heartbroken when their forwardness is rebuffed. But why shouldn't it be? Men know what they want. No one has to ask *them* to lunch.

So, the short of it is that if you meet men professionally, you still have to do *The Rules.* You must wait until he brings up lunch or anything else beyond business. As we explain in *Rule #17,* the man must take the lead. Even if you are making the same amount of money as a man you are interested in, he must bring up lunch. If you refuse to accept that men and women are different romantically, even though they may be equal professionally, you will behave like men—talk to them first, ask for their phone number, invite them to discuss the case over dinner at your place—and drive them away. Such forwardness is very risky; sometimes we have seen it work, most of the time it doesn't and it *always* puts the woman through hell emotionally. By not accepting the concept that the man must pursue the woman, women put themselves in jeopardy of being rejected or ignored, if not at the moment, then at some point in the future. We hope you never have to endure the following torture:

Our dentist friend Pam initiated a friendship with Robert when they met in dental school several years ago by asking him out to lunch. *She spoke to him first.* Although they later became lovers and even lived together, he never seemed really "in love" with her and her insecurity about the relationship never went away. Why would it? *She spoke to him first.* He recently broke up with her over something trivial. The truth is he never loved her. Had Pam followed *The Rules,* she would never have spoken to Robert or initiated anything in the first place. Had she followed *The Rules,* she might have met someone else who truly wanted her. She would not have wasted time. *Rules* girls don't waste time.

Here's another example of a smart woman who broke *The Rules:* Claudia, a confident Wall Street broker, spotted her future husband on the dance floor of a popular disco and planted herself next to him for a good five minutes. When he failed to make the first move, she told herself that he was probably shy or had two left feet and asked him to dance. The relationship has been filled with problems. She often complains that he's as "shy" in the bedroom as he was that night on the dance floor.

A word about dances. It's become quite popular these days for women to ask men to dance. Lest there is any doubt in your mind, this behavior is totally against *The Rules.* If a man doesn't bother to walk across the room to seek you out and ask you to dance, then he's obviously not interested and asking him to dance won't change his feelings or rather his lack of feelings for you. He'll probably be flattered that you asked and dance with you just to be polite and he might even want to have sex with you that night, but he won't be crazy about you. Either he didn't notice you or you made it too easy. He never got the chance to pursue you and this fact will always permeate the relationship even if he does ask you out.

We know what you're thinking: What am I supposed to do all night if no one asks me to dance? Unfortunately, the answer is to go to the bathroom five times if you have to, reapply your lipstick, powder your nose, order more water from the bar, think happy thoughts, walk around the room in circles until someone notices you, make phone calls from the lobby to your married friends for encouragement—in short, anything but ask a man to dance. Dances are not necessarily fun for us. They may be fun for other women who just want to go out and have a good time. But you're looking for love and marriage so you can't always do what you feel like. You have to do *The Rules*. That means that even when you're bored or lonely, you don't ask men to dance. Don't even stand next to someone you like, hoping he'll ask you, as many women do. You have to *wait* for someone to notice you. You might have to go home without having met anyone you liked or even danced one dance. But tell yourself that at least you got to practice *The Rules* and there's always another dance. You walk out with a sense of accomplishment that at least you didn't break *The Rules!*

If this sounds boring, remember the alternative is worse. Our good friend Sally got so resentful of having to dance with all the "losers" at a particular party that she finally decided to defy *The Rules* she knew only too well and asked the best-looking man in the room to dance. Not only was he flattered, but they danced for hours and he asked her out for the next three nights. "Maybe there are exceptions to *The Rules*," she thought triumphantly. She found out otherwise, of course. It seems Mr. Right was in town for just a few days on business and had a girlfriend on the West Coast. No wonder he hadn't asked anyone to dance that night. He probably just went to the party to have fun, not to find his future wife. The moral of the story: Don't figure out why someone hasn't asked you to dance—there's always a good reason.

Unfortunately, more women than men go to dances to meet "The One." Their eagerness and anxiety get the best of them and they end up talking to men first or asking them to dance. So you must condition yourself not to expect anything from a dance. View it simply as an excuse to put on high heels, apply a new shade of blush, and be around a lot of people. Chances are someone of the opposite sex will start to talk to *you* at some point in the evening. If and when he does, and you're not having such a great time, don't show it. For example, don't be clever or cynical and say, "I would have been better off staying home and watching *Seinfeld*." Men aren't interested in women who are witty in a negative way. If someone asks if you're having a good time, simply say yes and smile.

If you find all of this much too hard to do, then don't go to the dance. Stay home, do sit-ups, watch *Seinfeld,* and reread *The Rules*. It's better to stay home and read *The Rules* than go out and break them.

SAMANTHA DANIELS
20 Simple Tips for the Perfect Date

1. It's okay to suggest a drink instead of dinner for a first date. She dreads a boring four-course ordeal, too.
2. Call her by early evening on Monday to confirm a Tuesday get-together. (Weekends aren't for first dates.)
3. Leave your home and work numbers. No home number and she'll assume you have a wife or girlfriend.
4. If you want to keep the plans a surprise, at least clue her in as to what to wear. You do not want an overdressed, overstressed woman navigating the Talladega pits in high heels.
5. Yes, she'll notice if the date location you've chosen is conveniently around the block from your place.
6. Don't assume that just because you're out with a beautiful woman, she knows how pretty she looks—she wants to hear it from you.
7. Ask if she's too cold or too warm, and if changing the temperature is in your power, fix it.
8. Men judge women according to whether they can picture having sex with them; women judge men by whether they can imagine kissing them. White teeth, fresh breath, and unchapped lips make her more apt to pucker up.
9. Do not ask her, "So, what kind of music do you like?" The last 25 guys asked that. Be original.
10. She loves when you insist on ordering dessert. Sharing = extra sexy.
11. Tip well: Grab the check, mentally divide the bill by 10, double that number, and throw down the tip. Do it quickly but casually. Believe me, she'll be watching.
12. If she touches your arm, she's interested; if she touches your leg, she's interested tonight.
13. When in doubt, hold her hand.
14. Very small protective gestures go a long way and show her you're a gentleman: Offer your arm as she's stepping from a curb, direct her away from shards of broken glass. She'll notice if you wait until she's safely in her car or house before you leave. Wait the extra 90 seconds, and next time you might be going in with her.
15. She expects you to know her eye color after the first date.
16. Women need momentum—without it, they lose interest or wonder if you have. Momentum = a minimum of one date a week, plus a couple of phone calls in between.

17. She knows that when you invite her over for a homemade meal or to watch a movie, it's code for "tonight is hook-up night." Don't play this card any earlier than date three.
18. A Friday or Saturday night is required by date four. Otherwise, she'll wonder who else you're seeing.
19. Rule of Groping: If anything happens that couldn't be shown on prime-time TV, call her the next day. Otherwise, she'll feel cheap and used.
20. Don't say, "I'll call you," if you have no intention to. She'd prefer that you say nothing at all.

KATHY WILSON
Dude Looks Like a Lady

There oughta be a name for people like me.

You know, people straddling perception and reality because of interpretation.

This is about hair, breasts, and identity.

Let me tell you what it's like walking around as a black woman with barely there hair and 40 Cs. I mostly keep my hair buzzed short not out of any confusion over identity, self-hatred, or penis envy, but because I'm lazy and it's cool looking.

And I'm cute this way.

Yeah, I've got a pretty, round, brown face and dark eyes. Lest you think this is a singles ad, let me move on.

I had hair—lots of it, in fact. But it's overrated and sometimes a security blanket. I never felt freer than when I first cut my hair off in, I think, 1989. Even when I had hair, I never could relate to those commercials with flaxen-haired white girls throwing their manes around.

My point is, people get so twisted over female presentation and what exactly *is* feminine that my bald head is cause for pause.

People actually stop.

Their physicality changes.

Some stare and, when I attempt eye contact, look away.

Then there's the case of the two white guys—one we'll call Ice Cream Man, the other we'll call Redneck Man.

I'm addicted to those butter cookies at Graeter's, a local ice cream shop pedaling hand-dipped homemade ice cream. One day I was waiting in line with a 50ish, silver-haired matron at the Graeter's in Hyde Park, a toney, posh neighborhood where white people either jog or drive luxury SUVs everywhere.

The clerk—Ice Cream Man—was on the telephone while servicing patrons at the counter.

The lady perused the cases. Hyde Park Man, phone tucked between his ear and shoulder, glanced up at me. "What can I get ya, sir?" he said.

I'm accustomed to but not immune to this kind of hurried assumption.

"Just these," I said, handing over the bag of cookies for purchase.

"Oh . . . uh . . . uh . . . oh, I mean, ma'am. I'm sorry, ma'am." He fell all over himself.

What's best in instances like these is one quick apology.

Either that, or we should all just act like it never happened, like a booger hanging from a friend's nose, an impolite public fart, or the open zipper.

The lady next to me was outraged.

"I cannot *believe* that!" she snorted, her voice hushed like we were at the opera.

"There's no way you could be mistaken for a man. You have such a pretty round face. Those cookies should be free."

I giggled.

I love well-meaning whites.

"Forget the round face," I said, "What about the 40 Cs? How could you *not* see these?"

Unimpressed, she kept her focus on the pastry selection.

Weeks later I was walking into Joseph-Beth, an independent bookstore in a shopping center in Norwood, a working-class white neighborhood bordering Hyde Park.

It was mid-afternoon, so hot I felt delirious.

I thought a skate through the bookstore would inspire me to write.

Plus, I was killing time before returning to the barbershop.

Al, my barber, has an uncanny ability to estimate haircuts to the minute so there's rarely a backlog of uncut heads clogging the waiting area.

You come back, it's your turn.

I couldn't wait to get into the bookstore.

Like an outtake from *Deliverance* appeared a shirtless, raggedy white man driving a raggedy white van.

Yes, it was Redneck Man.

As I walked through the parking lot, we made eye contact.

He slowed down. I slowed down.

Aaaw, I thought. *Bring it on.*

Just as I set foot on the sidewalk to the bookstore, he yelled from his window.

"Take your boy-lookin' ass on somewhere!"

His timing was perfect. He'd waited 'til I'd reached a clearing so everyone within earshot could see the bald black bitch he'd caught in his sights.

I felt like I used to in the fourth grade when Robert, son of a Klansman, put pictures of black folks hanging from trees on my desk, trapping me and then smothering me.

I felt ambushed.

I was angry and confused.

How could he just yell out what he thought of me when I'd squelched my classification of him?

I wanted my say.

I turned and walked up the embankment, waiting for him to enter traffic and drive past on the main thoroughfare. Maybe he'd get caught at the light and I could have a word with him.

I remembered a long-ago image of my mother—tall, black, and proud with fists fitted on her waist like an Angela Davis action figure. Throughout my childhood, she was always somewhere setting someone straight. While it was thrilling to watch, it almost always left her drained.

And I caught myself about to disrespect the urban nobility of my mother's sass.

I was 'bout to be a straight nigga.

Then Redneck Man turned the other way. Lucky for both of us.

Laughing at the absurdity of Redneck Man's shout out to my presumed identity, I walked into the bookstore and cooled off. I couldn't shake it so easily, though. I seriously reconsidered cutting my hair again.

Then I stopped myself when I realized I almost let some fool have power over me.

I am a black woman whose bald head makes me invisible to some, boyish to others, and beautiful to me.

It makes me unfettered and unadorned.

Mostly it makes me free.

And without it my name is all woman.

FIROOZEH DUMAS
The "F Word"

My cousin's name, Farbod, means "Greatness." When he moved to America, all the kids called him "Farthead." My brother Farshid ("He Who Enlightens") became "Fartshit." The name of my friend Neggar means "Beloved," although it can be more accurately translated as "She Whose Name Almost Incites Riots." Her brother Arash ("Giver") initially couldn't understand why every time he'd say his name, people would laugh and ask him if it itched.

All of us immigrants knew that moving to America would be fraught with challenges, but none of us thought that our names would be such an obstacle. How could our parents have ever imagined that someday we would end up in a country where monosyllabic names reign supreme, a land where "William" is shortened to "Bill," where "Susan" becomes "Sue," and "Richard" somehow evolves into "Dick"? America is a great country, but nobody without a mask and a cape has a z in his name. And have Americans ever realized the great scope of the guttural sounds they're missing? Okay, so it has to do with linguistic roots, but I do believe this would be a richer country if all Americans could do a little tongue aerobics and learn to pronounce "kh," a sound more commonly associated in this culture with phlegm, or "gh," the sound usually made by actors in the final moments of a choking scene. It's like adding a few new spices to the kitchen pantry. Move over, cinnamon and nutmeg, make way for cardamom and sumac.

Exotic analogies aside, having a foreign name in this land of Joes and Marys is a pain in the spice cabinet. When I was twelve, I decided to simplify my life by adding an American middle name. This decision serves as proof that sometimes simplifying one's life in the short run only complicates it in the long run.

My name, Firoozeh, chosen by my mother, means "Turquoise" in Farsi. In America, it means "Unpronounceable" or "I'm Not Going to Talk to You Because I Cannot Possibly Learn Your Name and I Just Don't Want to Have to Ask You Again and Again Because You'll Think I'm Dumb or You Might Get Upset or Something." My father, incidentally, had wanted to name me Sara. I do wish he had won that argument.

To strengthen my decision to add an American name, I had just finished fifth grade in Whittier, where all the kids incessantly called me "Ferocious." That summer, my family moved to Newport Beach, where I looked forward to starting a new life. I wanted to be a kid with a name that didn't draw so much attention, a name that didn't come with a built-in inquisition as to when and why I had moved to America and how was it that I spoke English without an accent and was I planning on going back and what did I think of America?

My last name didn't help any. I can't mention my maiden name, because: "Dad, I'm writing a memoir."

"Great! Just don't mention our name."

Suffice it to say that, with eight letters, including a *z,* and four syllables, my last name is as difficult and foreign as my first. My first and last name together generally served the same purpose as a high brick wall. There was one exception to this rule. In Berkeley, and only in Berkeley, my name drew people like flies to baklava. These were usually people named Amaryllis or Chrysanthemum, types who vacationed in Costa Rica and to whom lentils described a type of burger. These folks were probably not the pride of Poughkeepsie, but they were refreshingly nonjudgmental.

When I announced to my family that I wanted to add an American name, they reacted with their usual laughter. Never one to let mockery or good judgment stand in my way, I proceeded to ask for suggestions. My father suggested "Fifi." Had I had a special affinity for French poodles or been considering a career in prostitution, I would've gone with that one. My mom suggested "Farah," a name easier than "Firoozeh" yet still Iranian. Her reasoning made sense, except that Farrah Fawcett was at the height of her popularity and I didn't want to be associated with somebody whose poster hung in every postpubescent boy's bedroom. We couldn't think of any American names beginning with *F,* so we moved on to *J,* the first letter of our last name. I don't know why we limited ourselves to names beginning with my initials, but it made sense at that moment, perhaps by the logic employed moments before bungee jumping. I finally chose the name "Julie" mainly for its simplicity. My brothers, Farid and Farshid, thought that adding an American name was totally stupid. They later became Fred and Sean.

That same afternoon, our doorbell rang. It was our new next-door neighbor, a friendly girl my age named Julie. She asked me my name and after a moment of hesitation, I introduced myself as Julie. "What a coincidence!" she said. I didn't mention that I had been Julie for only half an hour.

Thus I started sixth grade with my new, easy name and life became infinitely simpler. People actually remembered my name, which was an entirely refreshing new sensation. All was well until the Iranian Revolution, when I found myself with a new set of problems. Because I spoke English without an accent and was known as Julie, people assumed I was American. This meant that I was often privy to their real feelings about those "damn I-raynians." It was like having those X-ray glasses that let you see people undressed, except that what I was seeing was far uglier than people's underwear. It dawned on me that these people would have probably never invited me to their house had they known me as Firoozeh. I felt like a fake.

When I went to college, I eventually went back to using my real name. All was well until I graduated and started looking for a job. Even though I had graduated with honors from UC–Berkeley, I couldn't get a single interview. I was guilty of being a humanities major, but I began to suspect that there was more to my problems. After three months of rejections, I added "Julie" to my résumé. Call it coincidence, but the job offers started coming in. Perhaps it's the same kind of coincidence that keeps African Americans from getting cabs in New York.

Once I got married, my name became Julie Dumas. I went from having an identifiably "ethnic" name to having ancestors who wore clogs. My family and non-American friends continued calling me Firoozeh, while my coworkers and American friends called me Julie. My life became one big knot, especially when friends who knew me as Julie met friends who knew me as Firoozeh. I felt like those characters in soap operas who have an evil twin. The two, of course, can never be in the same room, since they're played by the same person, a struggling actress who wears a wig to play one of the twins and dreams of moving on to bigger and better roles. I couldn't blame my mess on a screenwriter; it was my own doing.

I decided to untangle the knot once and for all by going back to my real name. By then, I was a stay-at-home mom, so I really didn't care whether people remembered my name or gave me job interviews. Besides, most of the people I dealt with were in diapers and were in no position to judge. I was also living in Silicon Valley, an area filled with people named Rajeev, Avishai, and Insook.

Every once in a while, though, somebody comes up with a new permutation and I am once again reminded that I am an immigrant with a foreign name. I recently went to have blood drawn for a physical exam. The waiting room for blood work at our local medical clinic is in the basement of the building, and no matter how early one arrives for an appointment, forty coughing, wheezing people have gotten there first. Apart from reading *Golf Digest* and *Popular Mechanics,* there isn't much to do except guess the number of contagious diseases represented in the windowless room. Every ten minutes, a name is called and everyone looks to see which cough matches that name. As I waited patiently, the receptionist called out, "Fritzy, Fritzy!" Everyone looked around, but no one stood up. Usually, if I'm waiting to be called by someone who doesn't know me, I will respond to just about any name starting with an *F.* Having been called Froozy, Frizzy, Fiorucci, and Frooz and just plain "Uhhhh . . . ," I am highly accommodating. I did not, however, respond to "Fritzy" because there is, as far as I know, no *t* in my name. The receptionist tried again, "Fritzy, Fritzy DumbAss." As I stood up to this most linguistically original version of my name, I could feel all eyes upon me. The room was momentarily silent as all of these sick people sat united in a moment of gratitude for their own names.

MIM UDOVITCH
A Secret Society of the Starving

Claire is 18. She is a pretty teenager, with long strawberry-blond hair, and she is almost abnormally self-possessed for a girl from a small town who has suddenly been descended upon by a big-city reporter who is there to talk to her, in secret, about her secret life. She is sitting on the track that runs around the field of her high school's football stadium, wearing running shorts and a T-shirt and shivering a little because even though we are in Florida—in the kind of town where, according to Claire, during "season" when you see yet another car with New York plates, you just feel like running it down—there's an evening chill.

Claire's is also the kind of town where how the local high school does in sports matters. Claire herself plays two sports. Practice and team fund-raisers are a regular part of her life, along with the typical small-town-Florida teenage occupations—going to "some hick party," hanging out with friends in the parking lot of the Taco Bell, bowling, going to the beach.

Another regular part of her life, also a common teenage occupation, is anorexia—refusal to eat enough to maintain a minimally healthy weight. So she is possibly shivering because she hasn't consumed enough calories for her body to keep itself warm. Claire first got into eating disorders when she was 14 or 15 and a bulimic friend introduced her to them. But she was already kind of on the lookout for something: "I was gonna do it on my own, basically. Just because, like, exercise can only take you so far, you know? And I don't know, I just started to wonder if there was another way. Because they made it seem like, 'You do drugs, you die; be anorexic and you're gonna die in a year.' I knew that they kind of overplayed it and tried to frighten you away. So I always thought it can't be *that* bad for you."

Bulimia—binge eating followed by purging through vomiting or laxatives—didn't suit her, however, so after a little while she moved on to anorexia. But she is not, by her own lights, anorexic. And her name isn't Claire. She is, in her terms, "an ana" or "pro-ana" (shortened from pro-anorexia), and Claire is a variation of Clairegirl, the name she uses on the Web sites that are the fulcrum of the pro-ana community, which also includes people who are pro-mia (for bulimia) or simply pro-E.D., for eating disorder.

About one in 200 American women suffers from anorexia; two or three in 100 suffer from bulimia. Arguably, these disorders have the highest fatality rates of any mental illness, through suicide as well as the obvious health problems. But because they are not threatening to the passer-by, as psychotic disorders are, or likely to render people unemployable or criminal, as alcoholism and addiction are, and perhaps also because they are disorders that primarily afflict girls and women, they are not a proportionately imperative social priority.

And now there's pro-ana, in many ways an almost too lucid clarification of what it really feels like to be eating disordered. "Pain of mind is worse than pain of body" reads the legend on one Web site's live-journal page, above a picture of the Web mistress's arm, so heavily scored with what look like razor cuts that there is more open wound than flesh. "I'm already disturbed," reads the home page of another. "Please don't come in." The wish to conform to a certain external ideal for the external ideal's sake is certainly a component of anorexia and bulimia. But as they are experienced by the people who suffer from them, it is just that: a component, a stepping-off point into the abyss.

As the girls (and in smaller numbers, boys) who frequent the pro-E.D. sites know, being an ana is a state of mind — part addiction, part obsession, and part seesawing sense of self-worth, not necessarily correlating to what you actually weigh. "Body image is a major deal, but it's about not being good enough," says Jill M. Pollack, the executive director of the Center for the Study of Anorexia and Bulimia, "and they're trying to fix everything from the outside." Clairegirl, like many of the girls who include their stats — height, weight, and goal weight — when posting on such sites, would not receive a diagnosis of anorexia, because she is not 15 percent under normal weight for her height and age.

But she does have self-devised rules and restrictions regarding eating, which, if she does not meet them, make her feel that she has erred — "I kind of believe it is a virtue, almost," she says of pro-ana. "Like if you do wrong and you eat, then you sin." If she does not meet her goals, it makes her dislike herself, makes her feel anxiety and a sense of danger. If she does meet them, she feels "clean." She has a goal weight, lower than the weight she is now. She plays sports for two hours a day after school and tries to exercise at least another hour after she gets home. She also has a touch of obsessive-compulsive disorder regarding non-food-related things — cleaning, laundry, the numeral three. ("Both anorexia and bulimia are highly O.C.D.," says Pollack. "Highly.")

And she does spend between one and three hours a day online, in the world of pro-ana. Asked what she likes best about the sites, Claire says: "Just really, like at the end of the day, it would be really nice if you could share with the whole world how you felt, you know? Because truthfully, you just don't feel comfortable, you can't tell the truth. Then, like, if I don't eat lunch or something, people will get on my case about it, and I can't just come out and tell them I don't eat, or something like that. But at the end of the day, I can go online and talk to them there, and they know exactly what I'm going through and how I feel. And I don't have to worry about them judging me for how I feel."

Pro-ana, the basic premise of which is that an eating disorder is not a disorder but a lifestyle choice, is very much an ideology of the early twenty-first century, one that could not exist absent the anonymity and accessibility of the Internet, without which the only place large numbers of anorexics and bulimics would find themselves together would be at inpatient treatment. "Primarily, the sites reinforce the secretiveness and the 'specialness' of the disorder," Davis says. "When young women get into the grips of this disease, their thoughts become very distorted, and part of it is they believe they're unique and special. The sites are a way for them to connect with other girls and to basically talk about how special they are. And they become very isolated. Women with eating disorders really thrive in a lot of ways on being very disconnected. At the same time, of course, they have a yearning to be connected."

Perfectionism, attention to detail, and a sense of superiority combine to make the pro-ana sites the most meticulous and clinically fluent self-representations of a mental disorder you could hope to find, almost checklists of diagnostic criteria expressed in poignantly human terms. Starving yourself, just on the basis of its sheer difficulty, is a high-dedication ailment—to choose to be an ana, if choice it is, is to choose a way of life, a hobby, and a credo. And on the Web, which is both very public and completely faceless, the aspects of the disorder that are about attention-getting and secret-keeping are a resolved paradox. "I kind of want people to understand," Clairegirl says, "but I also like having this little hidden thing that only I know about, like—this little secret that's all yours."

Pro-ana has its roots in various newsgroups and lists deep inside various Internet service providers. Now there are numerous well-known-to-those-who-know sites, plus who knows how many dozens more that are just the lone teenager's Web page, with names that put them beyond the scope of search engines. And based on the two-week sign-up of 973 members to a recent message-board adjunct to one of the older and more established sites, the pro-ana community probably numbers in the thousands, with girls using names like Wannabeboney, Neverthinenuf, DiETpEpSi UhHuh! and Afraidtolookin-themirror posting things like: "I can't take it anymore! I'm fasting! I'm going out, getting all diet soda, sugar-free gum, sugar-free candy and having myself a 14-day fast. Then we'll see who is the skinny girl in the family!"

That ana and mia are childlike nicknames, names that might be the names of friends (one Web site that is now defunct was even called, with girlish fondness, "My Friend Ana"), is indicative. The pro-ana community is largely made up of girls or young women, most of whom are between the ages of 13 and 25. And it is a close community, close in the manner of close friendships of girls and young women. The members of a few sites send each other bracelets, like friendship bracelets, as symbols of solidarity and support. And like any ideology subscribed to by many individuals, pro-ana is not a monolithic system of belief.

At its most militant, the ideology is something along the lines of, as the opening page of one site puts it: "Volitional, proactive anorexia is not a disease or a disorder. . . . There are no VICTIMS here. It is a lifestyle that begins and ends with a particular faculty human beings seem in drastically short supply of today: the will. . . . Contrary to popular misconception, anorexics possess the most iron-cored, indomitable wills of all. Our way is not that of the weak. . . . If we ever *completely* tapped that potential in our midst . . . we could change the world. Completely. Maybe we could even rule it."

Mostly, though, the philosophical underpinnings of pro-ana thought are not quite so Nietzschean. The "Thin Commandments" on one site, which appear under a picture of Bugs Bunny smiling his toothy open-mouthed smile, leaning against a mailbox and holding a carrot with one bite taken out of it, include: "If thou aren't thin, thou aren't attractive"; "Being this is more important than being healthy"; "Thou shall not eat without feeling guilty"; "Thou shall not eat fattening food without punishing thyself afterward"; and "Being thin and not eating are signs of true willpower and success."

The "Ana Creed" from the same site begins: "I believe in Control, the only force mighty enough to bring order into the chaos that is my world. I believe that I am the most vile, worthless, and useless person ever to have existed on this planet."

In fact, to those truly "in the disorder"—a phrase one anonymous ana used to describe it, just as an anonymous alcoholic might describe being in A.A. as being "in the rooms"—pro-ana is something of a misnomer. It suggests the promotion of something, rather than its defense, for reasons either sad or militant. That it is generally understood otherwise and even exploited ("Anorexia: Not just for suicidal teenage white girls anymore" read the home page of Anorexic Nation, now a disabled site, the real purpose of which was to push diet drugs) is a source of both resentment and secret satisfaction to the true pro-ana community. Its adherents might be vile and worthless, but they are the elite.

The usual elements of most sites are pretty much the same, although the presentation is variable enough to suggest Web mistresses ranging from young women with a fair amount of programming know-how and editorial judgment to angry little girls who want to assert their right to protect an unhealthy behavior in the face of parental opposition and who happen to know a little HTML. But there are usually "tips" and "techniques"—on the face of it, the scariest aspect of pro-ana, but in reality, pretty much the same things that both dieters and anorexics have been figuring out on their own for decades. There are "thinspirational" quotes—"You can never be too rich or too thin"; "Hunger hurts but starving works"; "Nothing tastes as good as thin feels"; "The thinner, the winner!" There are "thinspirational" photo galleries, usually pretty much the same group of very thin models, actresses, and singers—Jodie Kidd, Kate Moss, Calista Flockhart, Fiona Apple. And at pro-ana's saddest extreme, balancing the militance on the scales of the double-digit goal weight, there are warnings of such severity that they might as well be the beginning of the third canto of Dante's "Inferno": "I am the way into the city of woe. I am the way to a forsaken people. I am the way into eternal sorrow." The pro-ana version of which, from one site, is:

> PLEASE NOTE: Anorexia is NOT a diet. Bulimia is NOT a weight-loss plan. These are dangerous, potentially life-threatening DISORDERS that you cannot choose, catch, or learn. If you do not already have an eating disorder, that's wonderful! If you're looking for a new diet, if you want to drop a few pounds to be slimmer or more popular or whatever, if you're generally content with yourself and just want to look a bit better in a bikini, GO AWAY. Find a Weight Watchers meeting. Better yet, eat moderate portions of healthy food and go for a walk.
>
> However.
>
> If you are half as emotionally scarred as I am, if you look in the mirror and truly loathe what you see, if your relationships with food and your body are already beyond "normal" parameters no matter what you weigh, then come inside. If you're already too far into this to quit, come in and have a look around. I won't tell you to give up what I need to keep hold of myself.

Most of the pro-ana sites also explicitly discourage people under 18 from entering, partly for moral and partly for self-interested reasons. Under pressure from the National Eating Disorders Association, a number of servers shut down the pro-ana sites they were hosting last fall. But obviously, pretty much anyone who wanted to find her way to these sites and into them could do so, irrespective of age. And could find there, as Clairegirl did, a kind of perverse support group, a place where a group of for the most part very unhappy and in some part very angry girls and women come together to support each other in sickness rather than in health.

Then there's Chaos—also her Web name—who like her friend Futurebird (ditto) runs an established and well-respected pro-E.D. site. Chaos, whom I met in Manhattan although that's not where she lives, is a very smart, very winning, very attractive 23-year-old who has been either bulimic or anorexic since she was 10. Recently she's been bingeing and purging somewhere between 4 and 10 times a week. But when not bingeing, she also practices "restricting"—she doesn't eat in front of people, or in public, or food that isn't sealed, or food that she hasn't prepared herself, or food that isn't one of her "safe" foods, which since they are a certain kind of candy and a certain kind of sugar-free gum, is practically all food. ("You're catching on quickly," she says, laughing, when this is remarked on.) Also recently, she has been having trouble making herself throw up. "I think my body's just not wanting to do it right now," she says. "You have the toothbrush trick, and usually I can just hit my stomach in the right spot, or my fingernails will gag me in the right spot. It just depends on what I've eaten. And if that doesn't work, laxis always do."

Chaos, like Clairegirl, is obsessive-compulsive about a certain number (which it would freak her out to see printed), and when she takes laxatives she either has to take that number of them, which is no longer enough to work, or that number plus 10, or that number plus 20, and so forth. The most she has ever taken is that number plus 60, and the total number she takes depends on the total number of calories she has consumed.

While it hardly needs to be pointed out that starving yourself is not good for you, bulimia is in its own inexorable if less direct way also a deadly disorder. Because of the severity of Chaos's bulimia, its long-standing nature, and the other things she does—taking ephedra or Xenadrine, two forms of, as she says, "legal speed," available at any health food or vitamin store; exercising in excess; fasting—she stands a very real chance of dying any time.

As it is, she has been to the emergency room more than half a dozen times with "heart things." It would freak her out to see the details of her heart things in print. But the kinds of heart things a severe bulimic might experience range from palpitations to cardiac arrest. And although Chaos hasn't had her kidney function tested in the recent past, it probably isn't great. Her spleen might also be near the point of rupturing.

Chaos is by no means a young woman with nothing going for her. But despite her many positive attributes, Chaos punishes herself physically on a regular basis, not only through bulimia but also through cutting—hers is the live-journal page with the picture of the sliced-up arm. To be beheld is, to Chaos, so painful that after meeting me in person, she was still vomiting and crying with fear over the possible consequences of cooperating with this story a week later. "Some days," she says of her bulimia, "it's all I have."

While in some moods Chaos says she would do anything to be free of her eating disorders, in others she has more excuses not to be than the mere lack of health insurance: She has a job, she is in school, she doesn't deserve help. And what she has, on all days, is her Web site, a place where people who have only their eating disorders can congregate, along with the people who *aspire* to having eating disorders—who for unknowable reasons of neurochemistry and personal experience identify with the self-lacerating worlds of anorexia and bulimia.

Futurebird, whom I also met in Manhattan, says that she has noticed a trend, repeating itself in new member after new member, of people who don't think they're anorexic *enough* to get treatment. And it's true, very much a func-tion of the Internet—its accessibility, its anonymity—that the pro-ana sites seem to have amplified an almost-diagnostic category: the subclinical eating disorder, for the girl who's anorexic on the inside, the girl who hates herself so much that she forms a virtual attachment to a highly traumatized body of women, in a place where through posts and the adoption of certain behaviors, she can make her internal state external.

Futurebird and Chaos are sitting in a little plaza just to the south of Washington Square Park, with the sun behind them. Futurebird is a small African-American woman. As she notes, and as she has experienced when being taken to the hospital, it is a big help being African-American if you don't want people to think you have anorexia, which is generally and inaccurately considered to be solely an affliction of the white middle class. Futurebird has had an eating disorder since she was in junior high school and is now, at 22, looking for a way to become what you might call a maintenance anorexic — eating a little bit more healthily, restricting to foods like fruits and whole-grain cereal and compensating for the extra calories with excessive exercising.

Like Chaos, she is opposed, in principle, to eating disorders in general and says that she hates anorexia with a blind and burning hatred. Although she also says she thinks she's fat, which she so emphatically is not that in the interest of not sounding illogical and irrational, she almost immediately amends this to: she's not as thin as she'd like to be.

Both she and Chaos would vigorously dispute the assertion that the sites can *give* anyone an eating disorder. You certainly can't give anyone without the vulnerability to it an eating disorder. But many adolescent girls teeter on the edge of vulnerability. And the sites certainly might give those girls the suggestion to . . . hey, what the hell, give it a try.

"What I'd like people to understand," Futurebird says, "is that it is very difficult for people who have an eating disorder to ask for help. What a lot of people are able to do is to say, well, I can't go to a recovery site and ask for help. I can't go to a doctor or a friend and ask for help. I can't tell anyone. But I can go to this site because it's going to quote-unquote make me worse. And instead what I hope they find is people who share their experience and that they're able to just simply talk. And I've actually tested this. I've posted the same thing that I've posted on my site on some recovery sites, and I've read the reactions, and in a lot of ways it's more helpful."

In what ways?

"The main difference is that if you post — if someone's feeling really bad, like, I'm so fat, et cetera, on a recovery site, they'll say, that's not recovery talk. You have to speak recovery-speak."

"Fat is not a feeling," Chaos says, in tones that indicate she is echoing a recovery truism.

"And they'll use this language of recovery," Futurebird continues. "Which does work at some point in the negative thinking patterns that you have. But one tiny thing that I wish they would do is validate that the feeling does exist. To say, yes, I understand that you might feel that way. And you get not as much of that. A lot of times people just need to know that they aren't reacting in a completely crazy way."

The problem is that by and large, the people posting on these sites are reacting in a completely crazy way. There are many, many more discussions answering questions like, "What do you guys do about starvation headaches?"

DAVID BERREBY
It Takes a Tribe

When the budding pundit Walter Lippmann coined the term "stereotype" back in 1922, he offered several examples from the America of his time: "Agitator." "Intellectual." "South European." "From the Back Bay." You know, he told the reader, when a glimpse and a word or two create a full mental picture of a whole group of people. As in "plutocrat." Or "foreigner." Or "Harvard man."

Harvard man? We know, thanks to Lippmann, that stereotypes are part of serious problems like racism, prejudice, and injustice. What is Lippmann's alma mater doing on such a list? (He even added: "How different from the statement, 'He is a Yale man.'")

Spend time on a campus in coming weeks, though, and you'll see what he meant.

At colleges across the country, from Ivy League to less exclusive state schools, students who are mispronouncing the library's name this month will soon feel truly and deeply a part of their college. They'll be singing their school songs and cherishing the traditions (just as soon as they learn what they are). They'll talk the way "we" do. (Going to Texas A&M? Then greet people with a cheerful "howdy.") They'll learn contempt for that rival university — Oklahoma to their Texas, Sacramento State to their U.C. Davis, Annapolis to their West Point.

They may come to believe, too, that an essential trait separates them from the rest of humanity — the same sort of feeling most Americans have about races, ethnic groups, and religions. As the writer Christopher Buckley said recently in his college's alumni magazine: "When I run into a Yale man I somehow feel that I am with a kindred spirit. A part of that kindred-ness comes from his gentility and his not being all jumped up about it. It's a certain sweetness of character."

All this sentiment comes on fast (a study last year at Ivy League campuses found freshmen even more gung-ho than older students). Yet college loyalty, encouraged by alumni relations offices, can last a lifetime — as enduring as the Princeton tiger tattooed on the buttock of former Secretary of State George P. Shultz, or the Yale sweater sported by evil Mr. Burns on "The Simpsons," a number of whose writers went to Harvard.

New identities are forged within the university as well, in elite groups like Skull and Bones at Yale or the Corps of Cadets at Texas A&M or Michigamua at the University of Michigan; in sororities and fraternities; even in particular majors and particular labs. Students don't just attend a college; they join its tribes.

"What endlessly impresses me is people losing sight of how arbitrary it is," says Robert M. Sapolsky, a Stanford biologist who specializes in the links between social life and stress. "Students understand how readily they could have wound up at another school or wound up in another lab." Yet every year, he adds, "they fall for it." For most, what Professor Sapolsky calls that "nutty but palpable" onset of college tribalism is just a part of campus life. For social scientists, it's an object of research, offering clues to a fundamental and puzzling aspect of human nature: People need to belong, to feel a part of "us." Yet a sense of "us" brings with it a sense of "them."

Human beings will give a lot, including their lives, for a group they feel part of—for "us," as in "our nation" or "our religion." They will also harm those labeled "them," including taking their lives. Far as genocide and persecution seem from fraternity hazings and Cal versus Stanford, college tribes may shed light on the way the mind works with those other sorts of groups, the ones that shape and misshape the world, like nation, race, creed, caste, or culture.

After all, a college campus is full of people inventing a sense of "us" and a sense of "them." As one junior at the University of California, Los Angeles, told her school paper before a game against the University of Southern California: "School spirit is important because it gives us a sense of belonging and being a part of something bigger. Besides," she said, "U.S.C. sucks in every way."

In an e-mail interview, Professor Sapolsky writes that "Stanford students (and faculty) do tons of this, at every possible hierarchical level." For instance, he says, they see Stanford versus Harvard, and Stanford versus the University of California at Berkeley. "Then, within Stanford, all the science wonks doing tribal stuff to differentiate themselves from the fuzzies—the humanities/social science types. Then within the sciences, the life science people versus the chemistry/physics/math geeks." Within the life sciences, he adds, the two tribes are "bio majors and majors in what is called 'human biology'—former deprecated as being robotic pre-meds, incapable of thinking, just spitting out of factoids; latter as fuzzies masquerading as scientists."

Recent research on students suggests these changes in perception aren't trivial. A few years ago, a team of social psychologists asked students at the University of California at Santa Barbara to rank various collections of people in terms of how well they "qualify as a group." In their answers, "students at a university" ranked above "citizens of a nation." "Members of a campus committee" and "members of a university social club" ranked higher than "members of a union" or "members of a political party," romantic couples, or office colleagues working together on a project. For that matter, "students at a university" and "members of a campus committee" ranked well above blacks and Jews in the students' estimation of what qualifies as a group.

Much of this thinking, researchers have found, is subconscious. We may think we care about our college ties for good and sensible reasons—wonderful classes! dorm-room heart-to-hearts! job connections!—when the deeper causes are influences we didn't notice.

Some 20 years ago, researchers asked students at Rutgers to describe themselves using only words from a set of cards prepared in advance. Some cards contained words associated with Rutgers, like "scarlet," the school color, and "knight," the name of its athletic teams. Others, like "orange," were associated with archrival Princeton. Some students took the test in a room decorated with a Rutgers pennant; others took it under a Princeton flag. A third group saw only a New York Yankees banner.

Students who saw a Princeton or Rutgers emblem were more likely to use Rutgers-related words to describe themselves. They also mentioned that they were students at Rutgers earlier than those who saw only the neutral flag. They didn't consciously decide to stand up for Rutgers. Outside their conscious minds, though, that identity was in place, ready to be released by symbols of the tribe.

More recently, three social psychologists at Harvard looked at another example of subconscious tribal beliefs. Mahzarin R. Banaji, who led the study, argues that people in similar, equivalent groups will place those groups into a hierarchy, from best to worst, even when there is no rational basis for ranking them. The psychologists tested Yale sophomores, juniors, and seniors, who live and eat together in "residential colleges." Students know that these colleges are effectively all alike and that people are assigned to them at random. Still, the team found, Yalies did indeed rank them from best to worst. (In the interests of peace and comity, the colleges were kept anonymous.) Moreover, students assigned to the less prestigious units were less enthusiastic about their homes than those from the ones with a better reputation.

What this suggests, Professor Banaji says, is that taking one's place in a tribe, and accepting the tribe's place in a larger society, are mental acts that happen regardless of the group's purpose or meaning. Once people see that they've been divided into groups, they'll act accordingly, even if they know that the divisions are as meaningless as, oh, the University of Arizona versus Arizona State. "We know that human beings identify with social groups, sometimes sufficiently to kill or die on their behalf," she says. "What is not as well known is that such identity between self and group can form rapidly, often following a psychological route that is relatively subconscious. That is, like automata, we identify with the groups in which we are accidentally placed."

Not all researchers agree that people care about so-called nonsense groups with the same passion they give to religion, politics, or morals. Another theory holds that the subconscious mind can distinguish which groups matter and how much. One example comes from a much-cited experiment, performed, naturally, on college students.

In 1959, the social psychologists Elliot Aronson and Judson Mills asked undergraduate women to join a discussion group after a short initiation. For one set of participants the initiation required reciting a few mild sexual words. The other group had to say a list of much saltier words about sex, which embarrassed them no end (remember, this was 1959). The discussion group was dull as dishwater, but the women who suffered to join rated it as much more valuable than those who had a mild initiation (and higher than a control group that didn't have to do anything).

A subconscious clue for perceiving a tribe as real and valuable, then, may be expending sweat, tears, and embarrassment to get in. The political activist Tom Hayden recently recalled just such a rite at the University of Michigan, in an article on the left-wing Web site alternet.org. He was complaining about the lock that Skull and Bones has on November's election (President Bush and the Democratic nominee, Senator John Kerry, are members).

"As a junior, I was tapped for the Druids," Mr. Hayden wrote about his own campus clan, "which involved a two-day ritual that included being stripped to my underpants, pelted with eggs, smeared with red dye, and tied to a campus tree. These humiliations signified my rebirth from lowly student journalist to Big Man on Campus."

As for Professor Aronson, had he not wanted tight control over the experiment, he writes in his widely used textbook, *The Social Animal,* he and Professor Mills could simply have studied an initiation outside the lab—at a campus fraternity or sorority.

That kind of lumping together—studying one group to explain another—drives scholars in other fields to distraction. To them, a pep rally is different from a political rally. Historians, trained to see big generalizations as meaningless, are often aghast at the way psychologists' theories about groups ignore the difference between, say, today's two-gendered, multiethnic, and meritocratic Harvard College and the one that gave Lippmann his degree in 1909. And anthropologists for generations have disdained psychology for ignoring cultural differences.

But one fact is clear, and college groups exemplify it well: While many creatures live in groups, humanity's are unlike anything else found in nature. Peter Richerson, a biologist at Sacramento State's rival, the University of California at Davis, likes to point out that his students, sitting quietly together on the first day of class, are an amazing exception to the general rules of animal behavior. Put chimpanzees or monkeys that don't know one another in a room, and they would be in hysterics. People team up with strangers easily.

Professor Richerson and his longtime collaborator, Robert Boyd, an anthropologist at U.S.C.'s hated enemy, U.C.L.A., argue that we will sign up for membership in tribelike groups for the same reason birds sing: It feels right because we evolved to do it. "We want to live in tribes," Professor Richerson says. Humans are "looking to be told what group they belong to, and then once they do that, they want to know, 'What are the rules?'"

The tricky part, says Professor Sapolsky of Stanford, Cal-Berkeley's bitter rival, is that humans alone among animals can think about what a tribe is and who belongs. "Humans actually think about who is an 'us' and who is a 'them' rather than just knowing it," he says. "The second it becomes a cognitive process, it is immensely subject to manipulation."

And, of course, studying the phenomenon won't make you immune. "I'm true blue," says Professor Banaji, who taught at Yale from 1986 until 2002, when she joined the Harvard faculty. "I was physically unable to sit through a women's basketball game between Harvard and Yale on the Harvard side."

ADAM STERNBERGH
Britney Spears: The Pop Tart in Winter

A few months ago, Lynne Spears wrote in an online column that her daughter Britney's new video—for the single "My Prerogative"—possessed "an element of old Hollywood glamour and mystery." Her statement may puzzle some viewers; namely, those with eyes. In the video, Britney drives her car into a swimming pool; emerges from the water, dripping and squirming; writhes on a bed in her undies; and poses in lingerie and garters, stroking herself while a man puffing a cigar ogles her. That final scene, in particular, is a uniquely Spearsian take on adult-child arousal: all smoke and leerers.

Sadly, the singer herself seems unaroused. "My Prerogative" arrives along with a disarmingly candid message on Spears' Web site. In this self-described "Letter of Truth," the pop star declares her need for a break. "My prerogative right now is to just chill & let all of the other overexposed blondes on the cover of *Us Weekly* be your entertainment. GOOD LUCK GIRLS!!" She continues, "I understand now what they mean when they talk about child stars. . . . It's amazing what advisors will push you to do, even if it means taking a naive, young, blonde girl & putting her on the cover of every magazine."

Spears has already taken a lot of flack for her vigorously punctuated *cri de coeur.* But the fact is, she's absolutely right. She *is* tragically overexposed. Perhaps it's time for the pop tart to go home and eat some Pop-Tarts (which she has publicly longed for), and ponder what happened to her—or her publicists'—masterful navigation of the fine line between self-exposure and self-destruction. Having made an art of inviting viewers to wonder just how knowingly she has participated in her own hyper-sexualization, Spears can't find anyone willing to cut her the break accorded to most young naifs in the world of showbiz.

From the start, Spears' career was built on her ability to be authentically inauthentic. When the 17-year-old Spears first showed up on MTV in 1999—a pig-tailed, kilt-wearing kitten who purred, "Hit me, baby, one more time"—it seemed unlikely she'd wind up as the most scrutinized pop star of her era. Critics never regarded her as much more than a singer of middling talent. And she's hardly a beauty for the ages—she's pretty in the way the best-looking girl at your high school was (ask her first husband, Jason Alexander).

But, unlike, say, Ashlee Simpson, whose *Saturday Night Live* meltdown was a mere gaffe, Spears has elevated inauthenticity to a Warholian level. She's never had to take responsibility for her sexy persona because she refuses to acknowledge she has a persona, sexy or otherwise. Consider the evidence: "[T]he record label wanted me to do certain kinds of songs, and I was like, 'Look, if you want me to be some kind of sex thing, that's not me.'" This is Spears, quoted in an *Esquire,* alongside photos of her naked, save for white panties and strings of pearls that magically conceal (with the apparent aid of an airbrush) her nipples and little else. "I'm not gonna come out on this record and show my crotch or anything. That's not me. I would never do anything like that." This from an issue of *Rolling Stone,* in which Spears appeared topless on the cover, humping a wall. "I don't want to be part of someone's Lolita thing. It kind of freaks me out." This in response to questions about her first *Rolling Stone* photo shoot, in 1999, in which the 17-year-old Britney stood in a bedroom in short-shorts and a push-up bra, surrounded by baby dolls.

Spears didn't invent sexual doublespeak—every teen star does the dance of posing in her underwear while talking up her chastity. But she speaks it more fluently than most. Her jujitsu-like ability to deflect all criticism by turning it back on the accuser—if you ask her about her Lolita-esque antics, you're the one who's a perv—has allowed her to exploit contradictions that have felled lesser stars.

Spears learned her lessons from her acknowledged master, Madonna. Madonna stirred controversy by attaching herself to (some might say exploiting) marginalized subcultures: voguing drag queens, S & M fetishists, etc. Madonna was interested—however glancingly—in contradictions: in, say, dressing as a man and grabbing her crotch. But there was never any doubt that she was calling the shots, working the levers of her own career. Spears, on the other hand, has managed to adopt a "What? Me? Duplicitous?" pose. Spears just *is* a series of contradictions. As such, she can only peel her own layers away.

Which makes her "letter of truth" and her video cry for freedom all the more interesting. The girl who always claimed she'd never been packaged now says she wants to break free of her packaging. Perhaps Spears senses that the perma-bubble of cognitive dissonance surrounding her has finally been punctured—that there are only so many times you can invite viewers to wonder just how knowing you are before they decide, in fact, that you should know better. (It's never a good sign when a look-alike of you is killed in a movie promo, to great cheers, as Britney is in the trailer for the upcoming *Seed of Chucky.*) The problem, now, is that just when she wants to point to her own innocence—her manipulation at the hands of her PR staff—the public is likely to conclude that even her declaration of desperation smacks of a stay-on-message memo. She's referred to her online missive as "The Letter of Truth: I Hope You Can Handle It," which echoes oddly the opening words of the "Prerogative" video: "They can never take away your truth. The question is: Can you handle mine?" It seems Britney can break free from everything except her own talking points. But then, that's always been her greatest trick: She strips and strips and strips, yet never reveals a thing.

DAVID STERRITT
Face of an Angel

What do the films *Bruce Almighty* and *The Green Mile* have in common with *The Family Man,* the *Matrix* movies, and *Ghost?*

All feature black characters whose main function is to help a white hero through magical or supernatural means. These are Hollywood's "black angels," whose popularity has surged in recent years—so much so that in a recent episode of *The Simpsons,* Homer mistook a black man in a white suit for an angelic visitor, all because (according to his embarrassed wife) he'd been seeing too many movies lately.

Of course, there are many films aimed at African-Americans that star blacks in a variety of parts, from villainous to heroic. But casting blacks as angelic characters has become an increasingly common trend in mainstream movies.

For their part, many African-Americans see this heavenly designation as less than beatific. Filmmakers like Spike Lee have spoken out against such roles, calling them patronizing and unrealistic.

"Black-angel movies appeal to a genuine desire for reconciliation among whites and blacks. But they also exploit a distorted fascination with blacks that many whites have," says film historian Krin Gabbard, who explores this subject in his book *Black Magic: White Hollywood and African-American Culture* [2004]. "In vast amounts of entertainment and culture, whites have trouble regarding blacks as real people. That's depressing, but true."

The record supports Dr. Gabbard's charge. In one tradition of American filmmaking, dating to D. W. Griffith's epic *The Birth of a Nation* in 1915, black people are portrayed as villains and monsters—like the lust-crazed Gus who forces Mae Marsh's character to choose death before dishonor.

This practice lives on in many films that still cast black performers as criminals or thugs. Denzel Washington played a crooked cop in *Training Day*— and won an Oscar for it. (Halle Berry also won in 2002, causing many to hope that African-Americans had finally written themselves a bigger part in Hollywood.)

In another tradition, exemplified by *Gone with the Wind* in 1939, blacks are often lovable, but also ignorant and subservient, like the characters played by Butterfly McQueen and Hattie McDaniel. In the most common tradition of all, African-Americans are excluded altogether or allowed a few seconds of screen time to lend local color or comic relief. They may also be depicted as anonymous hordes, as in war pictures such as *Zulu* and *Black Hawk Down.*

94

For decades, most film historians agreed that these traditions served to reinforce the racial prejudices of their times, and that little or nothing can be said in their favor. More recently, revisionist critics have noted that at least such roles allowed black performers to hold careers in the entertainment industry and to display their talents for large audiences.

"Why should I complain about making $7,000 a week playing a maid?" asked Ms. McDaniel, referring to the character type that dominated her career. "If I didn't, I'd be making $7 a week being one."

Viewed in this context, black-angel movies can be seen as an attempt at compromise, giving on-screen blacks more dignity—without taking much of the action away from the white hero. Key examples include *The Green Mile,* where black death-row inmate John Coffey heals a white prison guard and his wife before marching obediently to his execution, and the *Matrix* series, where a black "oracle" (the late Gloria Foster) dispenses prophecy and wisdom to the white "chosen one" (Keanu Reeves). The *Matrix* films, however, can't be accused of tokenism, since they also feature African-American actors, such as Laurence Fishburne and Jada Pinkett-Smith, in prominent roles.

And overall, African-American stars, from Queen Latifah to Will Smith, are commanding higher salaries and headlining more movies than in the past. (Certainly, no one is going to claim that Bill Pullman and Randy Quaid were the main heroes of *Independence Day.*)

But the list of heavenly visitations could stretch all the way down the Walk of Fame. In 1998's *What Dreams May Come,* Cuba Gooding Jr. plays an angel who leads Robin Williams, who is in heaven, on a quest to rescue his wife from hell. That same year Andre Braugher provided comfort to fallen angel Nicolas Cage in *City of Angels.* A seminal film was *Ghost,* where a psychic played by Whoopi Goldberg helps a murder victim (Patrick Swayze) communicate with his widow, Demi Moore. Ms. Goldberg won an Oscar for her role.

"Hollywood has to tread a very fine line," Gabbard says. "It can't keep putting blacks into subservient positions . . . because that would turn off the huge black audience. So in these [black-angel] movies, at some moments [a black character] gets to have total control over the white people. That way blacks don't feel demeaned, and whites don't feel . . . threatened, because the blacks aren't really from their world, they're from heaven."

"And heaven appears to be administered by white people," he adds, "because the black people [in these films] only give their help to whites. John Coffey only helps one character who isn't a white person in *The Green Mile,* and that's a mouse!"

The racial dimensions of films like *The Green Mile* have deep roots in U.S. culture, says Linda Williams, author of *Playing the Race Card: Melodramas of Black and White from Uncle Tom to O.J. Simpson.*

"They come from the tradition of melodrama," Dr. Williams explains, "where to suffer is to acquire virtue. The person who suffers is Christlike and has the moral authority to forgive and offer absolution. The black man's initials in [*The Green Mile*] are J.C., and he seems to exist for the purpose of serving and redeeming white people. You see similar things in *Bruce Almighty,* where a black person redeems a white person, even though the white person's problems are of the most trivial kind."

Williams says the "black angel" movies can be traced back 200 years to *Uncle Tom's Cabin.* "That novel came out of a moment when a certain kind of strict Calvinism was in crisis, and the solution was a more loving kind of approach," she says. "Today . . . there is a feeling that we need some kind of spiritual redemption, and we turn to black people because they're the ones who have suffered."

A key quality of the black-angel movies is that they're not realistic stories but overt, often flamboyant fantasies. Hollywood's ideal black angel [has been] embodied by Morgan Freeman, whose many authoritative roles—the president in *Deep Impact,* a judge in *The Bonfire of the Vanities*—culminate in *Bruce Almighty,* where he plays God as a white-suited gentleman bent on making the life of a self-indulgent journalist (Jim Carrey) more fulfilling.

"There's an unspoken agreement in American culture that blacks are more spiritual, more in touch with the Divine than whites," Gabbard says. "Freeman manages to project that, along with an authenticity, a folksiness, a lack of pretension. He's a man of wisdom, but not an intellectual—a guy who feels the pain of the world. There's compassion in his face, his speech, his manner. . . . This suits our fantasies of how God would act."

Too patronizing? Gabbard points out that the film also gives Freeman's character an above-the-fray quality that other black angels share. Such figures are isolated from the black community, and also from the complicated world of politics, dissension, and difficult moral questions.

Hollywood's recent pattern of casting blacks in idealistic roles and evading "the real world," is exasperating, say many race-conscious critics and filmmakers. "These movies don't really deal with race," says Armond White, an African-American cultural critic for the *New York Press,* a weekly newspaper. "They deal with the desire of white filmmakers to patronize black people . . . by portraying them as kindly, beneficent helpmates."

"These aren't progressive ideas," he adds. "They're a fantasy sold mainly to people over 40, whose thinking is a vestige of the civil rights era. Younger people are less interested in this, because the commercial media encourage them to think racism doesn't exist anymore. 'Eminem showed anyone can be black!' But he's really Elvis redux—another white performer appropriating black styles to get fame and money." (As the rapper himself boasted in last year's hit song "Without Me.")

Another black observer with a critical view of black-angel movies is filmmaker Spike Lee, who expressed his outrage in a March 2001 interview with *Cineaste* magazine. He called Coffey of *The Green Mile* a reworking of the "old grateful slave," and showed even more anger at 2000's *The Legend of Bagger*

Vance, with Matt Damon as a (white) golfer who's supernaturally aided by his (black) caddy, played by Mr. Smith. Observing that the story takes place in the Deep South during the 1930s, when violence against blacks was common, Lee posed a pointed question: "If this magical black caddy has all these powers, why isn't he using them to try and stop some of the brothers from being lynched and [mutilated]? . . . I don't understand this!"

SAMUEL L. JACKSON
In Character

I think it's significant for the growth of the [movie] business that a black actor like me is being cast in race-neutral parts when 20 years ago I wouldn't have been. It's significant for young actors who have aspirations to be things other than criminals and drug dealers and victims and whatever rap artist they have to be to get into a film. The things I've done and Morgan's done and Denzel's done, that Fish has done, that Wesley's° done, everybody's done, have allowed us to achieve a level of success as other kinds of people. We've been successful in roles as doctors, lawyers, teachers, policemen, detectives, spies, monsters—anything that we have been able to portray on-screen in a very realistic way that made audiences say, I believe that, and that brought them into the theaters to see us do it. This has allowed young black actors the opportunity to become different kinds of characters in the cinematic milieu we're a part of.

Before, I used to pick up scripts and I was criminal number two and I looked to see what page I died on. We've now demonstrated a level of expertise, in terms of the care we give to our characters and in terms of our professionalism—showing up to work on time, knowing our lines, and bringing something to the job beyond the lines and basic characterizations. Through our accomplishments and the expertise we have shown, studios know there is a talent pool out there that wants to be like us, and hopefully, these young actors will take care to do the things we did.

As the fabric of our society changes in certain ways, the fabric of the cinematic world changes in the same ways. For a very long time, the people that were in power were white men. They tended to hire other white men, and when they saw a story, the people in those stories were white men or specific kinds of white women. As we get younger producers and younger people in the studios, we have a generation, or several generations, of people who have lived in a society where they have black friends. They have Asian friends. They have Hispanic friends who do a wide variety of jobs, who went into a wide variety of vocations. When the studio heads look at a script now, they can see their friend Juan or they can see their friend Kwong or they can see their friend Rashan. So all of a sudden you see a different look in the movies, as they reflect the way this younger generation of producers and studio executives live their lives. And consequently, through the worldwide network of cinema, you meet other top-quality actors from other cultures. The world of cinema brings us all together. And we've started to cast films in a whole other way that reflects

---

Fish . . . Wesley: refers to Laurence Fishburne and Wesley Snipes.

the way we live and the pattern of our society. Outside of *Spider-Man,* all the big action heroes now seem to be ethnic. The new Arnold Schwarzenegger is The Rock, and the new Bruce Willis is about to be Vin Diesel. So we're doing something right. But it's difficult to do a film that's of a serious nature and that does not have guns, sex, and explosions in it if it's ethnic.

There are many ways to answer the question whether Hollywood is racist. The direct and honest answer, I guess, is yes, only because Hollywood is anti anything that's not green. If something doesn't make money, they don't want to be bothered with it. Therefore, it's still difficult to get a movie about Hispanics made; it's difficult to get a movie about blacks made that doesn't have to do with hip-hop, drugs, and sex. You can get a black comedy made. Eddie Murphy's funny, Will Smith is funny, Martin Lawrence is funny. We have huge black comics. But getting a film like *Eve's Bayou* made is practically impossible. For five years, nobody knew what that movie was. Like, what is it? It's a family drama. Yeah, but how do we market that? Nobody wanted to be bothered with it. Or *Caveman's Valentine.* What is it? It's a mystery, a murder mystery. But it's a black murder mystery. No, there's white people in it; it just happens that a black person is the lead. So Hollywood is racist in its ideas about what can make money and what won't make money. They'll make Asian movies about people who jump across buildings and use swords and swing in trees, like *Crouching Tiger,* but we can't sell an Asian family drama. What do we do with that? Or if we're going to have Asian people in the film, they've got to be like the tong, or they're selling drugs and they got some guns and it's young gang members. It's got to be that. And Hollywood is sexist in its ideals about which women are appealing and which women aren't. It's a young woman's game. Women have got to be either real old or real young to be successful. If they're in the middle, it's like, what do we do with her? Put her in kids' movies, you know, with some kids.

Hollywood can be perceived as racist and sexist, because that's what audiences have said to them they will pay their money to come see. It's difficult to break that cycle, because it's a moneymaking business and it costs money to make films. Hollywood tends to copy things that make lots of money. The first thing they want to know is how many car chases are there and what's blowing up. They're over the how-many-people-die thing, because of 9/11. Now it's like, how many people can we kill and get away with it? We can't blow up anything right now unless it's in the right context. We can blow something up over there, and the bad guy can be a guy with a turban. So there's all kinds of things that go into what people say about Hollywood being racist. There have been times I had to go in a room and convince people I'm the right person for their script and the fact that I'm black will not impact on the script in a negative way. I've had to explain that my being black won't change the dynamics of the interaction; it won't change the dynamics of the story in terms of my character's interaction with the other characters. I'll just happen to be a black guy who's in that story doing those things.

We [African Americans] need to produce our own films. We need to own our own theaters in addition to producing our own films. The more theaters we own, the sooner we can have our own distribution chain. It's a matter of us having that kind of network [as major Hollywood studios do], so when we do make small films that we want to distribute to a specific group of people or to a wider audience, we're able to do it.

I want to be able to produce films for friends of mine who haven't had the opportunity to be seen in the way I've been seen. They're good at what they do, and they deserve an opportunity to be seen by a greater public.

CATHERINE G. LATTERELL
TV Families: The Partridges vs. The Osbournes

On the television show *The Partridge Family,* actress Shirley Jones portrayed the single mother and bandleader of five musically gifted and remarkably wholesome children. The show costarred David Cassidy as the heartthrob Keith, Susan Dey as the fresh-faced Lori, and Danny Bonaduce as the wise-cracking Danny, who, along with the band's bus driver and manager, Mr. Kincaid, represented the show's comic relief. The popularity of *The Partridge Family,* which premiered in September 1970, launched a number of hit records and a product line that included the ubiquitous Partridge-themed lunchbox.

In contrast to the Partridges are the Osbournes, a real and arguably self-promoting musical family. Starring as themselves on their notorious "reality" show, *The Osbournes,* Sharon and Ozzy, along with two of their children, Kelly and Jack, and various pooches, give us a look at the home life of the bleary-eyed, bat-biting, heavy-metal rocker Ozzy Osbourne. First airing in 2000 on MTV, the tagline of the show is "they put the funk into dysfunctional."

1. What do these very different portrayals of musical families—one from 1970 and one from 2000—suggest about changing our cultural attitudes toward family? What messages do these images suggest about popular notions of conformity and nonconformity?

2. Can you think of a contemporary TV family that is similar in some way to *The Partridge Family*? If so, compare the typical problems faced by the Partridges versus the modern TV family. How are the families' conflicts resolved? What conclusions can you draw about the different time periods that produced these shows?

3. Can you think of a TV family from the past that is parallel to *The Osbournes*? If so, choose an episode of each show and compare the plot lines and jokes. What are the differences and similarities between how the shows convey humor? Explain, using specific quotes.

ANDREW NELSON
Wilma Mankiller

San Francisco transformed many people living there during the 1960s. Its shabby, lunch-pail-toting neighborhoods became crucibles for a society recasting its values. The fire eventually caught a shy housewife and mother in her 20s named Mrs. Hugo Olaya and alchemized her into Wilma Pearl Mankiller, a symbol of both feminism and Native American self-determination.

In 1985 Mankiller, now 57, became the first female chief of the Cherokee Nation, the 220,000–member Native American tribe based in Tahlequah, Okla., to which she belongs. She did it not only by overcoming the usual barriers set against Native Americans, but also by vaulting the chauvinistic hurdles imposed by her fellow Cherokees, who had never been led by a woman.

Once chief, Mankiller took the traditional "women's issues" of education and health care and made them tribal priorities. She raised $20 million to build a much-needed infrastructure for schools and other projects, including an $8 million job-training center. The largest Cherokee health clinic was started under her tenure in Stilwell, Okla., and is now named in her honor. Mankiller also sought to reunite the Eastern Cherokee, a group based in North Carolina, with the larger Western division.

She ruled with grace and humor—she often teased patronizing Anglos by telling them her surname was due to her reputation; in fact, "Mankiller" is a Cherokee military term for a village protector—and with organizational smarts learned in the blue-collar neighborhoods of clapboard and "ethnic politics" that circled San Francisco Bay.

Her journey—from complacency to activism to political power—followed a familiar boomer[1] flight path, but hers was a working woman's ascendancy. It was born in the rural grit[2] of Adair County, Okla., and the tough industrial neighborhood of San Francisco's Hunters Point. Elite, tree-shaded suburbs like Pasadena or Grosse Pointe that shaped so many '60s radicals couldn't have been more remote to Mankiller.

Mankiller grew up on her father Charley's ancestral Oklahoma lands. "Dirt poor" was how she described her early life. The Mankillers frequently ate suppers of squirrel and other game. The house had no electricity. Her parents used coal oil for illumination.

In 1956 Charley Mankiller, eager to provide a better life for his growing family, moved them from Oklahoma to California as part of a Bureau of Indian

---

[1] **ESL boomer:** Shortened form of *baby boomer,* referring to a person born during an increase in population, especially the one following World War II.
[2] **ESL grit:** Toughness; determination.

Affairs (BIA) program, initiated by the same bureaucrats who had "relocated" Japanese-Americans during World War II. The program, a misguided experiment in social engineering, transplanted rural Native Americans to jobs in industrial cities, thus serving to weaken reservation ties and diffuse the little political clout the tribes held. It was another insult in a history of them stretching back two centuries.

In 1838 the Cherokee Nation was ripped from its ancestral homelands in the Carolinas, Tennessee and Georgia by U.S. Army troops acting under orders from the federal government. The forced march to the Oklahoma reservations, the famous "Trail of Tears," killed thousands of men, women and children. Buffeted by white assaults—both physical and legal—the Cherokees would spend more than 100 years as wards of the state. It wasn't until 1970 that Washington allowed the tribe to elect its leaders directly.

Wilma was 11 when the Mankillers arrived in San Francisco. Charley found work as a rope maker and the family settled down. Wilma had a difficult transition. She and her siblings were the proverbial hicks[3] in the big city. A kindly Mexican family showed them how to work a telephone and taught Wilma to roller skate. Charley Mankiller had instilled in his children a pride in their heritage, and San Francisco's Indian Center, located in the Mission District, fostered it. The center became Wilma's after-school refuge. The city's diversity exposed her to other things. In high school, African-American girlfriends influenced Mankiller's taste in popular culture. While white girls swooned over Fabian[4] and Elvis, Mankiller absorbed Etta James[5] and B.B. King.[6] Life in a poor black neighborhood, Mankiller told a Sweet Briar College audience in 1993, taught her other valuable lessons.

"What I learned from my experience in living in a community of almost all African-American people," she said, "is that poor people have a much, much greater capacity for solving their own problems than most people give them credit for."

Mankiller exhibited no appetite for intellectual ambition as a teenager. In her 1993 autobiography, *Mankiller: A Chief and Her People,* co-written with Michael Wallis, she recalled hating the classroom. When she graduated from high school in June 1963, she expected that to be the end of formal schooling. "There were never plans for me to go to college," she said. "That thought never even entered my head."

Instead, a tedious pink-collar job followed graduation, as did a fast courtship and marriage to a handsome Ecuadorean college student, Hugo Olaya, with whom Mankiller had two children. Olaya's family was middle-

---

[3]***ESL hicks:*** Derogatory term for unsophisticated and uncultured rural or small-town people.

[4]***Fabian:*** Fabian Forte, popular late 1950s and early 1960s American singer.

[5]***Etta James:*** Blues singer popular from the 1960s through today.

[6]***ESL B.B. King:*** Contemporary blues guitarist.

class; his prospects were good. At 17 the pretty girl, whose dark, flashing eyes gave her a resemblance to actress Natalie Wood, settled down to live the life of a California hausfrau[7] —replete with psychedelic pantsuits, baby strollers and European vacations.

The social protests of the '60s didn't touch Mankiller directly until the decade's last days. On Nov. 9, 1969, 19 Native Americans made their way out to Alcatraz Island, the abandoned federal prison in the middle of San Francisco Bay. The hunk of sandstone, in full view of San Francisco's corporate skyline, was supposed to be handed over to Texas oil tycoon Lamar Hunt and turned into a futuristic shopping mall and revolving restaurant. Instead, the 19 Native Americans claimed the island "in the name of Indians of All Tribes," transforming it into a symbol of Native American liberation.

Led by Mohawk tribesman Richard Oakes and Adam Nordwell, a Minnesota Chippewa, the protesters carried what they considered a fair price for the island: $24 worth of glass beads and red cloth. The beads and cloth were comparable to the ones the Europeans had used to buy Manhattan, but the federal government declined their offer. Coast Guard patrols escorted the protesters back to the mainland.

On Nov. 20 the protesters, now numbering 89, returned for another occupation of the island. This time they stayed 19 months. The rebellion soon bore all the trappings of a media circus. TV news crews hired speedboats to get close to the action, while tourists snapped photos from tour liners. Politicians dropped by. Jane Fonda and Anthony Quinn vowed solidarity. Candice Bergen showed up with a sleeping bag and crashed on the floor.

Mankiller didn't come to Alcatraz in those first two waves, and her siblings Richard, James and Vanessa got there ahead of her. She had stayed in the background, but when she finally arrived, Alcatraz became a pivotal point in her life. While she had been conscious of Native American issues before that time, these protests "flashed like bright comets."

"Every day that passed seemed to give me more self-respect and sense of pride," she wrote.

Pop culture discovered Native American issues around then, too, and glommed onto Red Pride. Dustin Hoffman played the Cheyenne-raised hero in Arthur Penn's film *Little Big Man,* released in 1970. Soon after, Cherokee injustices made the Top 40 with the Paul Revere and the Raiders' hit "Indian Reservation." Meanwhile, Mankiller found herself spending time at the Indian Center helping with fundraising and organizational efforts. She became acting director of East Oakland's Native American Youth Center.

Soon Mankiller's expanding idea of herself (she was now taking college classes in social work) clashed with the more traditional family her husband envisioned. He forbade her to buy a car; she got a little red Mazda with a stick shift and drove to tribal meetings all over the West Coast. Mankiller's favorite

---

[7]*hausfrau:* German for Housewife.

song now, and the one she liked to dance to with her daughters, was Aretha Franklin's "Respect."

She and Olaya divorced in 1974. Mankiller found a job as an Oakland social worker. When she decided to return to Oklahoma with her daughters, she left California in a U-Haul with $20 in her pocket.

"I came home in 1976," she says. "I had no job, very little money, no car, had no idea what I was going to do, but knew it was time to go home."

Mankiller soon found a position as a community coordinator in the Cherokee tribal headquarters. The tribe was beginning to operate with less dependence on the BIA. Reforming the BIA, observed one Creek chief, was like rotating four bald tires on a car: Nothing changed. There were other ways to wrest money from the government. Mankiller, now finishing her degree at the University of Arkansas, became adept in the art of organizing as well as grant and proposal writing. She was proving to be a formidable leader.

In 1979 a head-on car crash seriously injured Mankiller and killed the other driver. By awful coincidence that driver was Sherry Morris, one of Mankiller's best friends. Mankiller spent the next year in rehab wracked with physical pain and guilt. Then, in November 1980, she was diagnosed with the neuromuscular disease myasthenia gravis. An operation to remove her thymus[8] cured her of the illness and she returned to her job in January 1981 to supervise the rejuvenation of the Cherokee town of Bell, Okla. The job involved urban planning and constructing a 16-mile water pipeline, and Mankiller excelled at it. She also met her second husband, Charlie Soap. They married in 1986.

Just three years before, ruling Cherokee Chief Ross Swimmer had asked Mankiller to run as his deputy in the next tribal election. After much debate she accepted and was promptly criticized—not for her liberal Democratic politics but for her gender. Mankiller described herself as "stunned" by the hostility. Charley Mankiller's daughter toughened her hide.

"I expected my politics to be the issue," she said later. "They weren't. The issue was my being a woman, and I wouldn't have it. I simply told myself that it was a foolish issue, and I wouldn't argue with a fool."

Swimmer and Mankiller won the election. Ironically, it was Ronald Reagan, whose policies Mankiller opposed, who gave her the opportunity to become Cherokee chief when he appointed Swimmer head of the BIA in September 1985. Succeeding him, Mankiller served as chief for the next 10 years—winning her second term with 82 percent of the vote.

As chief, Mankiller oversaw a historic self-determination agreement, making the Cherokee Nation one of six tribes to assume responsibility for BIA funds formerly spent by the bureau. She oversaw an annual budget of more than $75 million and more than 1,200 employees. Much of her focus was on developing adequate health care for her tribe. *Ms.* magazine named her 1987's

---

[8] *thymus:* Gland involved with the body's immune system.

"Woman of the Year." She was becoming a national figure, hobnobbing[9] with Bill Clinton and other leaders.

"People are always enormously disappointed when they meet me," she said, "because I'm not handing out crystals or am not laden with Native American jewelry."

In 1995 Mankiller was diagnosed with lymphoma—it's now in remission—and did not seek another term. Joe Byrd was elected chief. His administration soon derailed over bitter tribal constitutional controversies. In 1999 Chad Smith, a legal scholar Mankiller endorsed, became chief and the political infighting abated.

Mankiller has remained in the public eye. In 1995 she received a Chubb Fellowship from Yale University, and in 1998 President Clinton presented her with the Presidential Medal of Freedom.

Illness continues to plague her. In 1990 and 1998 Mankiller underwent two kidney transplants, and in 1999 she was diagnosed with breast cancer. But she still lectures and stays active in the issues that have shaped so much of her life.

"If we're ever going to collectively begin to grapple with the problems that we have collectively," Mankiller has said, "we're going to have to move back the veil and deal with each other on a more human level."

With the courage to sweep old restrictions aside, Mankiller continues to be a warrior not just for the Cherokee but for humanity itself.

---

[9]*hobnobbing:* Associating with.

JON KATZ
How Boys Become Men

Two nine-year-old boys, neighbors and friends, were walking home from school. The one in the bright blue windbreaker was laughing and swinging a heavy-looking book bag toward the head of his friend, who kept ducking and stepping back. "What's the matter?" asked the kid with the bag, whooshing it over his head. "You chicken?"[1]

His friend stopped, stood still and braced himself. The bag slammed into the side of his face, the thump audible all the way across the street where I stood watching. The impact knocked him to the ground, where he lay mildly stunned for a second. Then he struggled up, rubbing the side of his head. "See?" he said proudly. "I'm no chicken."

No. A chicken would probably have had the sense to get out of the way. This boy was already well on the road to becoming a man, having learned one of the central ethics of his gender: Experience pain rather than show fear.

Women tend to see men as a giant problem in need of solution. They tell us that we're remote and uncommunicative, that we need to demonstrate less machismo and more commitment, more humanity. But if you don't understand something about boys, you can't understand why men are the way we are, why we find it so difficult to make friends or to acknowledge our fears and problems.

Boys live in a world with its own Code of Conduct, a set of ruthless, unspoken, and unyielding rules:

Don't be a goody-goody.[2]

Never rat.[3] If your parents ask about bruises, shrug.

Never admit fear. Ride the roller coaster, join the fistfight, do what you have to do. Asking for help is for sissies.

Empathy is for nerds.[4] You can help your best buddy, under certain circumstances. Everyone else is on his own.

Never discuss anything of substance with anybody. Grunt, shrug, dump on teachers, laugh at wimps,[5] talk about comic books. Anything else is risky.

Boys are rewarded for throwing hard. Most other activities—reading, befriending girls, or just thinking—are considered weird. And if there's one thing boys don't want to be, it's weird.

---

[1]*ESL chicken:* A slang mocking term for someone who is afraid of something.
[2]*ESL goody-goody:* A slang mocking term for someone who is eager to please.
[3]*ESL rat:* A slang mocking term for someone who gives away information.
[4]*ESL nerds:* A slang mocking term for unpopular people.
[5]*ESL wimps:* A slang mocking term for people who are afraid of doing something.

More than anything else, boys are supposed to learn how to handle themselves. I remember the bitter fifth-grade conflict I touched off by elbowing aside a bigger boy named Barry and seizing the cafeteria's last carton of chocolate milk. Teased for getting aced out by a wimp, he had to reclaim his place in the pack. Our fistfight, at recess, ended with my knees buckling and my lip bleeding while my friends, sympathetic but out of range, watched resignedly.

When I got home, my mother took one look at my swollen face and screamed. I wouldn't tell her anything, but when my father got home I cracked and confessed, pleading with them to do nothing. Instead, they called Barry's parents, who restricted his television for a week.

The following morning, Barry and six of his pals stepped out from behind a stand of trees. "It's the rat," said Barry.

I bled a little more. Rat was scrawled in crayon across my desk.

They were waiting for me after school for a number of afternoons to follow. I tried varying my routes and avoiding bushes and hedges. It usually didn't work.

I was as ashamed for telling as I was frightened. "You did ask for it," said my best friend. Frontier Justice has nothing on Boy Justice.

In panic, I appealed to a cousin who was several years older. He followed me home from school, and when Barry's gang surrounded me, he came barreling toward us. "Stay away from my cousin," he shouted, "or I'll kill you."

After they were gone, however, my cousin could barely stop laughing. "You were afraid of them?" he howled. "They barely came up to my waist."

Men remember receiving little mercy as boys; maybe that's why it's sometimes difficult for them to show any.

"I know lots of men who had happy childhoods, but none who have happy memories of the way other boys treated them," says a friend. "It's a macho marathon from third grade up, when you start butting each other in the stomach."

"The thing is," adds another friend, "you learn early on to hide what you feel. It's never safe to say, 'I'm scared.' My girlfriend asks me why I don't talk more about what I'm feeling. I've gotten better at it, but it will never come naturally."

You don't need to be a shrink[6] to see how the lessons boys learn affect their behavior as men. Men are being asked, more and more, to show sensitivity, but they dread the very word. They struggle to build their increasingly uncertain work lives but will deny they're in trouble. They want love, affection, and support but don't know how to ask for them. They hide their weaknesses and fears from all, even those they care for. They've learned to be wary of intervening when they see others in trouble. They often still balk at being stigmatized as weird.

---

[6]**ESL shrink:** A slang term for psychiatrist.

Some men get shocked into sensitivity — when they lose their jobs, their wives, or their lovers. Others learn it through a strong marriage, or through their own children.

It may be a long while, however, before male culture evolves to the point that boys can learn more from one another than how to hit curve balls. Last month, walking my dog past the playground near my house, I saw three boys encircling a fourth, laughing and pushing him. He was skinny and rumpled, and he looked frightened. One boy knelt behind him while another pushed him from the front, a trick familiar to any former boy. He fell backward.

When the others ran off, he brushed the dirt off his elbows and walked toward the swings. His eyes were moist and he was struggling for control.

"Hi," I said through the chain-link fence. "How ya doing?"

"Fine," he said quickly, kicking his legs out and beginning his swing.

DAVID CARR

On Covers of Many Magazines, a Full Racial Palette Is Still Rare

Halle Berry, in her role as the sexy superspy Jinx in *Die Another Day,* helps James Bond save the world from certain doom. But Ms. Berry may be performing an even more improbable feat as the cover model of the December issue of *Cosmopolitan* magazine.

Ms. Berry became only the fifth black to appear on the cover of *Cosmopolitan* since the magazine began using cover photographs in 1964, and she is the first since Naomi Campbell in 1990. Ms. Berry is evidently one of a tiny cadre of nonwhite celebrities who are deemed to have enough crossover appeal to appear on the cover of mass consumer magazines.

There are signs that the freeze-out may be beginning to thaw, as the continuing explosion of hip-hop has pushed many black artists into prominence, and as teenagers' magazines that are less anxious about race are bringing more diversity. But in many broad-circulation magazines, the unspoken but routinely observed practice of not using nonwhite cover subjects—for fear they will depress newsstand sales—remains largely in effect.

A survey of 471 covers from 31 magazines published in 2002—an array of men's and women's magazines, entertainment publications and teenagers' magazines—conducted two weeks ago by the *New York Times* found that about one in five depicted minority members. Five years ago, according to the survey, which examined all the covers of those 31 magazines back through 1998, the figure was only 12.7 percent. And fashion magazines have more than doubled their use of nonwhite cover subjects.

But in a country with a nonwhite population of almost 30 percent, the incremental progress leaves some people unimpressed.

"The magazine industry has been slow and reluctant to embrace the change in our culture," said Roy S. Johnson, editorial director of Vanguarde Media and editor in chief of *Savoy,* a magazine aimed at black men. "The change is broad and profound, and in many ways is now the mainstream."

The absence of cover-model diversity could reflect the industry's racial homogeneity. Four years ago, the trade publication *Mediaweek* found that only 6.1 percent of the magazine industry's professional staff was nonwhite.

"We do not see ourselves in magazines," said Diane Weathers, editor in chief of *Essence,* a monthly magazine for black women. "Considering what the country we live in looks like today, I think it's appalling."

The women's category has seen the most profound changes, largely as a result of *O,* the Oprah magazine, whose cover repeatedly hosts Oprah Winfrey[1] and has a large white readership.

Both *Cosmo* and *O* are published by Hearst magazines. As a newsstand giant, selling two million copies a month, *Cosmo* uses a near scientific blend of sex and Middle American beauty on its covers — a formula that does not seem to include black women. *O* magazine, in contrast, transcends race with a new, spiritually based female empowerment.

Publishing is a conservative industry, one that has been known to define risk as using a cover model with dark hair instead of blond. But a wave of Latina superstars like Jennifer Lopez, along with genre-breaking athletes like Tiger Woods[2] and the Williams sisters,[3] have redefined what a celebrity looks like. And the audience is changing as well. In the last five years, the nonwhite audience for magazines has increased to 17 percent from 15 percent, according to Mediamark Research Inc.

Yet, even as black and Hispanic women slowly make their way onto the covers of magazines of various genres, black males still find themselves mainly confined to a ghetto of music and sports magazines.

"When it comes to magazine covers, my client, who is one of the busiest guys in Hollywood, can't get arrested," said an agent for an A-list[4] Hollywood actor who declined to give her name or the name of her client for fear of making a bad situation even worse. "Magazines are in trouble and they are fearful of offending their audience of Middle Americans," she said. "But those same people are buying tickets to his movies."

Daniel Peres, editor of *Details,* a men's magazine owned by Fairchild Publications, said there was pressure to stick with outdated conventions because newsstands now display so many more titles competing for the consumer's attention.

"Everyone is terrified of a misstep," he said. "While most people in the business would prefer it go unspoken because they are horrified at being perceived as racist, it is a well-known legend that blacks, especially black males, do not help generate newsstand sales."

Christina Kelly, now editor in chief of *YM,* a teenagers' magazine owned by Gruner & Jahr USA, recalls a struggle with the circulation people when she worked as an editor in 1993 at the now-closed *Sassy* magazine.

"We wanted to put Mecca from the band Digable Planets on the cover because she was huge at the time and gorgeous," she recalled. "The circulation guys hated the idea, but we just went ahead and did it. The magazine was

---

[1] *ESL Oprah Winfrey:* Successful television talk show host.
[2] *ESL Tiger Woods:* One of the top golfers in America today.
[3] *ESL the Williams sisters:* Serena and Venus Williams, American star tennis players.
[4] *ESL A-list:* The most sought-after and hence most highly paid celebrities.

bagged with a separate beauty booklet, which was usually placed in the back, but this time, it was bagged in front. It just happened to have a picture of a blond, blue-eyed woman on it."

Today, magazines like *Teen People* and *YM* feature cover subjects of a variety of hues. In the last year, *YM* has had covers that included nonwhite artists like Ashanti and Enrique Iglesias. And in August, *Teen People* chose Usher, a black R&B singer, as its No. 1 "hot guy" and featured him on the cover.

"Race is a much more fluid concept among teens," said Barbara O'Dair, managing editor of *Teen People*.

Magazines for teenagers, because of their reliance on the heavily integrated music industry, use 25 percent nonwhite subjects on their covers. If white teenagers are crossing over to embrace minority artists, many artists are meeting them halfway in terms of style.

Fashion, previously a very segregated world, has become transracial, with young white women adopting street fashion while black artists wear long, flowing tresses. Certain totems[5] of beauty—blond hair, among other things—can now be seamlessly situated on almost anyone regardless of race. The singers Shakira, Beyoncé Knowles, and Christina Aguilera, all nonwhite, have at times worn blond hair that is indiscernible from that of Britney Spears.

There is virtually no stigma attached to black celebrities changing their hair as there has been in the past," said Leon E. Wynter, author of *American Skin: Pop Culture, Big Business, and the End of White America* (Crown Publishers, 2002). "The hair thing is completely over."

And race itself has become more complicated and less definable, said Mr. Wynter. He suggests that many of the Latin superstars like Jennifer Lopez are often seen not as minorities by young white teenagers, but as a different kind of white person. Very few of the breakout artists[6] featured on covers are dark skinned.

The growing acceptance of nonwhite cover subjects is not restricted to teenaged girls. Men's magazines, for example, are not as racially monolithic[7] as they once were. *GQ*, which has a nonwhite readership of 18 percent, has always had more diverse images by featuring minority athletes and actors.

But a newer generation of men's magazines seem to find ethnicity sexy. In the last year, five of the twelve women featured on the cover of *Maxim,* the spectacularly successful young men's magazine owned by Dennis Publishing USA, were other than white.

"It doesn't stem from any political motivation," said Keith Blanchard, editor in chief of *Maxim*. His readers, mostly white young men, "are listening to Shakira and Beyoncé. They are cheering for Lucy Liu kicking butt in *Charlie's Angels*. And I think there is a certain attraction to exotic women."

---

[5]*totems:* Things treated with the kind of respect normally reserved for religious icons.
[6]*ESL breakout artists:* People who become stars quickly and sometimes unexpectedly.
[7]*monolithic:* Uniform in character and slow to change.

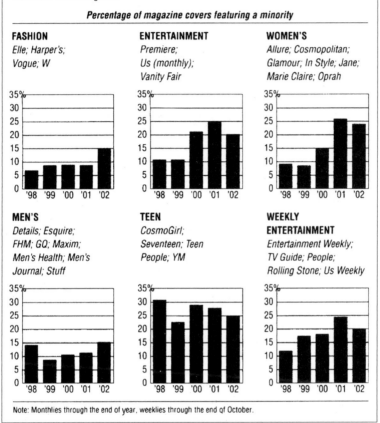

Cover Census

According to the United States Census Bureau, almost 30 percent of America's population belongs to minority groups. Over the last five years, however, the images on the covers of mass-market consumer magazines featured members of a minority less than 25 percent of the time in most categories.

Percentage of magazine covers featuring a minority

FASHION
Elle; Harper's; Vogue; W

ENTERTAINMENT
Premiere; Us (monthly); Vanity Fair

WOMEN'S
Allure; Cosmopolitan; Glamour; In Style; Jane; Marie Claire; Oprah

MEN'S
Details; Esquire; FHM; GQ; Maxim; Men's Health; Men's Journal; Stuff

TEEN
CosmoGirl; Seventeen; Teen People; YM

WEEKLY ENTERTAINMENT
Entertainment Weekly; TV Guide; People; Rolling Stone; Us Weekly

Note: Monthlies through the end of year, weeklies through the end of October.

But there are those who would argue that equal opportunity objectification of women does not represent progress. "What is attractive is socially constructed," said Robin D.G. Kelley, a professor of history at New York University who has written extensively about race and black culture. "I think that race still matters, and many times what is happening is that these poly-racial figures are used to fulfill fantasies. It's the Jezebel[8] phenomenon."

---

[8] *Jezebel:* In the Hebrew scriptures, a ninth-century B.C. queen who married Ahab and promoted idol worship; in general, an immoral woman.

As for the December *Cosmopolitan,* Kate White, the magazine's editor in chief, said Ms. Berry was on her cover simply because she meets all the criteria of a typical *Cosmo* girl. "She is beautiful, powerful, successful, and she can open a movie," Ms. White said, suggesting that Ms. Berry has the kind of wattage[9] that can draw people into a movie, or to buy a magazine. Ms. White said the absence of nonwhite women on the cover of *Cosmo* reflected the celebrities that Hollywood produces, not the magazine's preferences.

Still, when the magazine uses a model instead of a celebrity, it almost invariably chooses a white person. "We choose models who have already started to gain critical mass,[10] regardless of hair or eye color," said a Hearst spokeswoman in response. "We want the reader to have a sense of having seen them before."

It probably helps, in terms of both newsstand and advertising, that Ms. Berry's face is everywhere now that she has been selected as a spokeswoman for the cosmetics company Revlon. There are important business, as well as cultural reasons, why after so many years that black, at least in some magazines, may be beautiful.

"Part of what is going on is that the beauty industry woke up and realized there was a big market there," said Roberta Myers, editor in chief of *Elle,* a women's fashion magazine that is uncommonly diverse in cover selections. "The old assumptions that there was only one kind of beauty, the typical blond, blue-eyed Christie Brinkley[11] type, are gone."

While editors sweat over the consequences of diversifying their cover mix, they may fall behind a coming generation of young consumers who have decided that race is much less important than how hot a given celebrity's latest record or film is.

"The list of who is acceptable or hot is slowly expanding," said Mr. Wynter. "In the current generation, there is an underlying urge, an aspiration, to assert one's common humanity. You can't see it in the magazines that are on the shelves now, but it is coming to the fore."

---

[9] *ESL* **wattage:** Star power.

[10] **critical mass:** The amount necessary to have a significant effect.

[11] **ESL Christie Brinkley:** American supermodel during the 1970s and 1980s.

JOHN H. McWHORTER
How Hip-Hop Holds Blacks Back

Not long ago, I was having lunch in a KFC[1] in Harlem, sitting near eight African-American boys, aged about 14. Since 1) it was 1:30 on a school day, 2) they were carrying book bags, and 3) they seemed to be in no hurry, I assumed they were skipping school. They were extremely loud and unruly, tossing food at one another and leaving it on the floor.

Black people ran the restaurant and made up the bulk of the customers, but it was hard to see much healthy "black community" here. After repeatedly warning the boys to stop throwing food and keep quiet, the manager finally told them to leave. The kids ignored her. Only after she called a male security guard did they start slowly making their way out, tauntingly circling the restaurant before ambling off. These teens clearly weren't monsters, but they seemed to consider themselves exempt from public norms of behavior—as if they had begun to check out of mainstream society.

What struck me most, though, was how fully the boys' music—hard-edged rap, preaching bone-deep dislike of authority—provided them with a continuing soundtrack to their antisocial behavior. So completely was rap ingrained in their consciousness that every so often, one or another of them would break into cocky, expletive-laden rap lyrics, accompanied by the angular, bellicose gestures typical of rap performance. A couple of his buddies would then join him. Rap was a running decoration in their conversation.

Many writers and thinkers see a kind of informed political engagement, even a revolutionary potential, in rap and hip-hop. They couldn't be more wrong. By reinforcing the stereotypes that long hindered blacks, and by teaching young blacks that a thuggish adversarial stance is the properly "authentic" response to a presumptively racist society, rap retards black success.

The venom that suffuses rap had little place in black popular culture—indeed, in black attitudes—before the 1960s. The hip-hop ethos can trace its genealogy to the emergence in that decade of a black ideology that equated black strength and authentic black identity with a militantly adversarial stance toward American society. In the angry new mood, captured by Malcolm X's upraised fist, many blacks (and many more white liberals) began to view black crime and violence as perfectly natural, even appropriate, responses to the supposed dehumanization and poverty inflicted by a racist society. Briefly, this militant spirit, embodied above all in the Black Panthers,[2] infused black popular

---

[1] **ESL KFC:** An acronym for Kentucky Fried Chicken, a fast-food restaurant.
[2] **Black Panthers:** Members of a militant group of African Americans who were active in the 1960s and 1970s.

culture, from the plays of LeRoi Jones to "blaxploitation" movies, like Melvin Van Peebles's *Sweet Sweetbacks' Baadasssss Song,* which celebrated the black criminal rebel as a hero.

But blaxploitation and similar genres burned out fast. The memory of whites blatantly stereotyping blacks was too recent for the typecasting in something like *Sweet Sweetbacks' Baadasssss Song* not to offend many blacks. Observed black historian Lerone Bennett: "There is a certain grim white humor in the fact that the black marches and demonstrations of the 1960s reached artistic fulfillment" with "provocative and ultimately insidious reincarnations of all the Sapphires and Studds of yesteryear."

Early rap mostly steered clear of the Sapphires and Studds, beginning not as a growl from below but as happy party music. The first big rap hit, the Sugar Hill Gang's 1978 "Rapper's Delight," featured a catchy bass groove that drove the music forward, as the jolly rapper celebrated himself as a ladies' man and a great dancer. Soon, kids across America were rapping along with the nonsense chorus:

> I said a hip, hop, the hippie, the hippie,
> to the hip-hip hop, ah you don't stop
> the rock it to the bang bang boogie, say
> up jump the boogie,
> to the rhythm of the boogie, the beat.

A string of ebullient raps ensued in the months ahead. At the time, I assumed it was a harmless craze, certain to run out of steam soon.

But rap took a dark turn in the early 1980s, as this "bubble gum" music gave way to a "gangsta" style that picked up where blaxploitation left off. Now top rappers began to write edgy lyrics celebrating street warfare or drugs and promiscuity. Grandmaster Flash's ominous 1982 hit, "The Message," with its chorus, "It's like a jungle sometimes, it makes me wonder how I keep from going under," marked the change in sensibility. It depicted ghetto life as profoundly desolate:

> You grow in the ghetto, living second rate
> And your eyes will sing a song of deep hate.
> The places you play and where you stay
> Looks like one great big alley way.
> You'll admire all the numberbook takers,
> Thugs, pimps and pushers, and the big money makers.

Music critics fell over themselves to praise "The Message," treating it as the poetry of the streets—as the elite media has characterized hip-hop ever since. The song's grim fatalism struck a chord; twice, I've heard blacks in audiences for talks on race cite the chorus to underscore a point about black victimhood. So did the warning it carried: "Don't push me, 'cause I'm close to the edge," menacingly raps Melle Mel. The ultimate message of "The Message"— that ghetto life is so hopeless that an explosion of violence is both justified and imminent—would become a hip-hop mantra in the years ahead.

The angry, oppositional stance that "The Message" reintroduced into black popular culture transformed rap from a fad into a multi-billion-dollar industry that sold more than 80 million records in the U.S. in 2002—nearly 13 percent of all recordings sold. To rap producers like Russell Simmons, earlier black pop was just sissy music. He despised the "soft, unaggressive music (and non-threatening images)" of artists like Michael Jackson or Luther Vandross. "So the first chance I got," he says, "I did exactly the opposite."

In the two decades since "The Message," hip-hop performers have churned out countless rap numbers that celebrate a ghetto life of unending violence and criminality. Schooly D's "PSK What Does It Mean?" is a case in point:

> Copped my pistols, jumped into the ride.
> Got at the bar, copped some flack,
> Copped some cheeba-cheeba, it wasn't wack.
> Got to the place, and who did I see?
> A sucka-ass nigga tryin to sound like me.
> Put my pistol up against his head—
> I said, "Sucka-ass nigga, I should shoot you dead."

The protagonist of a rhyme by KRS-One (a hip-hop star who would later speak out against rap violence) actually pulls the trigger:

> Knew a drug dealer by the name of Peter—
> Had to buck him down with my 9 millimeter.

Police forces became marauding invaders in the gangsta-rap imagination. The late West Coast rapper Tupac Shakur expressed the attitude:

> Ya gotta know how to shake the snakes, nigga,
> 'Cause the police love to break a nigga,
> Send him upstate 'cause they straight up hate the nigga.

Shakur's anti-police tirade seems tame, however, compared with Ice-T's infamous "Cop Killer":

> I got my black shirt on.
> I got my black gloves on.
> I got my ski mask on.
> This shit's been too long.
>
> I got my 12-gauge sawed-off.
> I got my headlights turned off.
> I'm 'bout to bust some shots off.
> I'm 'bout to dust some cops off. . . .
>
> I'm 'bout to kill me somethin'
> A pig stopped me for nuthin'!
> Cop killer, better you than me.
> Cop killer, fuck police brutality! . . .

Die, die, die pig, die!
Fuck the police! . . .
Fuck the police yeah!

Rap also began to offer some of the most icily misogynistic music human history has ever known. Here's Schooly D again:

Tell you now, brother, this ain't no joke,
She got me to the crib, she laid me on the bed,
I fucked her from my toes to the top of my head.
I finally realized the girl was a whore,
Gave her ten dollars, she asked me for some more.

Jay-Z's "Is That Yo Bitch?" mines similar themes:

I don't love 'em, I fuck 'em.
I don't chase 'em, I duck 'em.
I replace 'em with another one. . . .
She be all on my dick.

Or, as N.W.A. (an abbreviation of "Niggers with Attitude") tersely sums up the hip-hop worldview: "Life ain't nothin' but bitches and money."

Rap's musical accompaniment mirrors the brutality of rap lyrics in its harshness and repetition. Simmons fashions his recordings in contempt for euphony.[3] "What we used for melody was implied melody, and what we used for music was sounds—beats, scratches, stuff played backward, nothing pretty or sweet." The success of hip-hop has resulted in an ironic reversal. In the seventies, screaming hard rock was in fashion among young whites, while sweet, sinuous funk and soul ruled the black airwaves—a difference I was proud of. But in the eighties, rock quieted down, and black music became the assault on the ears and soul. Anyone who grew up in urban America during the eighties won't soon forget the young men strolling down streets, blaring this sonic weapon from their boom boxes, with defiant glares daring anyone to ask them to turn it down.

Hip-hop exploded into popular consciousness at the same time as the music video, and rappers were soon all over MTV, reinforcing in images the ugly world portrayed in rap lyrics. Video after video features rap stars flashing jewelry, driving souped-up[4] cars, sporting weapons, angrily gesticulating at the camera, and cavorting with interchangeable, mindlessly gyrating, scantily clad women.

Of course, not all hip-hop is belligerent or profane—entire CDs of gang-bangin', police-baiting, woman-bashing invective would get old fast to most listeners. But it's the nastiest rap that sells best, and the nastiest cuts that make a career. As I write, the top ten best-selling hip-hop recordings are 50

---

[3] *euphony:* A pleasing combination of sounds.
[4] *ESL souped-up:* Modified for greater speed.

Cent (currently with the second-best-selling record in the nation among all musical genres), Bone Crusher, Lil' Kim, Fabolous, Lil' Jon and the East Side Boyz, Cam'ron Presents the Diplomats, Busta Rhymes, Scarface, Mobb Deep, and Eminem. Every one of these groups or performers personifies willful, staged opposition to society—Lil' Jon and crew even regale us with a song called "Don't Give a Fuck"—and every one celebrates the ghetto as "where it's at." Thus, the occasional dutiful songs in which a rapper urges men to take responsibility for their kids or laments senseless violence are mere garnish. Keeping the thug front and center has become the quickest and most likely way to become a star.

No hip-hop luminary[5] has worked harder than Sean "P. Diddy" Combs, the wildly successful rapper, producer, fashion mogul, and CEO of Bad Boy Records, to cultivate a gangsta image—so much so that he's blurred the line between playing the bad boy and really being one. Combs may have grown up middle-class in Mount Vernon, New York, and even have attended Howard University for a while, but he's proven he can gang-bang with the worst. Cops charged Combs with possession of a deadly weapon in 1995. In 1999, he faced charges for assaulting a rival record executive. Most notoriously, police charged him that year with firing a gun at a nightclub in response to an insult, injuring three bystanders, and with fleeing the scene with his entourage (including then-pal Jennifer "J. Lo" Lopez). Combs got off, but his young rapper protege Jamal "Shyne" Barrow went to prison for firing the gun.

Combs and his crew are far from alone among rappers in keeping up the connection between "rap and rap sheet,"[6] as critic Kelefa Sanneh artfully puts it. Several prominent rappers, including superstar Tupac Shakur, have gone down in hails of bullets—with other rappers often suspected in the killings. Death Row Records producer Marion "Suge" Knight just finished a five-year prison sentence for assault and federal weapons violations. Current rage 50 Cent flaunts his bullet scars in photos; cops recently arrested him for hiding assault weapons in his car. Of the top ten hip-hop sellers mentioned above, five have had scrapes with the law. In 2000, at least five different fights broke out at the Source Hiphop Awards—intended to be the rap industry's Grammys. The final brawl, involving up to 100 people in the audience and spilling over onto the stage, shut the ceremony down—right after a video tribute to slain rappers. Small wonder a popular rap website goes by the name rapsheet.com.

Many fans, rappers, producers, and intellectuals defend hip-hop's violence, both real and imagined, and its misogyny as a revolutionary cry of frustration from disempowered youth. For Simmons, gangsta raps "teach listeners something about the lives of the people who create them and remind them that these people exist." 50 Cent recently told *Vibe* magazine, "Mainstream America can look at me and say, 'That's the mentality of a young man from the

---

[5]***luminary:*** A celebrity.
[6]***ESL rap sheet:*** A list of crimes that a criminal has committed.

'hood.'" University of Pennsylvania black studies professor Michael Eric Dyson has written a book-length paean[7] to Shakur, praising him for "challenging narrow artistic visions of black identity" and for "artistically exploring the attractions and limits of black moral and social subcultures"—just one of countless fawning treatises on rap published in recent years. The National Council of Teachers of English, recommending the use of hip-hop lyrics in urban public school classrooms (as already happens in schools in Oakland, Los Angeles, and other cities), enthuses that "hip-hop can be used as a bridge linking the seemingly vast span between the streets and the world of academics."

But we're sorely lacking in imagination if in 2003—long after the civil rights revolution proved a success, at a time of vaulting opportunity for African Americans, when blacks find themselves at the top reaches of society and politics—we think that it signals progress when black kids rattle off violent, sexist, nihilistic lyrics, like Russians reciting Pushkin.[8] Some defended blaxploitation pictures as revolutionary, too, but the passage of time has exposed the silliness of such a contention. "The message of *Sweetback* is that if you can get it together and stand up to the Man, you can win," Van Peebles once told an interviewer. But win what? All Sweetback did, from what we see in the movie, was avoid jail—and it would be nice to have more useful counsel on overcoming than "kicking the Man's ass." Claims about rap's political potential will look equally gestural in the future. How is it progressive to describe life as nothing but "bitches and money"? Or to tell impressionable black kids, who'd find every door open to them if they just worked hard and learned, that blowing a rival's head off is "real"? How helpful is rap's sexism in a community plagued by rampant illegitimacy and an excruciatingly low marriage rate?

The idea that rap is an authentic cry against oppression is all the sillier when you recall that black Americans had lots more to be frustrated about in the past but never produced or enjoyed music as nihilistic as 50 Cent or N.W.A. On the contrary, black popular music was almost always affirmative and hopeful. Nor do we discover music of such violence in places of great misery like Ethiopia or the Congo—unless it's imported American hip-hop.

Given the hip-hop world's reflexive alienation, it's no surprise that its explicit political efforts, such as they are, are hardly progressive. Simmons has founded the "Hip-Hop Summit Action Network" to bring rap stars and fans together in order to forge a "bridge between hip-hop and politics." But HSAN's policy positions are mostly tired bromides.[9] Sticking with the long-discredited idea that urban schools fail because of inadequate funding from the stingy, racist white Establishment, for example, HSAN joined forces with the teachers' union to protest New York mayor Bloomberg's proposed education budget for its supposed lack of generosity. HSAN has also stuck it to President

---

[7]*paean:* A tribute.
[8]*Pushkin:* Alexander Pushkin, a nineteenth-century Russian poet.
[9]*bromides:* Tired, commonplace ideas.

Bush for invading Iraq. And it has vociferously protested the affixing of advisory labels on rap CDs that warn parents about the obscene language inside. Fighting for rappers' rights to obscenity: that's some kind of revolution!

Okay, maybe rap isn't progressive in any meaningful sense, some observers will admit; but isn't it just a bunch of kids blowing off steam and so nothing to worry about? I think that response is too easy. With music videos, DVD players, Walkmans, the Internet, clothes, and magazines all making hip-hop an accompaniment to a person's entire existence, we need to take it more seriously. In fact, I would argue that it is seriously harmful to the black community.

The rise of nihilistic rap has mirrored the breakdown of community norms among inner-city youth over the last couple of decades. It was just as gangsta rap hit its stride that neighborhood elders began really to notice that they'd lost control of young black men, who were frequently drifting into lives of gang violence and drug dealing. Well into the seventies, the ghetto was a shabby part of town, where, despite unemployment and rising illegitimacy, a healthy number of people were doing their best to "keep their heads above water," as the theme song of the old black sitcom *Good Times* put it.

By the eighties, the ghetto had become a ruleless war zone, where black people were their own worst enemies. It would be silly, of course, to blame hip-hop for this sad downward spiral, but by glamorizing life in the "war zone," it has made it harder for many of the kids stuck there to extricate themselves. Seeing a privileged star like Sean Combs behave like a street thug tells those kids that there's nothing more authentic than ghetto pathology, even when you've got wealth beyond imagining.

The attitude and style expressed in the hip-hop "identity" keeps blacks down. Almost all hip-hop, gangsta or not, is delivered with a cocky, confrontational cadence that is fast becoming—as attested to by the rowdies at KFC—a common speech style among young black males. Similarly, the arm-slinging, hand-hurling gestures of rap performers have made their way into many young blacks' casual gesticulations, becoming integral to their self-expression. The problem with such speech and mannerisms is that they make potential employers wary of young black men and can impede a young black's ability to interact comfortably with co-workers and customers. The black community has gone through too much to sacrifice upward mobility to the passing kick of an adversarial hip-hop "identity."

On a deeper level, there is something truly unsettling and tragic about the fact that blacks have become the main agents in disseminating debilitating—dare I say racist—images of themselves. Rap guru Russell Simmons claims that "the coolest stuff about American culture—be it language, dress, or attitude—comes from the underclass. Always has and always will." Yet back in the bad old days, blacks often complained—with some justification—that the media too often depicted blacks simply as uncivilized. Today, even as television and films depict blacks at all levels of success, hip-hop sends the message that blacks are . . . uncivilized. I find it striking that the cry-racism crowd doesn't condemn it.

For those who insist that even the invisible structures of society reinforce racism, the burden of proof should rest with them to explain just why hip-hop's bloody and sexist lyrics and videos and the criminal behavior of many rappers *wouldn't* have a powerfully negative effect upon whites' conception of black people.

Sadly, some black leaders just don't seem to care what lesson rap conveys. Consider Savannah's black high schools, which hosted the local rapper Camoflauge as a guest speaker several times before his murder earlier this year. Here's a representative lyric:

> Gimme the keys to tha car, I'm ready for war.
> When we ride on these niggas smoke that ass like a 'gar.
> Hit your block with a Glock, clear the set with a Tech. . . .
> You think I'm jokin, see if you laughing when tha pistol be smokin —
> Leave you head split wide open
> And you bones get broken. . . .

More than a few of the Concerned Black People inviting this "artist" to speak to the impressionable youth of Savannah would presumably be the first to cry out about "how whites portray blacks in the media."

Far from decrying the stereotypes rampant in rap's present-day blax-ploitation, many hip-hop defenders pull the "whitey-does-it-too" trick. They point to the *Godfather* movies or *The Sopranos* as proof that violence and vul-garity are widespread in American popular culture, so that singling out hip-hop for condemnation is simply bigotry. Yet such a defense is pitifully weak. No one really looks for a way of life to emulate or a political project to adopt in *The Sopranos.* But for many of its advocates, hip-hop, with its fantasies of revolution and community and politics, is more than entertainment. It forms a bedrock[10] of young black identity.

Nor will it do to argue that hip-hop isn't "black" music, since most of its buyers are white, or because the "hip-hop revolution" is nominally open to people of all colors. That whites buy more hip-hop recordings than blacks do is hardly surprising, given that whites vastly outnumber blacks nation-wide. More to the point, anyone who claims that rap isn't black music will need to reconcile that claim with the widespread wariness among blacks of white rappers like Eminem, accused of "stealing our music and giving it back to us."

At 2 a.m. on the New York subway not long ago, I saw another scene — more dispiriting than my KFC encounter with the rowdy rapping teens — that captures the essence of rap's destructiveness. A young black man entered the car and began to rap loudly — profanely, arrogantly — with the usual wild gestures.

---

[10]*bedrock:* A foundation.

This went on for five irritating minutes. When no one paid attention, he moved on to another car, all the while spouting his doggerel.[11]

This was what this young black man presented as his message to the world—his oratory, if you will.

Anyone who sees such behavior as a path to a better future—anyone, like Professor Dyson, who insists that hip-hop is an urgent "critique of a society that produces the need for the thug persona"—should step back and ask himself just where, exactly, the civil rights-era blacks might have gone wrong in lacking a hip-hop revolution. They created the world of equality, striving, and success I live and thrive in.

Hip-hop creates nothing.

---

[11]*doggerel:* Poor-quality poetry.

JAMILAH EVELYN

To the Academy with Love, from a Hip-Hop Fan

While putting together a cover story, a source asked me if I thought it was the academy's[1] responsibility to get to know and understand hip-hop—the music and its accompanying culture.

Pausing first, I replied: It may not be a professor's job to run out and buy the latest Jay-Z CD in order to better identify with her students. But the extent to which academe[2] can develop an empathetic rapport with the devotees of this cultural phenomenon is partly the extent to which academe's reach will be further enhanced. And yes, I do think it's the academy's responsibility to find new ways to extend its reach.

Too many potential students, potential dropouts and potential great black (and other) leaders are at stake.

For better or worse, hip-hop has molded several generations of college students—black, white, and every hue in between. With its vulgarities, its black political consciousness, its misogyny, and its soulful nourishment, this latest incarnation of black expression has quite simply taken the world by storm.

So love it or hate it. But do attempt to understand it.

As a member of the "hip-hop generation," and an admitted hip-hop fan, I too am distressed by any celebration of black sadism, ho-ism[3] and the effect such money-making demoralizing has on our youth. But the fact that violence sells is indicative more of American pop culture in general than of this one particular facet. The recipe for that disaster is easy to explain.

Perhaps what disappoints and confounds me more is seeing a cadre of scholars—often clever enough to be unmoved by the media's misplaced stereotypes—dismiss a whole genre of black music and its fans.

Where else besides higher education's forgiving, reflective and ideally inclusive sphere should we expect introspective exchanges on the music and the society that shapes it? Who else besides a professor, conscious of the thoughtful and intellectual side of kids otherwise cast as degenerates,[4] should we expect to give a ringing endorsement of hip-hop's prolific protégés?[5]

---

[1]*the academy:* Colleges and universities.
[2]*academe:* The academic world.
[3]*ho-ism:* Prostitution.
[4]*degenerates:* People who act in ways that many others feel are immoral.
[5]*protégés:* People whose careers are furthered by a person of experience or influence.

126

Hip-hop is so much more than the rump-shaking, "ice"-flossing,[6] gang-ster revelry that fuels the record industry's multibillion dollar sales every year.

That said, let us all keep in mind that even the dark and demoralized side of hip-hop is no more than a byproduct of the capitalist mindset that higher education often endorses.

We can accept and reach out to our students—the b-boys,[7] the hoochie mamas[8] and the thugged out[9] among them—without sanctioning the more destructive ethos[10] that unfortunately defines so much of the music today.

Truth be told, I was pleasantly surprised at the number of scholars I talked to who see hip-hop's redemptive aspects. Many even encourage their students to draw on its poetic, solicitous and uplifting facets to prepare their pa-pers, understand current events, indeed to change the world.

But I would encourage more of their colleagues to recognize that hip-hop's fruitage[11] includes the disengaged learner as well as the Rhodes Scholar.[12] It includes the kid who never even made it to college and the one who exceeded everyone's expectations.

It also includes the editor of a magazine devoted to making sure that higher education opens more doors, expands more minds and reaches out to ever more students who traditionally have been left out of the equation. Any-one committed to that mission has got to keep it real.

---

[6] *"ice"-flossing:* Flaunting expensive jewelry (ice).

[7] *b-boys:* Gang of men or boys, originally a basketball term.

[8] *hoochie mamas:* Slang for sexy women.

[9] *thugged out:* Gangster-like.

[10] *ethos:* The distinguishing character or guiding belief of a person, group, or institution.

[11] *fruitage:* The product or result.

[12] *Rhodes Scholar:* A recipient of one of numerous scholarships founded by Cecil J. Rhodes to allow gifted students to study at Oxford University in England.

LORRAINE ALI
Do I Look Like Public Enemy Number One?

You're not a terrorist, are you?" That was pretty much a stock question I faced growing up. Classmates usually asked it after they heard my last name: "Ali" sounded Arabic; therefore, I must be some kind of bomb-lobbing religious fanatic with a grudge against Western society. It didn't matter that just before my Middle Eastern heritage was revealed, my friend and I might have been discussing the merits of rock versus disco, or the newest flavor of Bonne Bell Lip Smacker.[1]

I could never find the right retort; I either played along ("Yeah, and I'm going to blow up the math building first") or laughed and shrugged it off. How was I going to explain that my background meant far more than buzz words like *fanatic* and *terrorist* could say? Back in the '70s and '80s, all Americans knew of the Middle East came from television and newspapers. "Arab" meant a contemptible composite of images: angry Palestinian refugees, irate Iranian hostage-takers, extremist leaders like Libya's Muammar al-Qaddafi or Iran's Ayatollah Khomeini, and long gas lines at home. What my limited teenage vernacular couldn't express was that an entire race of people was being judged by its most violent individuals.

Twenty years later, I'm still trying to explain. Not much has changed in the '90s. In fact, now that Russia has been outmoded as Public Enemy Number One, Arabs have been promoted into that position. Whenever a disaster strikes without a clear cause, fingers point toward Islam. When an explosion downed TWA Flight 800, pundits prematurely blamed "Arab terrorists." Early coverage following the Oklahoma City bombing featured experts saying it "showed Middle Eastern traits." Over the next six days there were 150 documented hate crimes against Arab Americans; phone calls to radio talk shows demanded detainment and deportation of Middle Easterners. Last fall, *The Siege* depicted Moslems terrorizing Manhattan, and TV's *Days of Our Lives* showed a female character being kidnapped by an Arabian sultan, held hostage in a harem, and threatened with death if she didn't learn how to belly dance properly. Whatever!

MY CHILDHOOD HAD NOTHING TO DO WITH BELLY DANCING

Defending my ethnicity has always seemed ironic to me because I consider myself a fake Arab. I am half of European ancestry and half Arab, and I grew up in the suburban sprawl of Los Angeles' San Fernando Valley. My skin is pale

---

[1] *ESL Bonne Bell Lip Smacker:* A brand of flavored lip gloss.

olive rather than smooth brown like my dad's, and my eyes are green, not black like my sisters' (they got all the Arab genes). Even my name, Lorraine Mahia Ali, saves all the Arab parts for last.

I also didn't grow up Moslem, like my dad, who emigrated from Baghdad, Iraq's capital, in 1956. In the old country he wore a galabiya (or robe), didn't eat pork, and prayed toward Mecca five times a day. To me, an American girl who wore short-shorts, ate Pop Rocks,[2] and listened to Van Halen,[3] his former life sounded like a fairy tale. The Baghdad of his childhood was an ancient city where he and his brothers swam in the Tigris River, where he did accounting on an abacus[4] in his father's tea shop, where his mother blamed his sister's polio on a neighbor's evil eye, where his entire neighborhood watched Flash Gordon[5] movies projected on the side of a bakery wall.

My father's world only started to seem real to me when I visited Iraq the summer after fifth grade and stayed in his family's small stucco house. I remember feeling both completely at home and totally foreign. My sister Lela and I spoke to amused neighbors in shoddy sign language, sat cross-legged on the floor in our Mickey Mouse T-shirts, rolling cigarettes to sell at market for my arthritic Bedouin[6] grandma, and sang silly songs in pidgin[7] Arabic with my Uncle Brahim. Afterward, I wrote a back-to-school essay in which I referred to my grandparents as Hajia and Haja Hassan, thinking their names were the Arab equivalent of Mary Ellen and Billy Bob. "You're such a dumb-ass," said Lela. "It just means grandma and grandpa." But she was wrong too. It actually meant they had completed their Haj duty — a religious journey to Mecca in Saudi Arabia that millions of Muslims embark on each year.

At home, my American side continued to be shamefully ignorant of all things Arab, but my Arab side began to notice some pretty hideous stereotypes. Saturday-morning cartoons depicted Arabs as ruthless, bumbling, and hygienically challenged. I'd glimpse grotesque illustrations of Arab leaders in my dad's paper. At the mall with my mom, we'd pass such joke items as an Arab face on a bull's-eye. She tried to explain to me that things weren't always this way, that there was a time when Americans were mesmerized by Arabia and Omar Sharif[8] made women swoon. A time when a WASP[9] girl like my mom, raised in a conservative, middle-class family, could be considered romantic and daring,

---

[2]*Pop Rocks:* A type of fizzy candy popular in the 1970s.

[3]*ESL Van Halen:* A rock musical group first popular in the 1980s.

[4]*abacus:* An ancient device for calculating numbers.

[5]*ESL Flash Gordon:* The hero of a comic book series that originated in 1934 about a space traveler battling evildoers.

[6]*Bedouin:* A tent dweller of the desert; a wanderer.

[7]*pidgin:* A simplified form of a language.

[8]*ESL Omar Sharif:* An Egyptian actor best known for his charismatic performances in the films *Lawrence of Arabia* and *Doctor Zhivago.*

[9]*ESL WASP:* Slang term for white Anglo-Saxon Protestant.

not subversive, for dating my dad. In effect, my mom belonged to the last generation to think sheiks were chic.

Not so in my generation. My mother tells me that when my oldest sister
was five, she said to a playmate that her dad "was an Arab, but not a bad one."
In elementary school, we forced smiles through taunts like, "Hey, Ali, where's
your oilcan?" Teachers were even more hurtful: During roll call on her first day
of junior high, Lela was made to sit through a twenty-minute lecture about the
bloodshed and barbarism of Arabs toward Israel and the world. As far as I knew,
Lela had never shed anyone's blood except for mine, when she punched me in
the nose over a pack of Pixie Sticks.[10] But that didn't matter. As Arabs, we were
guilty by association, even at the age of twelve.

BY HIGH SCHOOL, I WAS BEGINNING TO BELIEVE THE HYPE

It's awful to admit, but I was sometimes embarrassed by my dad.

I know it's every teen's job to think her parents are the most shameful
creatures to walk the planet, but this basic need to reject him was exacerbated by
the horrible images of Arabs around me. When he drove me to school, my dad
would pop in a cassette of Quran suras (recorded prayers) and recite the lines in
a language I didn't understand, yet somehow the twisting, weaving words
sounded as natural as the whoosh of the Santa Ana winds through the dusty hills
where we lived. His brown hands would rise off the steering wheel at high
points of the prayer, the sun illuminating the big white moons of his fingernails.
The mass of voices on tape would swell up and answer the Mezzuin[11] like a
gospel congregation responding to a preacher. It was beautiful, but I still made
my dad turn it down as we approached my school. I knew I'd be identified as
part of a culture that America loved to hate.

My dad must have felt this, too. He spoke his native tongue only in the
company of Arabic friends and never taught my sisters or me the language,
something he would regret until the day he died. His background was a mystery to me. I'd pester him for answers: "Do you dream in English or Arabic?" I'd
ask, while he was busy doing dad work like fixing someone's busted Schwinn[12]
or putting up Christmas lights. "Oh, I don't know," he'd answer playfully. "In
dreams, I can't tell the difference."

Outside the safety of our home, he could. He wanted respect; therefore,
he felt he must act American. Though he truly loved listening to Roberta
Flack[13] and wearing Adidas sweatsuits, I can't imagine he enjoyed making din-

---

[10]*Pixie Sticks:* A type of powdered candy that comes in a paper straw.
[11]*Mezzuin:* An Islamic cantor who sings to lead worshipers in prayer.
[12]*ESL Schwinn:* A popular bicycle manufacturer.
[13]*ESL Roberta Flack:* A jazz and pop singer who first gained popularity in the early
1970s.

ner reservations under pseudonyms like Mr. Allen. He knew that as Mr. Ali, he might never get a table.

DESERT STORM WARNING

Fifteen years later, "Ali" was still not a well-received name. We were at war with the Middle East. It was January 16, 1991, and Iraq's Saddam Hussein had just invaded Kuwait. I will never forget the night CNN's Bernard Shaw lay terrified on the floor of his Baghdad hotel as a cameraman shot footage of the brand-new war outside his window. I was twenty-six and working for a glossy music magazine called *Creem*. When the news broke that we were bombing Baghdad in an operation called Desert Storm, I went home early and sat helpless in my Hollywood apartment, crying. Before me on the TV was a man dressed in a galabiya, just like the kind my dad used to wear around the house, aiming an ancient-looking gun turret toward our space-age planes in the sky. He looked terrified, too. With every missile we fired, I watched the Baghdad I knew slip away and wondered just who was being hit. Was it Aunt Niama? My cousin Afrah?

Back at work, I had to put up with "funny" faxes of camels, SCUD missiles, and dead Arabs. To my colleagues, the Arabs I loved and respected were now simply targets. Outside the office, there was a virtual free-for-all of racist slogans. Arab-hating sentiment came out on bumper stickers like "Kick Their Ass and Take Their Gas." Military footage even documented our pilots joking as they bombed around fleeing civilians. They called it a turkey shoot. A turkey shoot? Those were people.

Arabs bleed and perish just like Americans. I know, because two years before we started dropping bombs on Baghdad, I watched my father die. He did not dissolve like a cartoon character, nor defy death like a Hollywood villain. Instead, chemotherapy shrunk his 180-pound body down to 120, turned his beautiful skin from brown to ashen beige, and rendered his opalescent[14] white fingernails a dull shade of gray. When he finally let go, I thought he took all the secrets of my Arabness with him, all the good things America didn't want me to know. But I look in the mirror and see my father's wide nose on my face and Hajia's think lines forming between my brows. I also see my mom's fair skin, and her mother's high cheekbones. I realize it's my responsibility to somehow forge an identity between dueling cultures, to focus on the humanity, not the terror, that bridges both worlds.

---

[14]*opalescent:* Reflecting an iridescent light.

JOAN T. MIMS AND ELIZABETH M. NOLLEN
Families Yesterday and Today

Norman Rockwell's art for *The Saturday Evening Post* has long been considered a staple of American popular culture. This New England artist rendered the everyday moments that have defined our society, catching our humanity and our frailty in a way that everyone can relate to and few other artists can match. In this iconic 1943 painting, *Freedom from Want,* Rockwell captures a moment familiar to many Americans, the extended family gathered around the table

Freedom from Want

One Big Happy Family

celebrating Thanksgiving. The song lyrics "Over the river and through the woods to Grandmother's house we go" may come to mind as we seem to be invited into this happy gathering by the smiling figures around the table.

This contemporary drawing by Charlie Powell titled *One Big Happy Family* accompanied a November 19, 2004, article in *Salon.com* that commented on the recent, divisive presidential elections. It captures a "family" moment that is similar to Rockwell's but that has a different artistic style and cast of characters. *One Big Happy Family* lacks the trademark photographic quality of Norman Rockwell's "Kodak moment" on canvas, but it is eye-catching in its own way. As we examine these modern figures gathered around the table for their own turkey feast, we find ourselves composing our own story about the scene depicted in the drawing as we imagine the table conversation and the connections among the guests. The faces have certainly changed, but many similarities remain between these two images.

Both of these images celebrate what many call the most "American" of holidays, Thanksgiving. What is ironic about this? Who is missing from each of these pictures? What important cultural group is not represented?

As you examine these images, consider these questions: What images of America do these two visuals represent? How do they reflect the changes in American culture during the more than sixty years that separate them? What has stayed the same? What has changed? How accurate are the titles of both images, considering when each was created? To what extent do these two visuals reflect Thanksgiving celebrations that you have experienced? How do your family's cultural traditions compare with those depicted in the two images?

●

○

H. D.
Dying to Be Bigger

I was only fifteen years old when I first started maiming my body with the abuse of anabolic steroids.[1] I was always trying to fit in with the "cool" crowd in junior high and high school. Willingly smoking or buying pot when offered, socially drinking in excess, displaying a macho image—and, of course, the infamous "kiss and tell" were essentials in completing my insecure mentality.

Being an immature, cocky kid from a somewhat wealthy family, I wasn't very well liked in general. In light of this, I got beat up a lot, especially in my first year of public high school.

I was one of only three sophomores to get a varsity letter in football. At five-foot-nine and 174 pounds, I was muscularly inferior to the guys on the same athletic level and quite conscious of the fact. So when I heard about this wonderful drug called steroids from a teammate, I didn't think twice about asking to buy some. I could hardly wait to take them and start getting bigger.

I bought three months' worth of Dianobol (an oral form of steroids and one of the most harmful). I paid fifty-five dollars. I was told to take maybe two or three per day. I totally ignored the directions and warnings and immediately started taking five per day. This is how eager I was to be bigger and possibly "cooler."

Within only a week, everything about me started to change. I was transforming mentally and physically. My attention span became almost nonexistent. Along with becoming extremely aggressive, I began to abandon nearly all academic and family responsibilities. In almost no time, I became flustered and agitated with simple everyday activities. My narcissistic ways brought me to engage in verbal as well as physical fights with family, friends, teachers, but mostly strangers.

My bodily transformations were clearly visible. In less than a month, I took the entire three-month supply. I gained nearly thirty pounds. Most of my weight was from water retention, although at the time I believed it to be muscle. Instead of having pimples like the average teenager, my acne took the form of grotesque, cystlike blood clots that would occasionally burst while I was lifting weights. My nipples became the size of grapes and hurt severely, which is

---
[1] *anabolic steroids:* Hormones used by athletes to temporarily increase muscle size and metabolism.

common among male steroid users. My hormonal level was completely out of whack.[2]

At first I had such an overload of testosterone that I would have to masturbate daily, at minimum, in order to prevent having "wet dreams." Obviously these factors enhanced my lust, which eventually led to acute perversion. My then almost-horrifying physique prevented me from having any sexual encounters.

All of these factors led to my classification as a wretched menace. My parents grew sick and tired of all the trouble I began to get in. They were scared of me, it seemed. They cared so much about my welfare, education, and state of mind that they sent me to a boarding school that summer.

I could not obtain any more steroids there, and for a couple of months it seemed I had subtle withdrawal symptoms and severe side effects. Most of the time that summer I was either depressed or filled with intense anger, both of which were uncontrollable unless I was in a state of intoxication from any mind-altering drug.

After a year of being steroid-free, things started to look promising for me, and I eventually gained control over myself. Just when I started getting letters from big-name colleges to play football for them, I suffered a herniated disc. I was unable to participate in any form of physical activity the entire school year.

In the fall, I attended a university in the Northeast, where I was on the football team but did not play due to my injury. I lifted weights with the team every day. I wasn't very big at the time, even after many weeks of working out. Once again I found myself to be physically inferior and insecure about my physique. And again I came into contact with many teammates using steroids.

My roommate was a six-foot-three, 250-pound linebacker who played on the varsity squad as a freshman. As the weeks passed, I learned of my roommate's heavy steroid use. I was exposed to dozens of different steroids I had never even heard of. Living in the same room with him, I watched his almost daily injections. After months of enduring his drug offerings, I gave in.

By the spring of my freshman year, I had become drastically far from normal in every way. My body had stopped producing hormones due to the amount of synthetic testosterone I injected into my system. At five-foot-eleven, 225 pounds, disproportionately huge, acne-infested, outrageously aggressive, and nearing complete sterility, I was in a terrible state of body and mind. Normal thoughts of my future (not pertaining to football), friends, family, reputation, moral status, etc., were entirely beyond me. My whole entire essence had become one of a primitive barbarian. This was when I was taking something called Sustunon (prepackaged in a syringe labeled "For equine use

---

[2]**ESL out of whack:** Not normal.

only") containing four types of testosterone. I was "stacking" (a term used by steroid users which means mixing different types) to get well-cut definition along with mass.

It was around this time when I was arrested for threatening a security guard. When the campus police came to arrest me, they saw how aggressive and large my roommate and I were. So they searched our room and found dozens of bottles and hundreds of dollars' worth of steroids and syringes. We had a trial, and the outcome was that I could only return the next year if I got drug-tested on a monthly basis. I certainly had no will-power or desire to quit my steroid abuse, so I transferred schools.

After a summer of even more heavy-duty abuse, I decided to attend a school that would cater to my instinctively backward ways. That fall I entered a large university in the South. Once again I simply lifted weights without being involved in competition or football. It was there that I finally realized how out of hand I'd become with my steroid problem.

Gradually I started to taper down my dosages. Accompanying my reduction, I began to drink more and more. My grades plummeted again. I began going to bars and keg parties on a nightly basis.

My celibacy, mental state, aggressiveness, lack of athletic competition, and alcohol problem brought me to enjoy passing my pain onto others by means of physical aggression. I got into a fight almost every time I drank. In the midst of my insane state, I was arrested for assault. I was in really deep this time. Finally I realized how different from everybody else I'd become, and I decided not to taper off but to quit completely.

The average person seems to think that steroids just make you bigger. But they are a drug, and an addictive one at that. This drug does not put you in a stupor or in a hallucinogenic state but rather gives you an up, all-around "bad-ass" mentality that far exceeds that of either normal life or any other narcotic I've tried with not taking steroids. Only lately are scientists and researchers discovering how addictive steroids are — only now, after hundreds of thousands may have done such extreme damage to their lives, bodies, and minds.

One of the main components of steroid addiction is how unsatisfied the user is with his overall appearance. Although I was massive and had dramatic muscular definition, I was never content with my body, despite frequent compliments. I was always changing types of steroids, places of injection, workouts, diet, etc. I always found myself saying, "This one oughta do it" or "I'll quit when I hit 230 pounds."

When someone is using steroids, he has psychological disorders that increase when usage stops. One disorder is anxiety from the loss of the superior feeling you get from the drug. Losing the muscle mass, high energy level, and superhuman sensation that you're so accustomed to is terrifying.

Another ramification of taking artificial testosterone over time is the effect on the natural testosterone level (thus the male sex drive). As a result of my steroid use, my natural testosterone level was ultimately depleted to the point where my sex drive was drastically reduced in comparison to the average twenty-one-year-old male. My testicles shriveled up, causing physical pain as well as extreme mental anguish. Thus I desired girls less. This however did lead me to treat them as people, not as objects of my desires. It was a beginning step on the way to a more sane and civil mentality.

The worst symptoms of my withdrawal after many months of drug abuse were emotional. My emotions fluctuated dramatically, and I rapidly became more sensitive. My hope is that this feeling of being trailed by isolation and aloneness will diminish and leave me free of its constant haunting.

ALICE WALKER
Beauty: When the Other Dancer Is the Self

It is a bright summer day in 1947. My father, a fat, funny man with beautiful eyes and a subversive wit, is trying to decide which of his eight children he will take with him to the county fair. My mother, of course, will not go. She is knocked out[1] from getting most of us ready: I hold my neck stiff against the pressure of her knuckles as she hastily completes the braiding and then beribboning of my hair.

My father is the driver for the rich old white lady up the road. Her name is Miss Mey. She owns all the land for miles around, as well as the house in which we live. All I remember about her is that she once offered to pay my mother thirty-five cents for cleaning her house, raking up piles of her magnolia leaves, and washing her family's clothes, and that my mother—she of no money, eight children, and a chronic earache—refused it. But I do not think of this in 1947. I am two and a half years old. I want to go everywhere my daddy goes. I am excited at the prospect of riding in a car. Someone has told me fairs are fun. That there is room in the car for only three of us doesn't faze me at all. Whirling happily in my starchy frock, showing off my biscuit-polished[2] patent-leather[3] shoes and lavender socks, tossing my head in a way that makes my ribbons bounce, I stand, hands on hips, before my father. "Take me, Daddy," I say with assurance, "I'm the prettiest!"

Later, it does not surprise me to find myself in Miss Mey's shiny black car, sharing the back seat with the other lucky ones. Does not surprise me that I thoroughly enjoy the fair. At home that night I tell the unlucky ones all I can remember about the merry-go-round,[4] the man who eats live chickens, and the teddy bears, until they say: that's enough, baby Alice. Shut up now, and go to sleep.

It is Easter Sunday, 1950. I am dressed in a green, flocked,[5] scalloped-hem dress (handmade by my adoring sister, Ruth) that has its own smooth satin petticoat and tiny hot-pink roses tucked into each scallop. My shoes, new T-strap patent leather, again highly biscuit-polished. I am six years old and have learned one of the longest Easter speeches to be heard that day, totally unlike the speech I

---

[1]*ESL knocked out:* Fatigued; tired out; exhausted.
[2]*ESL biscuit-polished:* Greased with a biscuit and made shiny.
[3]*ESL patent leather:* Leather with a hard, shiny surface.
[4]*ESL merry-go-round:* An amusement park ride featuring brightly colored animals to sit on; a carousel.
[5]*flocked:* Having a raised velvety pattern.

said when I was two: "Easter lilies/pure and white/blossom in/the morning light." When I rise to give my speech I do so on a great wave of love and pride and expectation. People in the church stop rustling their new crinolines.[6] They seem to hold their breath. I can tell they admire my dress, but it is my spirit, bordering on sassiness (womanishness), they secretly applaud.

"That girl's a little *mess*," they whisper to each other, pleased.

Naturally I say my speech without stammer or pause, unlike those who stutter, stammer, or, worst of all, forget. This is before the word "beautiful" exists in people's vocabulary, but "Oh, isn't she the *cutest* thing!" frequently floats my way. "And got so much sense!" they gratefully add . . . for which thoughtful addition I thank them to this day.

It was great fun being cute. But then, one day, it ended.

I am eight years old and a tomboy.[7] I have a cowboy hat, cowboy boots, checkered shirt and pants, all red. My playmates are my brothers, two and four years older than I. Their colors are black and green, the only difference in the way we are dressed. On Saturday nights we all go to the picture show, even my mother; Westerns are her favorite kind of movie. Back home, "on the ranch," we pretend we are Tom Mix,[8] Hopalong Cassidy,[9] Lash LaRue[10] (we've even named one of our dogs Lash LaRue); we chase each other for hours rustling cattle, being outlaws, delivering damsels from distress. Then my parents decide to buy my brothers guns. These are not "real" guns. They shoot "BBs," copper pellets my brothers say will kill birds. Because I am a girl, I do not get a gun. Instantly I am relegated to the position of Indian. Now there appears a great distance between us. They shoot and shoot at everything with their new guns. I try to keep up with my bow and arrows.

One day while I am standing on top of our makeshift "garage" — pieces of tin nailed across some poles — holding my bow and arrow and looking out toward the fields, I feel an incredible blow in my right eye. I look down just in time to see my brother lower his gun.

Both brothers rush to my side. My eye stings, and I cover it with my hand. "If you tell," they say, "we will get a whipping. You don't want that to happen, do you?" I do not. "Here is a piece of wire," says the older brother, picking it up from the roof; "say you stepped on one end of it and the other flew up and hit you." The pain is beginning to start. "Yes," I say. "Yes, I will say

---

[6]*crinolines:* Stiff petticoats designed to make a skirt stand out.
[7]*ESL tomboy:* A young girl who enjoys vigorous activities traditionally associated with males.
[8]*Tom Mix:* An actor in 1930s Western films.
[9]*Hopalong Cassidy:* An actor in Western films and television series from the 1930s through the 1950s.
[10]*Lash LaRue:* An actor in Western films in the 1940s, known as the King of the Bullwhip.

that is what happened." If I do not say this is what happened, I know my brothers will find ways to make me wish I had. But now I will say anything that gets me to my mother.

Confronted by our parents we stick to the lie agreed upon. They place me on a bench on the porch and I close my left eye while they examine the right. There is a tree growing from underneath the porch that climbs past the railing to the roof. It is the last thing my right eye sees. I watch as its trunk, its branches, and then its leaves are blotted out by the rising blood.

I am in shock. First there is intense fever, which my father tries to break using lily leaves bound around my head. Then there are chills: my mother tries to get me to eat soup. Eventually, I do not know how, my parents learn what has happened. A week after the "accident" they take me to see a doctor. "Why did you wait so long to come?" he asks, looking into my eye and shaking his head. "Eyes are sympathetic," he says. "If one is blind, the other will likely become blind too."

This comment of the doctor's terrifies me. But it is really how I look that bothers me most. Where the BB pellet struck there is a glob of whitish scar tissue, a hideous cataract, on my eye. Now when I stare at people—a favorite pastime, up to now—they will stare back. Not at the "cute" little girl, but at her scar. For six years I do not stare at anyone, because I do not raise my head.

Years later, in the throes[11] of a mid-life crisis, I ask my mother and sister whether I changed after the "accident." "No," they say, puzzled. "What do you mean?"

What do I mean?

I am eight, and, for the first time, doing poorly in school, where I have been something of a whiz since I was four. We have just moved to the place where the "accident" occurred. We do not know any of the people around us because this is a different county. The only time I see the friends I knew is when we go back to our old church. The new school is the former state penitentiary. It is a large stone building, cold and drafty, crammed to overflowing with boisterous, ill-disciplined children. On the third floor there is a huge circular imprint of some partition that has been torn out.

"What used to be here?" I ask a sullen girl next to me on our way past it to lunch.

"The electric chair," says she.

At night I have nightmares about the electric chair, and about all the people reputedly "fried" in it. I am afraid of the school, where all the students seem to be budding criminals.

"What's the matter with your eye?" they ask, critically.

When I don't answer (I cannot decide whether it was an "accident" or not), they shove me, insist on a fight.

---

[11]*throes:* Difficult or painful struggles.

My brother, the one who created the story about the wire, comes to my rescue. But then brags so much about "protecting" me, I become sick.

After months of torture at the school, my parents decide to send me back to our old community, to my old school. I live with my grandparents and the teacher they board. But there is no room for Phoebe, my cat. By the time my grandparents decide there *is* room, and I ask for my cat, she cannot be found. Miss Yarborough, the boarding teacher, takes me under her wing, and begins to teach me to play the piano. But soon she marries an African—a "prince," she says—and is whisked away to his continent.

At my old school there is at least one teacher who loves me. She is the teacher who "knew me before I was born" and bought my first baby clothes. It is she who makes life bearable. It is her presence that finally helps me turn on the one child at the school who continually calls me "one-eyed bitch." One day I simply grab him by his coat and beat him until I am satisfied. It is my teacher who tells me my mother is ill.

My mother is lying in bed in the middle of the day, something I have never seen. She is in too much pain to speak. She has an abscess in her ear. I stand looking down on her, knowing that if she dies, I cannot live. She is being treated with warm oils and hot bricks held against her cheek. Finally a doctor comes. But I must go back to my grandparents' house. The weeks pass but I am hardly aware of it. All I know is that my mother might die, my father is not so jolly, my brothers still have their guns, and I am the one sent away from home.

"You did not change," they say.

Did I imagine the anguish of never looking up?

I am twelve. When relatives come to visit I hide in my room. My cousin Brenda, just my age, whose father works in the post office and whose mother is a nurse, comes to find me. "Hello," she says. And then she asks, looking at my recent school picture, which I did not want taken, and on which the "glob," as I think of it, is clearly visible, "You still can't see out of that eye?"

"No," I say, and flop back on the bed over my book.

That night, as I do almost every night, I abuse my eye. I rant and rave at it, in front of the mirror. I plead with it to clear up before morning. I tell it I hate and despise it. I do not pray for sight. I pray for beauty.

"You did not change," they say.

I am fourteen and baby-sitting for my brother Bill, who lives in Boston. He is my favorite brother and there is a strong bond between us. Understanding my feelings of shame and ugliness he and his wife take me to a local hospital, where the "glob" is removed by a doctor named O. Henry. There is still a small bluish crater where the scar tissue was, but the ugly white stuff is gone. Almost immediately I become a different person from the girl who does not raise her head. Or so I think. Now that I've raised my head I win the boyfriend of my dreams.

Now that I've raised my head I have plenty of friends. Now that I've raised my head classwork comes from my lips as faultlessly as Easter speeches did, and I leave high school as valedictorian,[12] most popular student, and *queen,* hardly believing my luck. Ironically, the girl who was voted most beautiful in our class (and was) was later shot twice through the chest by a male companion, using a "real" gun, while she was pregnant. But that's another story in itself. Or is it?

"You did not change," they say.

It is now thirty years since the "accident." A beautiful journalist comes to visit and to interview me. She is going to write a cover story for her magazine that focuses on my latest book. "Decide how you want to look on the cover," she says. "Glamorous, or whatever."

Never mind "glamorous," it is the "whatever" that I hear. Suddenly all I can think of is whether I will get enough sleep the night before the photography session: if I don't, my eye will be tired and wander, as blind eyes will.

At night in bed with my lover I think up reasons why I should not appear on the cover of a magazine. "My meanest critics will say I've sold out," I say. "My family will not realize I write scandalous books."

"But what's the real reason you don't want to do this?" he asks.

"Because in all probability," I say in a rush, "my eye won't be straight."

"It will be straight enough," he says. Then, "Besides, I thought you'd made your peace with that."

And I suddenly remember that I have.

I remember:

I am talking to my brother Jimmy, asking if he remembers anything unusual about the day I was shot. He does not know I consider that day the last time my father, with his sweet home remedy of cool lily leaves, chose me, and that I suffered and raged inside because of this. "Well," he says, "all I remember is standing by the side of the highway with Daddy, trying to flag down[13] a car. A white man stopped, but when Daddy said he needed somebody to take his little girl to the doctor, he drove off."

I remember:

I am in the desert for the first time. I fall totally in love with it. I am so overwhelmed by its beauty, I confront for the first time, consciously, the meaning of the doctor's words years ago: "Eyes are sympathetic. If one is blind, the other will likely become blind too." I realize I have dashed about the world madly, looking at this, looking at that, storing up images against the fading of the light. *But I might have missed seeing the desert!* The shock of that possibility—

---

[12]**ESL valedictorian:** The student who has the highest rank in his or her class and delivers the graduation speech.

[13]**ESL flag down:** To signal to stop.

and gratitude for over twenty-five years of sight—sends me literally to my knees. Poem after poem comes—which is perhaps how poets pray.

On Sight

I am so thankful I have seen
The Desert
And the creatures in the desert
And the desert Itself.

The desert has its own moon
Which I have seen
With my own eye.
There is no flag on it.

Trees of the desert have arms
All of which are always up
That is because the moon is up
The sun is up
Also the sky
The stars
Clouds
None with flags.

If there *were* flags, I doubt
the trees would point.
Would you?

But mostly, I remember this:
 I am twenty-seven, and my baby daughter is almost three. Since her birth I have worried about her discovery that her mother's eyes are different from other people's. Will she be embarrassed? I think. What will she say? Every day she watches a television program called *Big Blue Marble*. It begins with a picture of the earth as it appears from the moon. It is bluish, a little battered-looking, but full of light, with whitish clouds swirling around it. Every time I see it I weep with love, as if it is a picture of Grandma's house. One day when I am putting Rebecca down for her nap, she suddenly focuses on my eye. Something inside me cringes, gets ready to try to protect myself. All children are cruel about physical differences, I know from experience, and that they don't always mean to be is another matter. I assume Rebecca will be the same.
 But no-o-o-o. She studies my face intently as we stand, her inside and me outside her crib. She even holds my face maternally between her dimpled little hands. Then, looking every bit as serious and lawyerlike as her father, she says, as if it may just possibly have slipped my attention: "Mommy, there's a *world* in your eye." (As in, "Don't be alarmed, or do anything crazy.") And then, gently, but with great interest: "Mommy, where did you *get* that world in your eye?"

For the most part, the pain left then. (So what, if my brothers grew up to buy even more powerful pellet guns for their sons and to carry real guns themselves. So what, if a young "Morehouse man"[14] once nearly fell off the steps of Trevor Arnett Library because he thought my eyes were blue.) Crying and laughing I ran to the bathroom, while Rebecca mumbled and sang herself off to sleep. Yes indeed, I realized, looking into the mirror. There *was* a world in my eye. And I saw that it was possible to love it: that in fact, for all it had taught me of shame and anger and inner vision, I *did* love it. Even to see it drifting out of orbit in boredom, or rolling up out of fatigue, not to mention floating back at attention in excitement (bearing witness, a friend has called it), deeply suitable to my personality, and even characteristic of me.

That night I dream I am dancing to Stevie Wonder's[15] song "Always" (the name of the song is really "As," but I hear it as "Always"). As I dance, whirling and joyous, happier than I've ever been in my life, another bright-faced dancer joins me. We dance and kiss each other and hold each other through the night. The other dancer has obviously come through all right, as I have done. She is beautiful, whole and free. And she is also me.

---

[14]*Morehouse man:* A student at Morehouse College, Atlanta, Georgia, the only all-male, historically black institution of higher learning in the United States.

[15]*ESL Stevie Wonder:* An African-American singer, pianist, and songwriter who is blind.

PATRICIA McLAUGHLIN
Venus Envy

It used to be that what mattered in life was how women looked and what men did—which, to many women and other right-thinking people, didn't seem fair. Now, thanks to the efforts of feminists (and a lot of social and economic factors beyond their control) what women do matters more.

Meanwhile, in a development that's almost enough to make you believe in the Great Seesaw of Being, how men look is also beginning to carry more weight. Men are having plastic surgery to get rid of their love handles[1] and tighten their eye bags and beef up their chins and flatten their bellies and even (major wince) bulk up their penises. They're dyeing their hair to hide the gray. They're buying magazines to find out how to lose those pesky last five pounds.

Naturally, women who always envied the way men never had to suffer to be beautiful think they're making a big mistake. (What next: too-small shoes with vertiginous heels?) But maybe they don't exactly have a choice.

The key to how men feel about how they look, says Michael Pertschuk, who's writing a book about it, is social expectation: What do they think folks expect them to look like? And how far do folks expect them to go to look that way?

You think of anorexia and bulimia as disorders that strike teenage girls, but men get them, too—not many, but "a bit more" than used to, according to Pertschuk, a psychiatrist who sees patients (including men) with eating disorders. Because eating disorders virtually always start with a "normal" desire to lose weight and look slimmer, the increase among men suggests that men are worrying about their looks more than they used to.

Pertschuk has also worked with the dermatologists and plastic surgeons at the Center for Human Appearance at the University of Pennsylvania to screen candidates for cosmetic surgery, and he says "there are certainly more male plastic surgery patients," which suggests the same thing: "It's become more culturally accepted or expected for men to be concerned about their appearance."

And no wonder, when you look at the media. Stephen Perrine, articles editor at *Men's Health,* a magazine that in the last six years has built a circulation as big as *Esquire*'s and *GQ*'s put together, says the mass media "in the last five to seven years has really changed the way it portrays men." Whether you look at Calvin Klein's[2] underwear ads or that Diet Coke commercial where the

---

[1]*love handles:* Excess fat around the waist; also called a spare tire.
[2]*ESL Calvin Klein:* An American fashion designer known for his classic style.

girls in the office ogle the shirtless construction hunk, "men are more and more portrayed as sex objects. So they're feeling the way women have for many, many years: 'Oh, that's what's expected of me? That's what I'm supposed to look like?'" And they—some of them, anyway—rush to live up to those expectations.

Which—wouldn't you know?—turns out to be a heck of a lot easier for them than it ever was for women: "It's easier for men to change their bodies," Perrine says, "easier to build muscle, easier to burn fat." Besides, the male physical ideal is more realistic to begin with: A man "who's healthy and works out . . . will look like Ken, but a woman can exercise till she's dead, and she's not going to look like Barbie," Perrine says.

Ken? Is that really what women want?

Maybe some women. Me, I get all weak in the knees when I see a guy running a vacuum, or unloading a dishwasher without being asked. Not that Calvin Klein is ever going to advertise his underwear on a cute guy with a nice big electric broom.

But what women want isn't the point.

Used to be, Pertschuk says, men who had plastic surgery said they were doing it for their careers: They wouldn't get promoted if they looked old and fat and tired. Now they say the same thing women do: "I want to feel better about myself." In other words, they look at their love handles or eye bags or pot bellies or saggy chins and feel inadequate and ugly and unworthy, just the way women have been feeling all along about their hips, stomachs, thighs, breasts, wrinkles, etc.

That's new: For more men, self-regard has come to hinge not just on what they do, but on what they see in the mirror. And it's easier to change that than the values that make them feel bad about it.

JOAN T. MIMS AND ELIZABETH M. NOLLEN
Female Body Image Yesterday and Today

In the early twentieth century, when the French Impressionist Auguste Renoir painted this nude, big was indeed beautiful. An ample, full-bodied woman was the feminine ideal; a thinner figure was suspect and suggested an impoverished existence. In the 1990s Body Shop ad, we again see the luscious curves of Renoir's beauty. However, this time we are no longer looking at a human model but at a plus-sized Barbie doll.

How has female body image changed since the Barbie doll was first introduced in 1959?

What do most supermodels look like today? How does today's feminine ideal of beauty differ from that presented in these two visuals? What message does The Body Shop, a body products company, send by using this image? What target audience is The Body Shop hoping to reach?

When Big Was Beautiful

147

There are **3 billion** women who **don't** look like **supermodels** and **only 8** who **do.**

A Real-Life Barbie Doll

LORRAINE ALI
Same Old Song

All the controversy, criticism and praise surrounding Eminem's recent release *The Marshall Mathers LP* finally caused a fiftyish coworker of mine to go out and buy the album to see what all the commotion was about. It's not as if he was treading on totally foreign terrain—he did, after all, love N.W.A.'s *Straight Outta Compton* when it came out a dozen years ago, and has avid interest in most anything that rubs people the wrong way. He just needed to know what the newest source of outrage was all about. He locked himself in his office and came out an hour later. "Wow," he said. "This sure isn't for adults."

He was right. And that's the point: pop music is an esthetic and consumer product targeted at kids between grade school and grad school, and often designed to irk their elders. It's been that way since young Frank Sinatra crooned[1] to screaming girls in the 1940s, Little Richard camped and gyrated in the '50s, the Beatles championed free love in the '60s, the Sex Pistols spat on fans in the '70s and Public Enemy instilled fear of a black planet in 1990. Throughout each trend and era, parents have been deeply concerned and kids have done their best to keep them that way.

Things get ratcheted up a notch with every generation. You're not rebelling if you're listening to the same stuff your parents did; you're embarrassing yourself. Remember Jim Morrison's hammy Oedipal[2] psychodrama[3] in the Doors' "The End" (1967): "Father, I want to kill you! Mother, I want to . . . arrgh!" Eminem's cartoonish "Kill You" moves the ball forward by collapsing both parents into a single Bad Mommy to be raped and murdered. Those parental warning stickers may really be for parents, as if to say, "Hey, there's stuff in here your kid will understand and you won't."

There's a hitch. As every book about raising kids will tell you, children need limits—in part to protect them, and in part to give them boundaries to smash and trample. Generation after generation of iconoclasts,[4] from Joyce and Picasso to Elvis and Marilyn to punks and gangstas, have gradually pushed the limits a little further. When N.W.A. dropped "F—k Tha Police" in 1988, it was a shocking moment. When DMX conveys essentially the same sentiments, who really notices? Even N.W.A.'s raps about killing rivals "like it ain't no thang"

---

[1] *crooned:* Sang in a gentle, murmuring manner.
[2] *Oedipal:* Characterized by sexual attraction of a son toward his mother and hostile or jealous feelings toward his father.
[3] *psychodrama:* A dramatic narrative or event characterized by psychological overtones.
[4] *iconoclasts:* People who attack settled beliefs or institutions.

149

weren't so far from Johnny Cash's in "Folsom Prison Blues," where he sang of shooting a man in Reno "just to watch him die."

But in some ways, it is different. Johnny may have sung about doing hard time—and other things you wouldn't want your mama to know about—but his fantasy seems tame compared with the sex-and-violence-saturated lyrics that proliferate and dominate the *Billboard*[5] charts today. It's a change that hasn't gone unnoticed. With hip-hop's current debate over whether rap has gone too far, insiders are once again trying to decipher what the dividing line is between true artistic value and provocative schlock.[6] The answers will come in retrospect, but in order for the genre to continue growing, it's an important debate that needs to start now.

At the moment, the new frontier of rebellion seems to be against political correctness—the well-intentioned fear of offending any person or "group." In the 1960s and '70s, the fashionably rebellious attitude was to celebrate differences, to elevate the condition of women, minorities and gays ("Come on people now, smile on your brother"). That precursor to the P.C.[7] ethos has now become the cultural mainstream; this election year, Democrats with their many-colors-of-Benetton[8] constituency and Republicans with their many-colors-of-Benetton convention are eagerly trying to top each other in their respect for each and every group that might be induced to vote for them. But in popular entertainment, and especially music, women are being debased in ever more degrading ways, excess and greed are extolled as worthy attributes and gay-bashing serves as a mark of deep-down daring. To be a counterculture rebel now, all you have to do is retool the vilest prejudices of your grandparents' day in the vilest language of your own. What's being promoted as the slaughter of sacred cows is McBigotry, with a state-of-the-art beat and no beef at all.

The result? Mainstream rap and hard rock, addicted to ever-escalating doses of defiance, can now feel as predictable as bad Hollywood action flicks. Part of the problem is that no really new style or scene has busted out of the gate since gangsta rap revolutionized hip-hop in the late '80s and grunge revitalized rock back in the early '90s. If there was anything out there in whatever today's equivalents might be of Compton, Calif., or Seattle, the entertainment corporations would have ferreted it out by now, exploited it and stamped it with their own trademarks. True, the Internet offers the promise of an under-the-radar musical bohemia[9] where an alternative sound might lie low long enough to flourish—the trouble is, most stuff on the Web is so far under the radar that a potentially supportive fan base can't find it. So pop music has fallen

---

[5] ***ESL Billboard:*** A weekly magazine of the music industry.
[6] *schlock:* Something of low quality or value.
[7] ***ESL P.C.:*** Politically correct.
[8] *many-colors-of-Benetton:* Slogan used by Benetton clothing to indicate wide appeal of its products.
[9] *bohemia:* A community of people such as writers or artists living an unconventional life.

back on the tried-and-true attention-getters—sex, violence, sex, consumerist excess and sex—and added the latest kinks in the Zeitgeist:[10] misogyny and homophobia as expressions of free-floating countercultural rage and anxiety.

Another part of the problem is that we risk becoming jaded and desensitized. When—as rappers and deliberately obnoxious bands like Limp Bizkit are proving every day—you can say absolutely anything you want, what's the point of saying anything? And how can you be outrageous enough to get anybody's attention when everybody is shouting at the same volume?

Of course, today's most vacuous pop—from bling-bling[11] to Britney to Blink-182—will pass away, either because it collapses under the weight of its own decadence like disco of the '70s and the hair bands of the '80s, or because it withers from sheer neglect. This happens to the vacuous pop of most every generation: the musical equivalents of Chia Pets give way to the musical equivalents of Razor scooters. The kids to whom these fads are marketed outgrow them and are replaced by new ranks of kids, snickering at yesterday's amusements and suckered in by tomorrow's. The great hope of pop music has always been that in these ruthless revolutions and counter-revolutions a terrible beauty will be born. It was with Public Enemy, with Nirvana—and with Elvis, too. We can only hope we'll get lucky again.

---

[10]*Zeitgeist:* The general intellectual, moral, and cultural climate of an era.
[11]*bling-bling:* Hip-hop slang for showy jewelry.

STEVEN LEVY
iPod Nation

Steve Jobs noticed something earlier this year in New York City. "I was on Madison," says Apple's CEO, "and it was, like, on every block, there was someone with white headphones, and I thought, 'Oh, my God, it's starting to happen.'" Jonathan Ive, the company's design guru, had a similar experience in London: "On the streets and coming out of the tubes, you'd see people fiddling with it." And Victor Katch, a 59-year-old professor of kinesiology[1] at the University of Michigan, saw it in Ann Arbor. "When you walk across campus, the ratio seems as high as 2 out of 3 people," he says.

They're talking about the sudden ubiquity of the iPod, the cigarette-box-size digital music player (and its colorful credit-card-size little sister, the Mini) that's smacked right into the sweet spot where a consumer product becomes something much, much more: an icon, a pet, a status indicator and an indispensable part of one's life. To 3 million-plus owners, iPods not only give constant access to their entire collection of songs and CDs, but membership into an implicit society that's transforming the way music will be consumed in the future. "When my students see me on campus with my iPod, they smile," says Professor Katch, whose unit stores everything from Mozart to Dean Martin. "It's sort of a bonding."

The glue for the bond is a tiny, limited-function computer with a capacious disk drive, decked in white plastic and loaded with something that until very recently was the province of ultrageeks and music pirates:[2] digital files that play back as songs. Apple wasn't the first company to come out with a player, but the earlier ones were either low-capacity toys that played the same few songs, or brick-size beasts with impenetrable controls. Apple's device is not only powerful and easy to use, but has an incandescent style that makes people go nuts about it. Or, in the case of 16-year-old Brittany Vendryes of Miami, to dub it "Bob the Music Machine." ("I wanted to keep it close to my heart and give it a name," she explains.)

Adding to the appeal is the cachet of A-list approbation. "I love it!" says songwriter Denise Rich. "I have my whole catalog on it and I take it everywhere." She is only one voice in a chorus of celebrity Podsters who sing the same praises voiced by ordinary iPod users, but add a dollop[3] of coolness to the device, as if it needed it. Will Smith has burbled[4] to Jay Leno and *Wired* magazine about his infatuation with "the gadget of the century." Gwyneth Paltrow

---

[1]*kinesiology:* The study of how parts of the body move.
[2]*ESL music pirates:* People who download music illegally.
[3]*dollop:* A small amount.
[4]*burbled:* Talked excitedly.

confided her Pod-love to *Vogue* (her new baby is named Apple — coincidence?). It's been seen on innumerable TV shows, movies and music videos, so much so that Fox TV recently informed Josh Schwartz, producer of its hit series *The O.C.*, that future depictions of music players would have to forgo the telltale white ear buds. Schwartz, himself a 27-year-old who still hasn't recovered from the shock of having his unit stolen from his BMW, was outraged. "It's what our audience uses and what our characters would use," he says.

People who actually create music are among the biggest fans: "The layout reminds the musician of music," says tunester John Mayer. And couture maven[5] Karl Lagerfeld's iPod collection is up to 60, coded in the back by laser etching so he can tell what's on them. "It's *the* way to store music," he says. Lagerfeld's tribute to the iPod is a $1,500 Fendi pink copper rectangular purse that holds 12 iPods. It is one of more than 200 third-party accessories ranging from external speakers, microphones and — fasten your seat belt — a special connector that lets you control your iPod from the steering wheel of a BMW.

Music hits people's emotions, and the purchase of something that opens up one's entire music collection — up to 10,000 songs in your pocket — makes for an intense relationship. When people buy iPods, they often obsess, talking incessantly about play lists and segues,[6] grumbling about glitches, fixating on battery life and panicking at the very thought of losing their new digital friend. "I'd be devastated if I lost it," says Krystyn Lynch, a Boston investment marketer.

Fans of the devices use it for more than music. "It's the limousine for the spoken word," says Audible CEO Don Katz, whose struggling digital audiobook company has been revitalized by having its products on Apple's iTunes store. (Podsters downloaded thousands of copies of Bill Clinton's autobiography within minutes of its 3 a.m. release last month.) And computer users have discovered that its vast storage space makes it a useful vault for huge digital files — the makers of the *Lord of the Rings* movies used iPods to shuttle dailies[7] from the set to the studio. Thousands of less-accomplished shutterbugs store digital photos on them.

iPods aren't conspicuous everywhere — their popularity seems centered on big cities and college towns — but sometimes it seems that way. "I notice that when I'm in the gym, as I look down the treadmills, that just about everybody in the row has one," says Scott Piro, a New York City book publicist. And the capper came earlier this year during the *Apple vs. Apple* case — wherein the Beatles' record company is suing the computer firm on a trademark issue. The judge wondered if he should recuse[8] himself — because he is an avid iPod user. (The litigants[9] had no objection to his staying on.)

---

[5]*couture maven:* An expert or knowledgeable enthusiast in designer fashions.
[6]*segues:* Smooth transitions.
[7]*dailies:* Rough, unedited clips of film that are reviewed on the same day they are shot.
[8]*recuse:* To remove from participation because of bias.
[9]*litigants:* People involved in a lawsuit.

In 1997, when Steve Jobs returned to the then struggling company he had cofounded, he says, there were no plans for a music initiative. In fact, he says, there wasn't a plan for anything. "Our goal was to revitalize and get organized, and if there were opportunities we'd see them," he says. "We just had to be ready to catch the ball when it's thrown by life." After some painful pink-slipping[10] and some joyous innovating, the company was solvent.

But in the flurry, Jobs & Co. initially failed to notice the impending revolution in digital music. Once that omission was understood, Apple compensated by developing a slick "jukebox" application known as iTunes. It was then that Apple's brain trust noticed that digital music players weren't selling. Why not? "The products stank," says Apple VP Greg Joswiak.

Life had tossed Jobs a softball, and early in 2001 he ordered his engineers to catch it. That February, Apple's hardware czar,[11] Jon Rubinstein, picked a team leader from outside the company—an engineer named Tony Fadell. "I was on the ski slopes in Vail when I got the call," says Fadell, who was told that the idea was to create a ground-breaking music player—and have it on sale for Christmas season that year. The requirements: A very fast connection to one's computer (via Apple's high-speed Firewire standard) so songs could be quickly uploaded. A close synchronization with the iTunes software to make it easy to organize music. An interface that would be simple to use. And gorgeous.

Fadell was able to draw on all of Apple's talents from Jobs on down. VP Phil Schiller came up with the idea of a scroll wheel that made the menus accelerate as your finger spun on it. Meanwhile, Apple's industrial designer Ive embarked on a search for the obvious. "From early on we wanted a product that would seem so natural and so inevitable and so simple you almost wouldn't think of it as having been designed," he says. This austerity extended to the whiteness of the iPod, a double-crystal polymer Antarctica, a blankness that screams in brilliant colors across a crowded subway. "It's neutral, but it is a bold neutral, just shockingly neutral," says Ive.

Assessing the final product, Jobs bestows, for him, the ultimate accolade: "It's as Apple as anything Apple has ever done."

The October 2001 launch was barely a month after 9/11, with the country on edge and the tech industry in the toilet.[12] Skeptics scoffed at the $399 price and the fact that only Macintosh users, less than a twentieth of the marketplace, could use it. But savvy Mac-heads saw the value, and the iPod was a hit, if not yet a sensation. What pushed it to the next level was a number of Apple initiatives beginning with a quick upgrade cycle that increased the number of songs (while actually lowering the price). Then Apple released a version that would run on Windows and Mac, dramatically increasing the potential market. Finally, after intense negotiations with the record labels, Apple licensed

---

[10]*ESL pink-slipping:* Firing from a job.
[11]*czar:* An absolute ruler; one with great authority and power to control.
[12]*ESL in the toilet:* In serious danger of failing.

hundreds of thousands of songs for its iTunes Music Store, which blended seamlessly with the iPod. As with the iPod itself, the legal-download store was not the first of its kind but was so felicitous and efficient that it leapt to a 70 percent market share.

Then sales began to spike. No one was surprised that Apple sold an impressive 733,000 iPods during the Christmas season last year, but the normally quiet quarter after that saw an increase to 807,000. And last week Apple announced that sales in the just-completed third quarter, traditionally another dead one—hit 860,000, up from 249,000 a year ago.

That total would have been higher had Apple not had problems getting parts for the latest iteration,[13] the iPod Mini. Though critics praised its compactness and its panache[14]—a burnished metallic surface made it look like a futuristic Zippo[15]—they sniffed at its relatively low capacity (only 1,000 songs!). But apparently there were lots of people like Los Angeles chiropractor Pat Dengler, who saw the Mini as a must. "At first I thought, I already have an iPod, I don't need it," she says. "But after I played with it, I thought, I really dig it. Now I use them both." Dengler was lucky, as many had to suffer through a month-long waiting list. To the delight of Apple (and the chagrin of Sony), the no-brainer description of the iPod is "the Walkman of the 21st century." And just as the Walkman changed the landscape of music and the soundscape of our lives, the iPod and the iTunes store are making their mark on the way we handle our music, and even the way we listen to it.

The store has proved that many people will pay for digital music (though certainly many millions of gigabytes of iPod space are loaded with tunes plucked from the dark side of the Internet). "The iPod and iTunes store are a shining light at a very bleak time in the industry," says Cary Sherman, president of the Record Industry Association of America. Since just about everybody feels that within a decade almost everybody will get their music from such places, this is very big.

An equally big deal is the way the iPod is changing our listening style. Michael Bull, a lecturer at the University of Sussex, has interviewed thousands of iPod users, finding that the ability to take your whole music collection with you changes everything. "People define their own narrative through their music collection," says Bull.

The primary way to exploit this ability is the iPod's "shuffle" feature. This takes your entire music collection, reorders it with the thoroughness of a Las Vegas blackjack dealer and then plays back the crazy-quilt mélange.[16] "Shuffle throws up almost anything—you don't know it's coming but you know you

---

[13]*iteration:* Version.
[14]*panache:* Style.
[15]*ESL Zippo:* A brand of cigarette lighter.
[16]*crazy-quilt mélange:* A mixture in random order.

like it," says Bull. "Because of this people often say, 'It's almost as if my iPod understands me.'"

Shuffle winds up helping people make connections between different genres of music. "People feel they're walking through musicology,"[17] says rocker John Mayer. These abilities have a predictable effect: people who use iPods wind up listening to more music, and with more passion.

And since the iTunes store encourages customers to eschew buying entire CDs, instead buying the best song or two for a buck a pop, it's easy to see why some think that the era of the CD is playing its final tracks, a circumstance many will lament. "The one cool thing about a CD is really getting to know an album," says iPod fan Wil-Dog Abers, bassist for the hip-hop collective Ozomatli. "I don't know what we're gonna do about that."

In Silicon Valley, the question is what Apple can do to maintain its dominant position in the field. While Apple execs say that they are surprised at how lame[18] the competition has been to date, it's reasonable to think that rivals might eventually close the gap. Almost all the hounds chasing Apple use technology from its longtime rival Microsoft. And Sony, whose initial efforts in the field were constrained by the copy-protection demands of its music unit, is introducing a new line of digital players this summer. "We feel that the experience is as good as Apple's, and we have the Walkman brand, which has sold 200 million units. We're in the game," says Sony America's CEO Howard Stringer. Meanwhile, the ultimate competition may come from services that stream unlimited music for a monthly fee, like Real Networks' Rhapsody. "The fat lady isn't even on the stage yet," says Chris Gorog, CEO of Napster.

But at the moment, the iPod *is* the category. And everything points to a humongous Christmas season for the iPod. The introduction of the new iPods this week extends the company's technology lead. If Apple, as promised, manages to get enough drives to satisfy the demand, the Mini iPod may achieve the ubiquity of its wide-bodied companion. And later this summer, when computer giant HP begins selling a cobranded version of the iPod, consumers will be able to get iPods in thousands of additional retail stores.

All this is infinitely gratifying for Steve Jobs, the computer pioneer and studio CEO who turns 50 next February. "I have a very simple life," he says, without a trace of irony. "I have my family and I have Apple and Pixar. And I don't do much else." But the night before our interview, Jobs and his kids sat down for their first family screening of Pixar's 2004 release *The Incredibles*. After that, he tracked the countdown to the 100 millionth song sold on the iTunes store. Apple had promised a prize to the person who moved the odometer to 10 figures, and as the big number approached, fortune seekers snapped up files at a furious rate. At around 10:15, 20-year-old Kevin Britten of Hays, Kans., bought a song by the electronica band Zero 7, and Jobs himself got

---

[17]*musicology:* The scholarly study of music.
[18]*lame:* Ineffective, weak.

on the phone to tell him that he'd won. Then Jobs asked a potentially embarrassing question: "Do you have a Mac or PC?"

"I have a Macintosh . . . *duh!*" said Britten.

Jobs laughs while recounting this. Even though Macintosh sales have gone up recently, he knows that the odds are small of anyone's owning a Mac as opposed to the competition. He doesn't want that to happen with his company's music player. "There are lots of examples where not the best product wins," he says. "Windows would be one of those, but there are examples where the best product wins. And the iPod is a great example of that." As anyone can see from all those white cords dangling from people's ears.

DEBORAH TANNEN
There Is No Unmarked Woman

Some years ago I was at a small working conference of four women and eight men. Instead of concentrating on the discussion I found myself looking at the three other women at the table, thinking how each had a different style and how each style was coherent.

One woman had dark brown hair in a classic style, a cross between Cleopatra and Plain Jane. The severity of her straight hair was softened by wavy bangs and ends that turned under. Because she was beautiful, the effect was more Cleopatra than plain.

The second woman was older, full of dignity and composure. Her hair was cut in a fashionable style that left her with only one eye, thanks to a side part that let a curtain of hair fall across half her face. As she looked down to read her prepared paper, the hair robbed her of bifocal vision and created a barrier between her and the listeners.

The third woman's hair was wild, a frosted blond avalanche falling over and beyond her shoulders. When she spoke she frequently tossed her head, calling attention to her hair and away from her lecture.

Then there was makeup. The first woman wore facial cover that made her skin smooth and pale, a black line under each eye and mascara that darkened already dark lashes. The second wore only a light gloss on her lips and a hint of shadow on her eyes. The third had blue bands under her eyes, dark blue shadow, mascara, bright red lipstick, and rouge; her fingernails flashed red.

I considered the clothes each woman had worn during the three days of the conference: In the first case, man-tailored suits in primary colors with solid-color blouses. In the second, casual but stylish black T-shirts, a floppy collarless jacket and baggy slacks or a skirt in neutral colors. The third wore a sexy jumpsuit; tight sleeveless jersey and tight yellow slacks; a dress with gaping armholes and an indulged tendency to fall off one shoulder.

Shoes? No. 1 wore string sandals with medium heels; No. 2, sensible, comfortable walking shoes; No. 3, pumps with spike heels. You can fill in the jewelry, scarves, shawls, sweaters—or lack of them.

As I amused myself finding coherence in these styles, I suddenly wondered why I was scrutinizing only the women. I scanned the eight men at the table. And then I knew why I wasn't studying them. The men's styles were unmarked.

The term "marked" is a staple of linguistic theory. It refers to the way language alters the base meaning of a word by adding a linguistic particle that has no

158

meaning on its own. The unmarked form of a word carries the meaning that goes without saying—what you think of when you're not thinking anything special.

The unmarked tense of verbs in English is the present—for example, *visit*. To indicate past, you mark the verb by adding *ed* to yield *visited*. For future, you add a word: *will visit*. Nouns are presumed to be singular until marked for plural, typically by adding *s* or *es*, so *visit* becomes *visits* and *dish* becomes *dishes*.

The unmarked forms of most English words also convey "male." Being male is the unmarked case. Endings like *ess* and *ette* mark words as "female." Unfortunately, they also tend to mark them for frivolousness. Would you feel safe entrusting your life to a doctorette? Alfre Woodard, who was an Oscar nominee for best supporting actress, says she identifies herself as an actor because "actresses worry about eyelashes and cellulite, and women who are actors worry about the characters we are playing." Gender markers pick up extra meanings that reflect common associations with the female gender: not quite serious, often sexual.

Each of the women at the conference had to make decisions about hair, clothing, makeup, and accessories, and each decision carried meaning. Every style available to us was marked. The men in our group had made decisions, too, but the range from which they chose was incomparably narrower. Men can choose styles that are marked, but they don't have to, and in this group none did. Unlike the women, they had the option of being unmarked.

Take the men's hair styles. There was no marine crew cut or oily longish hair falling into eyes, no asymmetrical, two-tiered construction to swirl over a bald top. One man was unabashedly bald; the others had hair of standard length, parted on one side, in natural shades of brown or gray or graying. Their hair obstructed no views, left little to toss or push back or run fingers through and, consequently, needed and attracted no attention. A few men had beards. In a business setting, beards might be marked. In this academic gathering, they weren't.

There could have been a cowboy shirt with string tie or a three-piece suit or a necklaced hippie in jeans. But there wasn't. All eight men wore brown or blue slacks and nondescript shirts of light colors. No man wore sandals or boots; their shoes were dark, closed, comfortable, and flat. In short, unmarked.

Although no man wore makeup, you couldn't say the men didn't wear makeup in the sense that you could say a woman didn't wear makeup. For men, no makeup is unmarked.

I asked myself what style we women could have adopted that would have been unmarked, like the men's. The answer was none. There is no unmarked woman.

There is no woman's hairstyle that can be called standard, that says nothing about her. The range of women's hairstyles is staggering, but a woman whose hair has no particular style is perceived as not caring about how she looks, which can disqualify her from many positions, and will subtly diminish her as a person in the eyes of some.

Women must choose between attractive shoes and comfortable shoes. When our group made an unexpected trek, the woman who wore flat, laced shoes arrived first. Last to arrive was the woman in spike heels, shoes in hand and a handful of men around her.

If a woman's clothing is tight or revealing (in other words, sexy), it sends a message — an intended one of wanting to be attractive, but also a possibly unintended one of availability. If her clothes are not sexy, that too sends a message, lent meaning by the knowledge that they could have been. There are thousands of cosmetic products from which women can choose and myriad ways of applying them. Yet no makeup at all is anything but unmarked. Some men see it as a hostile refusal to please them.

Women can't even fill out a form without telling stories about themselves. Most forms give four titles to choose from. "Mr." carries no meaning other than that the respondent is male. But a woman who checks "Mrs." or "Miss" communicates not only whether she has been married but also whether she has conservative tastes in forms of address — and probably other conservative values as well. Checking "Ms." declines to let on about marriage (checking "Mr." declines nothing since nothing was asked), but it also marks her as either liberated or rebellious, depending on the observer's attitudes and assumptions.

I sometimes try to duck these variously marked choices by giving my title as "Dr." — and in so doing risk marking myself as either uppity (hence sarcastic responses like "Excuse *me!*") or an overachiever (hence reactions of congratulatory surprise like "Good for you!").

All married women's surnames are marked. If a woman takes her husband's name, she announces to the world that she is married and has traditional values. To some it will indicate that she is less herself, more identified by her husband's identity. If she does not take her husband's name, this too is marked, seen as worthy of comment: She has *done* something; she has "kept her own name." A man is never said to have "kept his own name" because it never occurs to anyone that he might have given it up. For him using his own name is unmarked.

A married woman who wants to have her cake and eat it too may use her surname plus his, with or without a hyphen. But this too announces her marital status and often results in a tongue-tying string. In a list (Harvey O'Donovan, Jonathan Feldman, Stephanie Woodbury McGillicutty), the woman's multiple name stands out. It is marked.

I have never been inclined toward biological explanations of gender differences in language, but I was intrigued to see Ralph Fasold bring biological phenomena to bear on the question of linguistic marking in his book *The Sociolinguistics of Language.* Fasold stresses that language and culture are particularly unfair in treating women as the marked case because biologically it is the male that is marked. While two X chromosomes make a fe-male, two Y chromosomes make nothing. Like the linguistic markers *s, es,* or *ess,* the Y chromosome doesn't "mean" anything unless it is attached to a root form—an X chromosome.

Developing this idea elsewhere Fasold points out that girls are born with fully female bodies, while boys are born with modified female bodies. He invites men who doubt this to lift up their shirts and contemplate why they have nipples.

In his book, Fasold notes "a wide range of facts which demonstrates that female is the unmarked sex." For example, he observes that there are a few species that produce only females, like the whiptail lizard. Thanks to partheno-genesis, they have no trouble having as many daughters as they like. There are no species, however, that produce only males. This is no surprise, since any such species would become extinct in its first generation.

Fasold is also intrigued by species that produce individuals not involved in reproduction, like honeybees and leaf-cutter ants. Reproduction is handled by the queen and a relatively few males; the workers are sterile females. "Since they do not reproduce," Fasold said, "there is no reason for them to be one sex or the other, so they default, so to speak, to female."

Fasold ends his discussion of these matters by pointing out that if language reflected biology, grammar books would direct us to use "she" to include males and females and "he" only for specifically male referents. But they don't. They tell us that "he" means "he or she," and that "she" is used only if the referent is specif-ically female. This use of "he" as the sex-indefinite pronoun is an innovation in-troduced into English by grammarians in the eighteenth and nineteenth centuries, according to Peter Mühlhäusler and Rom Harré in *Pronouns and People.* From at least about 1500, the correct sex-indefinite pronoun was "they," as it still is in casual spoken English. In other words, the female was declared by grammari-ans to be the marked case.

Writing this article may mark me not as a writer, not as a linguist, not as an analyst of human behavior, but as a feminist—which will have positive or negative, but in any case powerful, connotations for readers. Yet I doubt that anyone reading Ralph Fasold's book would put that label on him.

I discovered the markedness inherent in the very topic of gender after writing a book on differences in conversational style based on geographical re-gion, ethnicity, class, age, and gender. When I was interviewed, the vast major-ity of journalists wanted to talk about the differences between women and men. While I thought I was simply describing what I observed—something I had learned to do as a researcher—merely mentioning women and men marked me as a feminist for some.

When I wrote a book devoted to gender differences in ways of speaking, I sent the manuscript to five male colleagues, asking them to alert me to any interpretation, phrasing, or wording that might seem unfairly negative toward men. Even so, when the book came out, I encountered responses like that of the television talk show host who, after interviewing me, turned to the audience and asked if they thought I was male-bashing.

Leaping upon a poor fellow who affably nodded in agreement, she made him stand and asked, "Did what she say accurately describe you?" "Oh, yes," he answered. "That's me exactly." "And what she said about women—does that sound like your wife?" "Oh yes," he responded. "That's her exactly." "Then why do you think she's male-bashing?" He answered, with disarming honesty, "Because she's a woman and she's saying things about men."

To say anything about women and men without marking oneself as either feminist or anti-feminist, male-basher or apologist for men seems as impossible for a woman as trying to get dressed in the morning without inviting interpretations of her character.

Sitting at the conference table musing on these matters, I felt sad to think that we women didn't have the freedom to be unmarked that the men sitting next to us had. Some days you just want to get dressed and go about your business. But if you're a woman, you can't, because there is no unmarked woman.

ERIC LIU
Notes of a Native Speaker

1

Here are some of the ways you could say I am "white":

I listen to National Public Radio.
I wear khaki Dockers.
I own brown suede bucks.
I eat gourmet greens.
I have few close friends "of color."
I married a white woman.
I am a child of the suburbs.
I furnish my condo à la Crate &Barrel.
I vacation in charming bed-and-breakfasts.
I have never once been the victim of blatant discrimination.
I am a member of several exclusive institutions.
I have been in the inner sanctums of political power.
I have been there as something other than an attendant.
I have the ambition to return.
I am a producer of the culture.
I expect my voice to be heard.
I speak flawless, unaccented English.
I subscribe to *Foreign Affairs.*
I do not mind when editorialists write in the first person plural.
I do not mind how white television casts are.
I am not too ethnic.
I am wary of minority militants.
I consider myself neither in exile nor in opposition.
I am considered "a credit to my race."

I never asked to be white. I am not literally white. That is, I do not have white skin or white ancestors. I have yellow skin and yellow ancestors, hundreds of generations of them. But like so many other Asian Americans of the second generation, I find myself now the bearer of a strange new status: white, by acclamation. Thus it is that I have been described as an "honorary white," by other whites, and as a "banana," by other Asians. Both the honorific and the epithet take as a given this idea: to the extent that I have moved away from the periphery and toward the center of American life, I have become white inside. *Some are born white, others achieve whiteness, still*

163

others have whiteness thrust upon them. This, supposedly, is what it means to assimilate.

There was a time when assimilation did quite strictly mean whitening. In fact, well into the first half of this century, mimicry of the stylized standards of the WASP gentry was the proper, dominant, perhaps even sole method of ensuring that your origins would not be held against you. You "made it" in society not only by putting on airs of anglitude, but also by assiduously bleaching out the marks of a darker, dirtier past. And this bargain, stifling as it was, was open to European immigrants almost exclusively; to blacks, only on the passing occasion; to Asians, hardly at all.

Times have changed, and I suppose you could call it progress that a Chinaman, too, may now aspire to whiteness. But precisely because the times have changed, that aspiration—and the *imputation* of the aspiration—now seems astonishingly outmoded. The meaning of "American" has undergone a revolution in the twenty-nine years I have been alive, a revolution of color, class, and culture. Yet the vocabulary of "assimilation" has remained fixed all this time: fixed in whiteness, which is still our metonym for power; and fixed in shame, which is what the colored are expected to feel for embracing the power.

I have assimilated. I am of the mainstream. In many ways I fit the psychological profile of the so-called banana: imitative, impressionable, rootless, eager to please. As I will admit in this essay, I have at times gone to great lengths to downplay my difference, the better to penetrate the "establishment" of the moment. Yet I'm not sure that what I did was so cut-and-dried as "becoming white." I plead guilty to the charges above: achieving, learning the ways of the upper middle class, distancing myself from radicals of any hue. But having confessed, I still do not know my crime.

To be an accused banana is to stand at the ill-fated intersection of class and race. And because class is the only thing Americans have more trouble talking about than race, a minority's climb up the social ladder is often willfully misnamed and wrongly portrayed. There is usually, in the portrayal, a strong whiff of betrayal: the assimilist is a traitor to his kind, to his class, to his own family. He cannot gain the world without losing his soul. To be sure, something *is* lost in any migration, whether from place to place or from class to class. But something is gained as well. And the result is always more complicated than the monochrome language of "whiteness" and "authenticity" would suggest.

My own assimilation began long before I was born. It began with my parents, who came here with an appetite for Western ways already whetted by films and books and music and, in my mother's case, by a father who'd been to the West. My parents, who traded Chinese formality for the more laissez-faire stance of this country. Who made their way by hard work and quiet adaptation. Who fashioned a comfortable life in a quiet development in a second-tier suburb. Who, unlike your "typical" Chinese parents, were not pushy, status-obsessed, rigid, disciplined, or prepared. Who were haphazard about passing down ancestral traditions and "lessons" to their children. Who did pass down, however, the sense that their children were entitled to mix and match, as they saw fit, whatever aspects of whatever cultures they encountered.

I was raised, in short, to assimilate, to claim this place as mine. I don't mean that my parents told me to act like an American. That's partly the point: they didn't tell me to do anything except to be a good boy. They trusted I would find my way, and I did, following their example and navigating by the lights of the culture that encircled me like a dome. As a function of my parents' own half-conscious, half-finished acculturation, I grew up feeling that my life was Book II of an ongoing saga. Or that I was running the second leg of a relay race. *Slap!* I was out of the womb and sprinting, baton in hand. Gradually more sure of my stride, my breathing, the feel of the track beneath me. Eyes forward, never backward.

Today, nearly seven years after my father's death and two years after my marriage into a large white family, it is as if I have come round a bend and realized that I am no longer sure where I am running or why. My sprint slows to a trot. I scan the unfamiliar vista that is opening up. I am somewhere else now, somewhere far from the China that yielded my mother and father; far, as well, from the modest horizons I knew as a boy. I look at my limbs and realize I am no longer that boy; my gait and grasp exceed his by an order of magnitude. Now I want desperately to see my face, to see what time has marked and what it has erased. But I can find no mirror except the people who surround me. And they are mainly pale, powerful.

How did I end up here, standing in what seems the very seat of whiteness, gazing from the promontory of social privilege? How did I cover so much ground so quickly? What was it, in my blind journey, that I felt I should leave behind? And what *did* I leave behind? This, the jettisoning of one mode of life to send another aloft, is not only the immigrant's tale; it is the son's tale, too. By coming to America, my parents made themselves into citizens of a new country. By traveling the trajectory of an assimilist, so did I.

2

As a child, I lived in a state of "amoebic bliss," to borrow the felicitous phrase of the author of *Nisei Daughter,* Monica Sone. The world was a gossamer web of wonder that began with life at home, extended to my friendships, and made the imaginary realm of daydream seem as immediate as the real. If something or someone was in my personal web of meaning, then color or station was irrelevant. I made no distinctions in fourth grade between my best friend, a black boy named Kimathi, and my next-best friend, a white boy named Charlie—other than the fact that one was number one, the other number two. I did not feel, or feel for, a seam that separated the textures of my Chinese life from those of my American life. I was not "bicultural" but omnicultural, and omnivorous, too. To my mind, I differed from others in only two ways that counted: I was a faster runner than most, and a better student. Thus did work blend happily with play, school with home, Western culture with Eastern: it was all the same to a self-confident boy who believed he'd always be at the center of his own universe.

As I approached adolescence, though, things shifted. Suddenly, I could no longer subsume the public world under my private concept of self. Suddenly, the public world was more complicated than just a parade of smiling teachers and a few affirming friends. Now I had to contend with the unstated, inchoate, but inescapable standards of *cool*. The essence of cool was the ability to conform. The essence of conformity was the ability to anticipate what was cool. And I wasn't so good at that. For the first time, I had found something that did not come effortlessly to me. No one had warned me about this transition from happy amoeboid to social animal; no one had prepared me for the great labors of fitting in.

And so in three adjoining arenas—my looks, my loves, my manners—I suffered a bruising adolescent education. I don't mean to overdramatize: there was, in these teenage banalities, usually something humorous and nothing particularly tragic. But in each of these realms, I came to feel I was not normal. And obtusely, I ascribed the difficulties of that age not to my age but to my color. I came to suspect that there was an order to things, an order that I, as someone Chinese, could perceive but not quite crack. I responded not by exploding in rebellion but by dedicating myself, quietly and sometimes angrily, to learning the order as best I could. I was never ashamed of being Chinese; I was, in fact, rather proud to be linked to a great civilization. But I was mad that my difference should matter now. And if it had to matter, I did not want it to defeat me.

Consider, if you will, my hair. For the first eleven years of my life, I sported what was essentially the same hairstyle: a tapered bowl cut, the handiwork of my mother. For those eleven joyful years, this low-maintenance do was entirely satisfactory. But in my twelfth year, as sixth grade got under way, I became aware—gradually at first, then urgently—that bangs were no longer the look for boys. This was the year when certain early bloomers first made the height-weight-physique distribution in our class seem startlingly wide—and when I first realized that I was lingering near the bottom. It was essential that I compensate for my childlike mien by cultivating at least a patina of teenage style.

This is where my hair betrayed me. For some readers the words "Chinese hair" should suffice as explanation. For the rest, particularly those who have spent all your lives with the ability to comb back, style, and part your hair *at will,* what follows should make you count your blessings. As you may recall, 1980 was a vintage year for hair that was parted straight down the middle, then feathered on each side, feathered so immaculately that the ends would meet in the back like the closed wings of angels. I dreamed of such hair. I imagined tossing my head back casually, to ease into place the one or two strands that had drifted from their positions. I dreamed of wearing the fluffy, tailored locks of the blessed.

Instead, I was cursed. My hair was straight, rigid, and wiry. Not only did it fail to feather back; it would not even bend. Worse still, it grew the wrong way. That is, it all emanated from a single swirl near the rear edge of my scalp. Parting my hair in any direction except back to front, the way certain balding men stage their final retreat, was a physical impossibility. It should go without saying that this was a disaster. For the next three years, I experimented with a variety of hairstyles that ranged from the ridiculous to the sublimely bad. There was the stringy pothead look. The mushroom do. Helmet head. Bangs folded back like curtains. I enlisted a blow-dryer, a Conair set on high heat, to force my hair into stiff postures of submission. The results, though sometimes innovative, fell always far short of cool.

I feigned nonchalance, and no one ever said anything about it. But make no mistake: this was one of the most consuming crises of my inner life as a young teen. Though neither of my parents had ever had such troubles, I blamed this predicament squarely on my Chinese genes. And I could not abide my fate. At a time when homogeneity was the highest virtue, I felt I stood out like a pigtailed Manchu.

My salvation didn't come until the end of junior high, when one of my buddies, in an epiphany as we walked past the Palace of Hair Design, dared me to get my head shaved. Without hesitation, I did it — to the tearful laughter of my friends and, soon afterward, the tearful horror of my mother. Of course, I had moments of doubt the next few days as I rubbed my peach-fuzzed skull. But what I liked was this: I had managed, without losing face, to rid myself of my greatest social burden. What's more, in the eyes of some classmates, I was now a bold (if bald) iconoclast. I've worn a crew cut ever since.

Well-styled hair was only one part of a much larger preoccupation during the ensuing years: wooing girls. In this realm I experienced a most frustrating kind of success. I was the boy that girls always found "sweet" and "funny" and "smart" and "nice." Which, to my highly sensitive ear, sounded like "leprous." Time and again, I would charm a girl into deep friendship. Time and again, as the possibility of romance came within reach, I would smash into what I took to be a glass ceiling.

The girls were white, you see; such were the demographics of my school. I was Chinese. And I was convinced that this was the sole obstacle to my advancement. It made sense, did it not? I was, after all, sweet and funny and smart and nice. Hair notwithstanding, I was not unattractive, at least compared with some of the beasts who had started "going out" with girls. There was simply no other explanation. Yet I could never say this out loud: it would have been the whining of a loser. My response, then, was to secretly scorn the girls I coveted. It was *they* who were subpar, whose small-mindedness and veiled prejudice made them unworthy.

My response, too, was to take refuge in my talents. I made myself into a Renaissance boy, playing in the orchestra but also joining the wrestling team, winning science prizes but also editing the school paper. I thought I was defying the stereotype of the Asian American male as a one-dimensional nerd. But in the eyes of some, I suppose, I was simply another "Asian overachiever."

In hindsight, it's hard to know exactly how great a romantic penalty I paid for being Chinese. There may have been girls who would have had nothing to do with me on account of my race, but I never knew them. There were probably girls who, race aside, simply didn't like me. And then there were girls who liked me well enough but who also shied from the prospect of being part of an interracial couple. With so many boys out there, they probably reasoned, why take the path of greater resistance? Why risk so many status points? Why not be "just friends" with this Chinese boy?

Maybe this stigma was more imagined than real. But being an ABC ("American-born Chinese," as our parents called us) certainly affected me another way. It made me feel like something of a greenhorn, a social immigrant. I wanted so greatly to be liked. And my earnestness, though endearing, was not the sort of demeanor that won girls' hearts. Though I was observant enough to notice how people talked when flirting, astute enough to mimic the forms, I was oblivious to the subterranean levels of courtship, blind to the more subtle rituals of "getting chicks" by spurning them. I held the view that if you were manifestly a good person, eventually someone of the opposite sex would do the rational thing and be smitten with you. I was clueless. Many years would pass before I'd wise up.

It wasn't just dating rituals that befuddled me as a youth. It was ritual of all kinds. Ceremony, protocol, etiquette—all these made me feel like an awkward stranger. Things that came as second nature to many white kids were utterly exotic to me. American-style manners, for instance. Chinese families often have their own elaborate etiquette, but "please" and "may I" weren't the sort of words ever heard around my house. That kind of formality seemed so beside the point. I was never taught by my parents to write thank-you notes. I didn't even have the breeding to *say* "Thank you" after sleeping over at a friend's house. I can recall the awful, sour feeling in my stomach when this friend told me his mother had been offended by my impoliteness. (At that point, I expressed my thanks.)

Eating dinner at the home of a *yangren* could be especially trying. The oaken furniture seemed scaled-up, chairs like thrones. The meal would begin with someone, usually the father, mumbling grace. Furtively, I'd steal a glance at the heads bowed in prayer. What if they asked me to say something? I looked back down and kept my mouth shut. Next was the question of silverware: which pieces to use, in which order, and so forth. I'd realize then that at home I ate by using chopsticks to shove rice and meat straight from bowl to slurping mouth. Then the whole thing about passing platters of food around the table, instead of just reaching over and getting what you wanted. I would hear myself ask, in too-high tones, "Would you please pass the carrots, please?" It was usually at that point that I would notice that my napkin was the only one still folded neatly on the table.

All this, of course, was in the context of being with my friends and having a nice time. But something made me feel vaguely sad while I sat there, swallowing huge servings of gravy-drenched food with this other family. These were the moments when I realized I was becoming something other than my parents. I wanted so badly then just to be home, in my own kitchen, taking in the aroma of stir-fry on the wok and the chattery sounds of Chinglish. And yet, like an amphibian that has just breached the shore, I could not stop inhaling this wondrous new atmosphere. My moist, blinking eyes opened wide, observing and recording the customs and predilections of these "regular" Americans. The more time I spent in their midst, the more I learned to be like them. To make their everyday idioms and idiosyncrasies familiar. To possess them.

This, the mundane, would be the locus of my conversion. It was through the small things that I made myself over. I wish, if only for storytelling purposes, that I could offer a more dramatic tale, a searing incident of racism that sent me into deep, self-abnegating alienation. The truth is, I can't. I was sometimes uncomfortable, but never really alienated. There were one or two occasions in seventh grade when the toughs in the back of the bus taunted me, called me *chink,* shot spitballs at me. I didn't like it. But each time, one of my friends—one of my white friends, in whose house I'd later eat dinner—would stand with me and fire back both spitballs and insults. Our insults were mean, too: scornful references to the trailer parks where these kids lived or the grubby clothes they wore or the crummy jobs their parents had. These skirmishes weren't just about race; they were also about mobility.

The same could be said, ultimately, about my own assimilation. To say simply that I became a banana, that I became white-identified, is somewhat simplistic. As an impressionable teen, I came to identify not with white people in general but with that subset of people, most of them white, who were educated, affluent: *going places.* It was their cues that I picked up, their judgments that I cared about. It was in their presence that old patterns of thought began to fall away like so much scaffolding around my psyche. It was in their presence that I began to imagine myself beyond race.

3

I recently dug up a photograph of myself from freshman year of college that made me smile. I have on the wrong shoes, the wrong socks, the wrong checkered shirt tucked the wrong way into the wrong slacks. I look like what I was: a boy sprung from a middlebrow burg who affected a secondhand preppiness. I look nervous. Compare that image to one from my senior-class dinner: now I am attired in a gray tweed jacket with a green plaid bow tie and a sensible button-down shirt, all purchased at the Yale Co-op. I look confident, and more than a bit contrived.

What happened in between those two photographs is that I experienced, then overcame, what the poet Meena Alexander has called "the shock of arrival."When I was deposited at the wrought-iron gates of my residential college as a freshman, I felt more like an outsider than I'd thought possible. It wasn't just that I was a small Chinese boy standing at a grand WASP temple; nor simply that I was a hayseed neophyte puzzled by the refinements of college style. It was *both:* color and class were all twisted together in a double helix of felt inadequacy.

For a while I coped with the shock by retreating to a group of my own kind—not fellow Asians, but fellow marginal public-school grads who resented the rah-rah Yalies to whom everything came so effortlessly. Aligning myself this way was bearable—I was hiding, but at least I could place myself in a long tradition of underdog exiles at Yale. Aligning myself by race, on the other hand, would have seemed too inhibiting.

I know this doesn't make much sense. I know also that college, in the multicultural era, is supposed to be where the deracinated minority youth discovers the "person of color" inside. To a point, I did. I studied Chinese, took an Asian American history course, a seminar on race politics. But ultimately, college was where the unconscious habits of my adolescent assimilation hardened into self-conscious strategy.

I still remember the moment, in the first week of school, when I came upon a table in Yale Station set up by the Asian American Student Association. The upperclassman staffing the table was pleasant enough. He certainly did not strike me as a fanatic. Yet, for some reason, I flashed immediately to a scene I'd witnessed days earlier, on the corner outside. Several Lubavitcher Jews, dressed in black, their faces bracketed by dangling side curls, were looking for fellow travelers at this busy crossroads. Their method was crude but memorable. As any vaguely Jewish-looking male walked past, the zealots would quickly approach, extend a pamphlet, and ask, "Excuse me, sir, are you Jewish?" Since most were not, and since those who weren't about to stop, the result was a frantic, nervous, almost comical buzz all about the corner: Excuse me, are you Jewish? Are you Jewish? Excuse me. Are you Jewish?

I looked now at the clean-cut Korean boy at the AASA table (I think I can distinguish among Asian ethnicities as readily as those Hasidim thought they could tell Gentile from Jew), and though he had merely offered an introductory hello and was now smiling mutely at me, in the back of my mind I heard only this: *Excuse me, are you Asian? Are you Asian? Excuse me. Are you Asian?* I took one of the flyers on the table, even put my name on a mailing list, so as not to appear impolite. But I had already resolved not to be active in any Asians-only group. I thought then: I would never *choose* to be so pigeonholed.

This allergic sensitivity to "pigeonholing" is one of the unhappy hallmarks of the banana mentality. What does the banana fear? That is, what did

I fear? The possibility of being mistaken for someone more Chinese. The possibility of being known only, or even primarily, for being Asian. The possibility of being written off by whites as a self-segregating ethnic clumper. These were the threats—unseen and, frankly, unsubstantiated—that I felt I should keep at bay.

I didn't avoid making Asian friends in college or working with Asian classmates; I simply never went out of my way to do so. This distinction seemed important—it marked, to my mind, the difference between self-hate and self-respect. That the two should have been so proximate in the first place never struck me as odd, or telling. Nor did it ever occur to me that the reasons I gave myself for dissociating from Asians as a group—that I didn't want to be part of a clique, that I didn't want to get absorbed and lose my individuality—were the very developments that marked my own assimilation. I simply hewed to my ideology of race neutrality and self-reliance. I didn't need that crutch, I told myself nervously, that crutch of racial affinity. What's more, I was vaguely insulted by the presumption that I might.

But again: Who was making the presumption? Who more than I was taking the mere existence of Korean volleyball leagues or Taiwanese social sets or pan-Asian student clubs to mean that *all* people of Asian descent, myself included, needed such quasi-kinship groups? And who more than I interpreted this need as infirmity, as a failure to fit in? I resented the faintly sneering way that some whites regarded Asians as an undifferentiated mass. But whose sneer, really, did I resent more than my own?

I was keenly aware of the unflattering mythologies that attach to Asian Americans: that we are indelibly foreign, exotic, math and science geeks, numbers people rather than people people, followers and not leaders, physically frail but devious and sneaky, unknowable and potentially treacherous. These stereotypes of Asian otherness and inferiority were like immense blocks of ice sitting before me, challenging me to chip away at them. And I did, tirelessly. All the while, though, I was oblivious to rumors of my *own* otherness and inferiority, rumors that rose off those blocks like a fog, wafting into my consciousness and chilling my sense of self.

As I had done in high school, I combated the stereotypes in part by trying to disprove them. If Asians were reputed to be math and science geeks, I would be a student of history and politics. If Asians were supposed to be feeble subalterns, I'd lift weights and go to Marine officer candidate school. If Asians were alien, I'd be ardently patriotic. If Asians were shy and retiring, I'd try to be exuberant and jocular. If they were narrow-minded specialists, I'd be a well-rounded generalist. If they were perpetual outsiders, I'd join every establishment outfit I could and show that I, too, could run with the swift.

I overstate, of course. It wasn't that I chose to do all these things with no other purpose than to cut against a supposed convention. I was neither so Pavlovian nor so calculating that I would simply remake myself into the opposite of what people expected. I actually *liked* history, and wasn't especially good at math. As the grandson of a military officer, I *wanted* to see what officer candidates school would be like, and I enjoyed it, at least once I'd finished. I am *by nature* enthusiastic and allegiant, a joiner, and a bit of a jingo.

At the same time, I was often aware, sometimes even hopeful, that others might think me "exceptional" for my race. I derived satisfaction from being the "atypical" Asian, the only Chinese face at OCS or in this club or that.

The irony is that in working so duteously to defy stereotype, I became a slave to it. For to act self-consciously against Asian "tendencies" is not to break loose from the cage of myth and legend; it is to turn the very key that locks you inside. What spontaneity is there when the value of every act is measured, at least in part, by its power to refute a presumption about why you act? The *typical Asian* I imagined, and the *atypical Asian* I imagined myself to be, were identical in this sense: neither was as much a creature of free will as a human being ought to be.

Let me say it plainly, then: I am not proud to have had this mentality. I believe I have outgrown it. And I expose it now not to justify it but to detoxify it, to prevent its further spread.

Yet it would be misleading, I think, to suggest that my education centered solely on the discomfort caused by race. The fact is, when I first got to college I felt deficient compared with people of *every* color. Part of why I believed it so necessary to achieve was that I lacked the connections, the wealth, the experience, the sophistication that so many of my classmates seemed to have. I didn't get the jokes or the intellectual references. I didn't have the canny attitude. So in addition to all my coursework, I began to puzzle over this, the culture of the influential class.

Over time, I suppose, I learned the culture. My interests and vocabulary became ever more worldly. I made my way onto what Calvin Trillin once described as the "magic escalator" of a Yale education. Extracurriculars opened the door to an alumni internship, which brought me to Capitol Hill, which led to a job and a life in Washington after commencement. Gradually, very gradually, I found that I was not so much of an outsider anymore. I found that by almost any standard, but particularly by the standards of my younger self, I was actually beginning to "make it."

It has taken me until now, however, to appraise the thoughts and acts of that younger self. I can see now that the straitening path I took was not the only or even the best path. For while it may be possible to transcend race, *it is not always necessary to try.* And while racial identity is sometimes a shackle, it is not *only* a shackle. I could have spared myself a great deal of heartache had I understood this earlier, that the choice of race is not simply "embrace or efface."

I wonder sometimes how I would have turned out had I been, from the start, more comfortable in my own skin. What did I miss by distancing myself from race? What friendships did I forgo, what self-knowledge did I defer? Had certain accidents of privilege been accidents of privation or exclusion, I might well have developed a different view of the world. But I do not know just how my view would have differed.

What I know is that through all those years of shadow-dancing with my identity, something happened, something that had only partially to do with color. By the time I left Yale I was no longer the scared boy of that freshman photo. I had become more sure of myself and of my place—sure enough, indeed, to perceive the folly of my fears. And in the years since, I have assumed a sense of expectation, of access and *belonging*, that my younger self could scarcely have imagined. All this happened incrementally. There was no clear tipping point, no obvious moment of mutation. The shock of arrival, it would seem, is simply that I arrived.

4

"The world is white no longer, and it will never be white again." So wrote James Baldwin after having lived in a tiny Swiss village where, to his knowledge, no black man had ever set foot. It was there, in the icy heart of whiteness, that the young expatriate began to comprehend the desire of so many of his countrymen to return to some state of nature where only white people existed. It was there too that he recognized just how impossible that was, just how intertwined were the fates and identities of the races in America. "No road whatever will lead Americans back to the simplicity of this European village where white men still have the luxury of looking on me as a stranger," he wrote. "I am not, really, a stranger any longer for any American alive."

That is precisely how I feel when I consider my own journey, my own family's travels. For here I am now, standing in a new country. Not as an expatriate or a resident alien, but as a citizen. And as I survey this realm—this Republic of Privilege—I realize certain things, things that my mother and father might also have realized about *their* new country a generation ago. I realize that my entry has yielded me great opportunities. I realize, as well, that my route of entry has taken a certain toll. I have neglected my ancestral heritage. I have lost something. Yes, I can speak some Mandarin and stir-fry a few easy dishes. I have been to China and know something of its history. Still, I could never claim to be Chinese at the core.

Yet neither would I claim, as if by default, to be merely "white inside." I do not want to be white. I only want to be integrated. When I identify with white people who wield economic and political power, it is not for their whiteness but for their power. When I imagine myself among white people who influence the currents of our culture, it is not for their whiteness but for their influence. When I emulate white people who are at ease with the world, it is not for their whiteness but for their ease. I don't like it that the people I should learn from tend so often to be white, for it says something damning about how opportunity is still distributed. But it helps not at all to call me white for learning from them. It is cruel enough that the least privileged Americans today have colored skin, the most privileged fair. It is crueler still that by our very language we should help convert this fact into rule. The time has come to describe assimilation as something other than the White Way of Being.

The time has also come, I think, to conceive of assimilation as more than a series of losses — and to recognize that what is lost is not necessarily sacred. I have, as I say, allowed my Chinese ethnicity to become diluted. And I often resolve to do more to preserve, to conserve, my inheritance. But have my acts of neglect thus far, my many omissions, been inherently wrong? G. K. Chesterton once wrote that "conservatism is based upon the idea that if you leave things alone, you leave them as they are. But you do not. If you leave a thing alone, you leave it to a torrent of change." I may have been born a Chinese baby, but it would have taken unremitting reinforcement, by my parents and by myself, for me to have remained Chinese. Instead, we left things alone. And a torrent of change washed over me.

This, we must remember, has been an act of creation as much as destruction. Something new is emerging from the torrent, in my case and the many millions like it. Something undeveloped, speaking the unformed tongue of an unformed nation. Something not white, and probably more Chinese than I know. Whatever it is that I am becoming, is it any less authentic for being an amalgam? Is it intrinsically less meaningful than what I might otherwise have been? In every assimilation, there is a mutiny against history — but there is also a destiny, which is to redefine history. What it means to be American — in spirit, in blood — is something far more borrowed and commingled than anything previous generations ever knew. Alongside the pain of migration, then, and the possibility, there is this truth: America is white no longer, and it will never be white again.

JON STEWART
Commencement Address

Thank you, Mr. President, I had forgotten how crushingly dull these cere-
monies are. Thank you.

My best to the choir. I have to say, that song never grows old for me.
Whenever I hear that song, it reminds me of nothing.

I am honored to be here. I do have a confession to make before we get
going that I should explain very quickly. When I am not on television, this is
actually how I dress. I apologize, but there's something very freeing about it. I
congratulate the students for being able to walk even a half a mile in this non-
breathable fabric in the Williamsburg heat. I am sure the environment that now
exists under your robes are the same conditions in which primordial life began
on this earth.

I know there were some parents that were concerned about my speech
here tonight, and I want to assure you that you will not hear any language that
is not common at, say, a dock workers' union meeting, or Tourrette's convention, or profanity seminar. Rest assured.

I am honored to be here and to receive this honorary doctorate. When
I think back to the people that have been in this position before me, from
Benjamin Franklin to Queen Noor of Jordan, I can't help but wonder what
has happened to this place.

Seriously, it saddens me. As a person, I am honored to get it; as an alum-
nus, I have to say I believe we can do better. And I believe we should. But it has
always been a dream of mine to receive a doctorate and to know that today,
without putting in any effort, I will. It's incredibly gratifying. Thank you. That's
very nice of you, I appreciate it.

I'm sure my fellow doctoral graduates—who have spent so long toiling
in academia, sinking into debt, sacrificing God knows how many years for
what, in truth, is a piece of parchment that in truth has been so devalued by our
instant gratification culture as to have been rendered meaningless—will join in
congratulating me. Thank you.

But today isn't about how my presence here devalues this fine institution.
It is about you, the graduates. I'm honored to be here to congratulate you today. Today is the day you enter into the real world, and I should give you a few
pointers on what it is. It's actually not that different from the environment here.
The biggest difference is you will now be paying for things, and the real world
is not surrounded by a three-foot brick wall. And the real world is not a
restoration. If you see people in the real world making bricks out of straw and
water, those people are not colonial reenactors—they are poor. Help them.

175

And in the real world, there is not as much candle lighting. I don't really know what it is about this campus and candle lighting, but I wish it would stop. We only have so much wax, people.

Let's talk about the real world for a moment. We had been discussing it earlier, and I . . . I wanted to bring this up to you earlier about the real world, and this is I guess as good a time as any. I don't really know how to put this, so I'll be blunt. We broke it.

Please don't be mad. I know we were supposed to bequeath to the next generation a world better than the one we were handed. So, sorry.

I don't know if you've been following the news lately, but it just kinda got away from us. Somewhere between the gold rush of easy Internet profits and an arrogant sense of endless empire, we heard kind of a pinging noise, and, uh, then the damn thing just died on us. So I apologize.

But here's the good news. You fix this thing, you're the next greatest generation, people. You do this—and I believe you can—you win this war on terror, and Tom Brokaw's kissing your ass from here to Tikrit, let me tell ya. And even if you don't, you're not gonna have much trouble surpassing my generation. If you end up getting your picture taken next to a naked-guy pile of enemy prisoners and don't give the thumbs up, you've outdone us.

We declared war on terror. We declared war on terror—it's not even a noun, so, good luck. After we defeat it, I'm sure we'll take on that bastard ennui.

But obviously that's the world. What about your lives? What piece of wisdom can I impart to you about my journey that will somehow ease your transition from college back to your parents' basement?

I know some of you are nostalgic today and filled with excitement and perhaps uncertainty at what the future holds. I know six of you are trying to figure out how to make a bong out of your caps. I believe you are members of Psi U. Hey, that did work, thank you for the reference.

So I thought I'd talk a little bit about my experience here at William and Mary. It was very long ago, and if you had been to William and Mary while I was here and found out that I would be the commencement speaker 20 years later, you would be somewhat surprised, and probably somewhat angry. I came to William and Mary because as a Jewish person I wanted to explore the rich tapestry of Judaica that is southern Virginia. Imagine my surprise when I realized "The Tribe" was not what I thought it meant.

In 1980 I was 17 years old. When I moved to Williamsburg, my hall was in the basement of Yates, which combined the cheerfulness of a bomb shelter with the prison-like comfort of the group shower. As a freshman I was quite a catch. Less than five feet tall, yet my head was the same size it is now. Didn't even really look like a head, it looked more like a container for a head. I looked like a *Peanuts* character. *Peanuts* characters had terrible acne. But what I lacked in looks I made up for with a repugnant personality.

In 1981 I lost my virginity, only to gain it back again on appeal in 1983. You could say that my one saving grace was academics where I excelled, but I did not.

And yet now I live in the rarified air of celebrity, of mega stardom. My life is a series of Hollywood orgies and Kabala center brunches with the cast of *Friends*. At least that's what my handlers tell me. I'm actually too valuable to live my own life and spend most of my days in a vegetable crisper to remain fake-news-anchor-fresh.

So I know that the decisions that I made after college worked out. But at the time I didn't know that they would. See, college is not necessarily predictive of your future success. And it's the kind of thing where the path that I chose obviously wouldn't work for you. For one, you're not very funny.

So how do you know what is the right path to choose to get the result that you desire? The honest answer is this: You won't. And accepting that greatly eases the anxiety of your life experience.

I was not exceptional here and am not now. I was mediocre here. And I'm not saying aim low. Not everybody can wander around in an alcoholic haze and then at 40 just, you know, decide to be president. You've got to really work hard to try to. I was actually referring to my father.

When I left William and Mary I was shell-shocked. Because when you're in college it's very clear what you have to do to succeed. And I imagine here everybody knows exactly the number of credits they needed to graduate, where they had to buckle down, which introductory psychology class would pad out the schedule. You knew what you had to do to get to this college and to graduate from it. But the unfortunate, yet truly exciting thing about your life is that there is no core curriculum. The entire place is an elective. The paths are infinite and the results uncertain. And it can be maddening to those who go here, especially here, because your strength has always been achievement. So if there's any real advice I can give you, it's this.

College is something you complete. Life is something you experience. So don't worry about your grade, or the results, or success. Success is defined in myriad ways, and you will find it, and people will no longer be grading you, but it will come from your own internal sense of decency, which I imagine, after going through the program here, is quite strong . . . although I'm sure downloading illegal files . . . but, nah, that's a different story.

Love what you do. Get good at it. Competence is a rare commodity in this day and age. And let the chips fall where they may.

And the last thing I want to address is the idea that somehow this new generation is not as prepared for the sacrifice and the tenacity that will be needed in the difficult times ahead. I have not found this generation to be cynical or apathetic or selfish. They are as strong and as decent as any people that I have met. And I will say this, on my way down here I stopped at Bethesda Naval, and when you talk to the young kids who are there that have just been back from Iraq and Afghanistan, you don't have the worry about the future that you hear from so many who are not a part of this generation but judging it from above.

And the other thing that I will say is, when I spoke earlier about the world being broke, I was somewhat being facetious, because every generation has its challenge. And things change rapidly, and life gets better in an instant.

I was in New York on 9-11 when the towers came down. I lived 14 blocks from the twin towers. And when they came down, I thought that the world had ended. And I remember walking around in a daze for weeks. And Mayor Giuliani had said to the city, "You've got to get back to normal. We've got to show that things can change and get back to what they were."

And one day I was coming out of my building, and on my stoop was a man who was crouched over, and he appeared to be in deep thought. And as I got closer to him I realized, he was playing with himself. And that's when I thought, "You know what, we're gonna be OK."

Thank you. Congratulations. I honor you. Good night.

MALCOLM X
Learning to Read

It was because of my letters that I happened to stumble upon starting to acquire some kind of a homemade education.

I became increasingly frustrated at not being able to express what I wanted
to convey in letters that I wrote, especially those to Mr. Elijah Muhammad. In the
street, I had been the most articulate hustler out there—I had commanded attention when I said something. But now, trying to write simple English, I not
only wasn't articulate, I wasn't even functional. How would I sound writing in
slang, the way I would *say* it, something such as "Look, daddy, let me pull your
coat about a cat, Elijah Muhammad—"

Many who today hear me somewhere in person, or on television, or
those who read something I've said, will think I went to school far beyond the
eighth grade. This impression is due entirely to my prison studies.

It had really begun back in the Charlestown Prison, when Bimbi first
made me feel envy of his stock of knowledge. Bimbi had always taken charge
of any conversation he was in, and I had tried to emulate him. But every book
I picked up had few sentences which didn't contain anywhere from one to
nearly all of the words that might as well have been in Chinese. When I just
skipped those words, of course, I really ended up with little idea of what the
book said. So I had come to the Norfolk Prison Colony still going through
only book-reading motions. Pretty soon, I would have quit even these motions, unless I had received the motivation that I did.

I saw that the best thing I could do was get hold of a dictionary—to
study, to learn some words. I was lucky enough to reason also that I should try
to improve my penmanship. It was sad. I couldn't even write in a straight line.
It was both ideas together that moved me to request a dictionary along with
some tablets and pencils from the Norfolk Prison Colony school.

I spent two days just riffling uncertainly through the dictionary's pages.
I'd never realized so many words existed! I didn't know *which* words I needed
to learn. Finally, just to start some kind of action, I began copying.

In my slow, painstaking, ragged handwriting, I copied into my tablet
everything printed on that first page, down to the punctuation marks.

I believe it took me a day. Then, aloud, I read back, to myself, everything
I'd written on the tablet. Over and over, aloud, to myself, I read my own handwriting.

I woke up the next morning, thinking about those words—immensely
proud to realize that not only had I written so much at one time, but I'd written words that I never knew were in the world. Moreover, with a little effort, I

also could remember what many of these words meant. I reviewed the words whose meanings I didn't remember. Funny thing, from the dictionary first page right now, that "aardvark" springs to my mind. The dictionary had a picture of it, a long-tailed, long-eared, burrowing African mammal, which lives off termites caught by sticking out its tongue as an anteater does for ants.

I was so fascinated that I went on—I copied the dictionary's next page. And the same experience came when I studied that. With every succeeding page, I also learned of people and places and events from history. Actually the dictionary is like a miniature encyclopedia. Finally the dictionary's A section had filled a whole tablet—and I went on into the B's. That was the way I started copying what eventually became the entire dictionary. It went a lot faster after so much practice helped me to pick up handwriting speed. Between what I wrote in my tablet, and writing letters, during the rest of my time in prison I would guess I wrote a million words.

I suppose it was inevitable that as my word-base broadened, I could for the first time pick up a book and read and now begin to understand what the book was saying. Anyone who has read a great deal can imagine the new world that opened. Let me tell you something: from then until I left that prison, in every free moment I had, if I was not reading in the library, I was reading on my bunk. You couldn't have gotten me out of books with a wedge. Between Mr. Muhammad's teachings, my correspondence, my visitors—usually Ella and Reginald—and my reading of books, months passed without my even thinking about being imprisoned. In fact, up to then, I never had been so truly free in my life.

The Norfolk Prison Colony's library was in the school building. A variety of classes was taught there by instructors who came from such places as Harvard and Boston universities. The weekly debates between inmate teams were also held in the school building. You would be astonished to know how worked up convict debaters and audiences would get over subjects like "Should Babies Be Fed Milk?"

Available on the prison library's shelves were books on just about every general subject. Much of the big private collection that Parkhurst had willed to the prison was still in crates and boxes in the back of the library—thousands of old books. Some of them looked ancient: covers faded, old-time parchment-looking binding. Parkhurst, I've mentioned, seemed to have been principally interested in history and religion. He had the money and the special interest to have a lot of books that you wouldn't have in general circulation. Any college library would have been lucky to get that collection.

As you can imagine, especially in a prison where there was heavy emphasis on rehabilitation, an inmate was smiled upon if he demonstrated an unusually intense interest in books. There was a sizable number of well-read inmates, especially the popular debaters. Some were said by many to be practically walking encyclopedias. They were almost celebrities. No university would ask any

student to devour literature as I did when this new world opened to me, of being able to read and *understand*.

I read more in my room than in the library itself. An inmate who was
known to read a lot could check out more than the permitted maximum
number of books. I preferred reading in the total isolation of my own room.

When I had progressed to really serious reading, every night at about ten
P.M. I would be outraged with the "lights out." It always seemed to catch me
right in the middle of something engrossing.

Fortunately, right outside my door was a corridor light that cast a glow
into my room. The glow was enough to read by, once my eyes adjusted to it. So
when "lights out" came, I would sit on the floor where I could continue reading in that glow.

At one-hour intervals the night guards paced past every room. Each time
I heard the approaching footsteps, I jumped into bed and feigned sleep. And as
soon as the guard passed, I got back out of bed onto the floor area of that light-
glow, where I would read for another fifty-eight minutes—until the guard approached again. That went on until three or four every morning. Three or four
hours of sleep a night was enough for me. Often in the years in the streets I had
slept less than that.

The teachings of Mr. Muhammad stressed how history had been
"whitened"—when white men had written history books, the black man simply had been left out. Mr. Muhammad couldn't have said anything that would
have struck me much harder. I had never forgotten how when my class, me and
all of those whites, had studied seventh-grade United States history back in
Mason, the history of the Negro had been covered in one paragraph, and the
teacher had gotten a big laugh with his joke, "Negroes' feet are so big that
when they walk, they leave a hole in the ground."

This is one reason why Mr. Muhammad's teachings spread so swiftly all
over the United States, among *all* Negroes, whether or not they became followers of Mr. Muhammad. The teachings ring true—to every Negro. You can
hardly show me a black adult in America—or a white one, for that matter—
who knows from the history books anything like the truth about the black
man's role. In my own case, once I heard of the "glorious history of the black
man," I took special pains to hunt in the library for books that would inform
me on details about black history.

I can remember accurately the very first set of books that really impressed
me. I have since bought that set of books and have it at home for my children
to read as they grow up. It's called *Wonders of the World*. It's full of pictures of
archeological finds, statues that depict, usually, non-European people.

I found books like Will Durant's *Story of Civilization*. I read H. G. Wells'
Outline of History. *Souls of Black Folk* by W. E. B. Du Bois gave me a glimpse into
the black people's history before they came to this country. Carter G. Woodson's

Negro History opened my eyes about black empires before the black slave was brought to the United States, and the early Negro struggles for freedom.

J. A. Rogers' three volumes of *Sex and Race* told about race-mixing before Christ's time; about Aesop being a black man who told fables; about Egypt's Pharaohs; about the great Coptic Christian Empires; about Ethiopia, the earth's oldest continuous black civilization, as China is the oldest continuous civilization.

Mr. Muhammad's teaching about how the white man had been created led me to *Findings in Genetics* by Gregor Mendel. (The dictionary's G section was where I had learned what "genetics" meant.) I really studied this book by the Austrian monk. Reading it over and over, especially certain sections, helped me to understand that if you started with a black man, a white man could be produced; but starting with a white man, you never could produce a black man—because the white gene is recessive. And since no one disputes that there was but one Original Man, the conclusion is clear.

During the last year or so, in the *New York Times,* Arnold Toynbee used the word "bleached" in describing the white man. (His words were: "White (i.e., bleached) human beings of North European origin. . . .") Toynbee also referred to the European geographic area as only a peninsula of Asia. He said there is no such thing as Europe. And if you look at the globe, you will see for yourself that America is only an extension of Asia. (But at the same time Toynbee is among those who have helped to bleach history. He has written that Africa was the only continent that produced no history. He won't write that again. Every day now, the truth is coming to light.)

I never will forget how shocked I was when I began reading about slavery's total horror. It made such an impact upon me that it later became one of my favorite subjects when I became a minister of Mr. Muhammad's. The world's most monstrous crime, the sin and the blood on the white man's hands, are almost impossible to believe. Books like the one by Frederick Olmstead opened my eyes to the horrors suffered when the slave was landed in the United States. The European woman, Fannie Kimball, who had married a Southern white slave owner, described how human beings were degraded. Of course I read *Uncle Tom's Cabin.* In fact, I believe that's the only novel I have ever read since I started serious reading.

Parkhurst's collection also contained some bound pamphlets of the Abolitionist Anti-Slavery Society of New England. I read descriptions of atrocities, saw those illustrations of black slave women tied up and flogged with whips; of black mothers watching their babies being dragged off, never to be seen by their mothers again; of dogs after slaves, and of the fugitive slave catchers, evil white men with whips and clubs and chains and guns. I read about the slave preacher Nat Turner, who put the fear of God into the white slavemaster. Nat Turner wasn't going around preaching pie-in-the-sky and "non-violent" freedom for the black man. There in Virginia one night in 1831, Nat and seven other slaves started out at his master's home and through the night they went from one plantation "big house" to the next, killing, until by the next morning 57 white people were dead and Nat had about 70 slaves following him. White people, terrified for their lives, fled from their homes, locked themselves up in public buildings, hid in the woods, and some even left the state. A small army of soldiers took two months to catch and hang Nat Turner. Somewhere I have read where Nat Turner's example is said to have inspired John Brown to invade Virginia and attack Harper's Ferry nearly thirty years later, with thirteen white men and five Negroes.

I read Herodotus, "the father of History," or, rather, I read about him. And I read the histories of various nations, which opened my eyes gradually, then wider and wider, to how the whole world's white men had indeed acted like devils, pillaging and raping and bleeding and draining the whole world's non-white people. I remember, for instance, books such as Will Durant's story of Oriental civilization, and Mahatma Gandhi's accounts of the struggle to drive the British out of India.

Book after book showed me how the white man had brought upon the world's black, brown, red, and yellow peoples every variety of the sufferings of exploitation. I saw how since the sixteenth century, the so-called "Christian trader" white man began to ply the seas in his lust for Asian and African empires, and plunder, and power. I read, I saw, how the white man never has gone among the non-white peoples bearing the Cross in the true manner and spirit of Christ's teachings—meek, humble, and Christ-like.

I perceived, as I read, how the collective white man had been actually nothing but a piratical opportunist who used Faustian machinations to make his own Christianity his initial wedge in criminal conquests. First, always "religiously," he branded "heathen" and "pagan" labels upon ancient non-white cultures and civilizations. The stage thus set, he then turned upon his non-white victims his weapons of war.

I read how, entering India—half a *billion* deeply religious brown people—the British white man, by 1759, through promises, trickery and manipulations, controlled much of India through Great Britain's East India Company. The parasitical British administration kept tentacling out to half of the subcontinent. In 1857, some of the desperate people of India finally mutinied—and, excepting the African slave trade, nowhere has history recorded any more unnecessary bestial and ruthless human carnage than the British suppression of the non-white Indian people.

Over 115 million African blacks—close to the 1930s population of the United States—were murdered or enslaved during the slave trade. And I read how when the slave market was glutted, the cannibalistic white powers of Europe next carved up, as their colonies, the richest areas of the black continent. And Europe's chancelleries for the next century played a chess game of naked exploitation and power from Cape Horn to Cairo.

Ten guards and the warden couldn't have torn me out of those books. Not even Elijah Muhammad could have been more eloquent than those books were in providing indisputable proof that the collective white man had acted like a devil in virtually every contact he had with the world's collective non-white man. I listen today to the radio, and watch television, and read the headlines about the collective white man's fear and tension concerning China. When the white man professes ignorance about why the Chinese hate him so, my mind can't help flashing back to what I read, there in prison, about how the blood forebears of this same white man raped China at a time when China was trusting and helpless. Those original white "Christian traders" sent into China millions of pounds of opium. By 1839, so many of the Chinese were addicts that China's desperate government destroyed twenty thousand chests of opium. The first Opium War was promptly declared by the white man. Imagine! Declaring *war* upon someone who objects to being narcotized! The Chinese were severely beaten, with Chinese-invented gunpowder.

The Treaty of Nanking made China pay the British white man for the destroyed opium; forced open China's major ports to British trade; forced China to abandon Hong Kong; fixed China's import tariffs so low that cheap British articles soon flooded in, maiming China's industrial development.

After a second Opium War, the Tientsin Treaties legalized the ravaging opium trade, legalized a British-French-American control of China's customs. China tried delaying that Treaty's ratification; Peking was looted and burned.

"Kill the foreign white devils!" was the 1901 Chinese war cry in the Boxer Rebellion. Losing again, this time the Chinese were driven from Peking's choicest areas. The vicious, arrogant white man put up the famous signs, "Chinese and dogs not allowed."

Red China after World War II closed its doors to the Western white world. Massive Chinese agricultural, scientific, and industrial efforts are described in a book that *Life* magazine recently published. Some observers inside Red China have reported that the world never has known such a hate-white campaign as is now going on in this non-white country where, present birthrates continuing, in fifty more years Chinese will be half the earth's population. And it seems that some Chinese chickens will soon come home to roost, with China's recent successful nuclear tests.

Let us face reality. We can see in the United Nations a new world order being shaped, along color lines—an alliance among the non-white nations. America's U.N. Ambassador Adlai Stevenson complained not long ago that in the United Nations "a skin game" was being played. He was right. He was facing reality. A "skin game" *is* being played. But Ambassador Stevenson sounded like Jesse James accusing the marshal of carrying a gun. Because who in the world's history ever has played a worse "skin game" than the white man?

Mr. Muhammad, to whom I was writing daily, had no idea of what a new world had opened up to me through my efforts to document his teachings in books.

When I discovered philosophy, I tried to touch all the landmarks of philosophical development. Gradually, I read most of the old philosophers, Occidental and Oriental. The Oriental philosophers were the ones I came to prefer; finally, my impression was that most Occidental philosophy had largely been borrowed from the Oriental thinkers. Socrates, for instance, traveled in Egypt. Some sources even say that Socrates was initiated into some of the Egyptian mysteries. Obviously Socrates got some of his wisdom among the East's wise men.

I have often reflected upon the new vistas that reading opened to me. I knew right there in prison that reading had changed forever the course of my life. As I see it today, the ability to read awoke inside me some long dormant craving to be mentally alive. I certainly wasn't seeking any degree, the way a college confers a status symbol upon its students. My homemade education gave me, with every additional book that I read, a little bit more sensitivity to the deafness, dumbness, and blindness that was afflicting the black race in America. Not long ago, an English writer telephoned me from London, asking questions. One was, "What's your alma mater?" I told him, "Books." You will never catch me with a free fifteen minutes in which I'm not studying something I feel might be able to help the black man.

Yesterday I spoke in London, and both ways on the plane across the Atlantic I was studying a document about how the United Nations proposes to insure the human rights of the oppressed minorities of the world. The American black man is the world's most shameful case of minority oppression. What makes the black man think of himself as only an internal United States issue is just a catch-phrase, two words, "civil rights." How is the black man going to get "civil rights" before first he wins his *human* rights? If the American black man will start thinking about his *human* rights, and then start thinking of himself as part of one of the world's great peoples, he will see he has a case for the United Nations.

I can't think of a better case! Four hundred years of black blood and sweat invested here in America, and the white man still has the black man begging for what every immigrant fresh off the ship can take for granted the minute he walks down the gangplank.

But I'm digressing. I told the Englishman that my alma mater was books, a good library. Every time I catch a plane, I have with me a book that I want to read—and that's a lot of books these days. If I weren't out here every day battling the white man, I could spend the rest of my life reading, just satisfying my curiosity—because you can hardly mention anything I'm not curious about. I don't think anybody ever got more out of going to prison than I did. In fact, prison enabled me to study far more intensively than I would have if my life had gone differently and I had attended some college. I imagine that one of the biggest troubles with colleges is there are too many distractions, too much panty-raiding, fraternities, and boola-boola and all of that. Where else but in a prison could I have attacked my ignorance by being able to study intensely sometimes as much as fifteen hours a day?

Fiction

●

○

ALICE WALKER
Everyday Use

for your grandmama

    I will wait for her in the yard that Maggie and I made so clean and wavy yesterday afternoon. A yard like this is more comfortable than most people know. It is not just a yard. It is like an extended living room. When the hard clay is swept clean as a floor and the fine sand around the edges lined with tiny, irregular grooves, anyone can come and sit and look up into the elm tree and wait for the breezes that never come inside the house.

    Maggie will be nervous until after her sister goes: she will stand hopelessly in corners, homely and ashamed of the burn scars down her arms and legs, eyeing her sister with a mixture of envy and awe. She thinks her sister has held life always in the palm of one hand, that "no" is a word the world never learned to say to her.

    You've no doubt seen those TV shows where the child who has "made it" is confronted, as a surprise, by her own mother and father, tottering in weakly from backstage. (A pleasant surprise, of course: What would they do if parent and child came on the show only to curse out and insult each other?) On TV mother and child embrace and smile into each other's faces. Sometimes the mother and father weep, the child wraps them in her arms and leans across the table to tell how she would not have made it without their help. I have seen these programs.

    Sometimes I dream a dream in which Dee and I are suddenly brought together on a TV program of this sort. Out of a dark and soft-seated limousine I am ushered into a bright room filled with many people. There I meet a smiling, gray, sporty man like Johnny Carson who shakes my hand and tells me what a fine girl I have. Then we are on the stage and Dee is embracing me with tears in her eyes. She pins on my dress a large orchid, even though she has told me once that she thinks orchids are tacky flowers.

In real life I am a large, big-boned woman with rough, man-working hands. In the winter I wear flannel nightgowns to bed and overalls during the day. I can kill and clean a hog as mercilessly as a man. My fat keeps me hot in zero weather. I can work outside all day, breaking ice to get water for washing; I can eat pork liver cooked over the open fire minutes after it comes steaming from the hog. One winter I knocked a bull calf straight in the brain between the eyes with a sledge hammer and had the meat hung up to chill before night-fall. But of course all this does not show on television. I am the way my daughter would want me to be: a hundred pounds lighter, my skin like an uncooked barley pancake. My hair glistens in the hot bright lights. Johnny Carson has much to do to keep up with my quick and witty tongue.

But that is a mistake. I know even before I wake up. Who ever knew a Johnson with a quick tongue? Who can even imagine me looking a strange white man in the eye? It seems to me I have talked to them always with one foot raised in flight, with my head turned in whichever way is farthest from them. Dee, though. She would always look anyone in the eye. Hesitation was no part of her nature.

"How do I look, Mama?" Maggie says, showing just enough of her thin body enveloped in pink skirt and red blouse for me to know she's there, almost hidden by the door.

"Come out into the yard," I say.

Have you ever seen a lame animal, perhaps a dog run over by some careless person rich enough to own a car, sidle up to someone who is ignorant enough to be kind to him? That is the way my Maggie walks. She has been like this, chin on chest, eyes on ground, feet in shuffle, ever since the fire that burned the other house to the ground.

Dee is lighter than Maggie, with nicer hair and a fuller figure. She's a woman now, though sometimes I forget. How long ago was it that the other house burned? Ten, twelve years? Sometimes I can still hear the flames and feel Maggie's arms sticking to me, her hair smoking and her dress falling off her in little black papery flakes. Her eyes seemed stretched open, blazed open by the flames reflected in them. And Dee. I see her standing off under the sweet gum tree she used to dig gum out of; a look of concentration on her face as she watched the last dingy gray board of the house fall in toward the red-hot brick chimney. Why don't you do a dance around the ashes? I'd wanted to ask her. She had hated the house that much.

I used to think she hated Maggie, too. But that was before we raised the money, the church and me, to send her to Augusta to school. She used to read to us without pity; forcing words, lies, other folks' habits, whole lives upon us two, sitting trapped and ignorant underneath her voice. She washed us in a river of make-believe, burned us with a lot of knowledge we didn't necessarily need to know. Pressed us to her with the serious way she read, to shove us away at just the moment, like dimwits, we seemed about to understand.

Dee wanted nice things. A yellow organdy dress to wear to her graduation from high school; black pumps to match a green suit she'd made from an old suit somebody gave me. She was determined to stare down any disaster in her efforts. Her eyelids would not flicker for minutes at a time. Often I fought off the temptation to shake her. At sixteen she had a style of her own: and knew what style was.

I never had an education myself. After second grade the school was closed down. Don't ask my why: in 1927 colored asked fewer questions than they do now. Sometimes Maggie reads to me. She stumbles along good-naturedly but can't see well. She knows she is not bright. Like good looks and money, quickness passed her by. She will marry John Thomas (who has mossy teeth in an earnest face) and then I'll be free to sit here and I guess just sing church songs to myself. Although I never was a good singer. Never could carry a tune. I was always better at a man's job. I used to love to milk till I was hooked in the side in '49. Cows are soothing and slow and don't bother you, unless you try to milk them the wrong way.

I have deliberately turned my back on the house. It is three rooms, just like the one that burned, except the roof is tin; they don't make shingle roofs any more. There are no real windows, just some holes cut in the sides, like the portholes in a ship, but not round and not square, with rawhide holding the shutters up on the outside. This house is in a pasture, too, like the other one. No doubt when Dee sees it she will want to tear it down. She wrote me once that no matter where we "choose" to live, she will manage to come see us. But she will never bring her friends. Maggie and I thought about this and Maggie asked me, "Mama, when did Dee ever *have* any friends?"

She had a few. Furtive boys in pink shirts hanging about on washday after school. Nervous girls who never laughed. Impressed with her they worshiped the well-turned phrase, the cute shape, the scalding humor that erupted like bubbles in lye. She read to them.

When she was courting Jimmy T she didn't have much time to pay to us, but turned all her faultfinding power on him. He *flew* to marry a cheap city girl from a family of ignorant flashy people. She hardly had time to recompose herself.

When she comes I will meet—but there they are!

Maggie attempts to make a dash for the house, in her shuffling way, but I stay her with my hand. "Come back here," I say. And she stops and tries to dig a well in the sand with her toe.

It is hard to see them clearly through the strong sun. But even the first glimpse of leg out of the car tells me it is Dee. Her feet were always neat-looking, as if God himself had shaped them with a certain style. From the other side of the car comes a short, stocky man. Hair is all over his head a foot long and hanging from his chin like a kinky mule tail. I hear Maggie suck in her breath. "Uhnnnh," is what it sounds like. Like when you see the wriggling end of a snake just in front of your foot on the road. "Uhnnnh."

Dee next. A dress down to the ground, in this hot weather. A dress so loud it hurts my eyes. There are yellows and oranges enough to throw back the light of the sun. I feel my whole face warming from the heat waves it throws out. Earrings gold, too, and hanging down to her shoulders. Bracelets dangling and making noises when she moves her arm up to shake the folds of the dress out of her armpits. The dress is loose and flows, and as she walks closer, I like it. I hear Maggie go "Uhnnnh" again. It is her sister's hair. It stands straight up like the wool on a sheep. It is black as night and around the edges are two long pig-tails that rope about like small lizards disappearing behind her ears.

"Wa-su-zo-Tean-o!" she says, coming on in that gliding way the dress makes her move. The short stocky fellow with the hair to his navel is all grin-ning and he follows up with "Asalamalakim, my mother and sister!" He moves to hug Maggie but she falls back, right up against the back of my chair. I feel her trembling there and when I look up I see the perspiration falling off her chin.

"Don't get up," says Dee. Since I am stout it takes something of a push. You can see me trying to move a second or two before I make it. She turns, showing white heels through her sandals, and goes back to the car. Out she peeks next with a Polaroid. She stoops down quickly and lines up picture after picture of me sitting there in front of the house with Maggie cowering behind me. She never takes a shot without making sure the house is included. When a cow comes nibbling around the edge of the yard she snaps it and me and Mag-gie *and* the house. Then she puts the Polaroid in the back seat of the car, and comes up and kisses me on the forehead.

Meanwhile Asalamalakim is going through motions with Maggie's hand. Maggie's hand is as limp as a fish, and probably as cold, despite the sweat, and she keeps trying to pull it back. It looks like Asalamalakim wants to shake hands but wants to do it fancy. Or maybe he don't know how people shake hands. Anyhow, he soon gives up on Maggie.

"Well," I say. "Dee."

"No, Mama," she says. "Not 'Dee,' Wangero Leewanika Kemanjo!"

"What happened to 'Dee'?" I wanted to know.

"She's dead," Wangero said. "I couldn't bear it any longer, being named after the people who oppress me."

"You know as well as me you was named after your aunt Dicie," I said. Dicie is my sister. She named Dee. We called her "Big Dee" after Dee was born.

"But who was *she* named after?" asked Wangero.

"I guess after Grandma Dee," I said.

"And who was she named after?" asked Wangero.

"Her mother," I said, and saw Wangero was getting tired. "That's about as far back as I can trace it," I said. Though, in fact, I probably could have carried it back beyond the Civil War through the branches.

"Well," said Asalamalakim, "there you are."

"Uhnnnh," I heard Maggie say.

"There I was not," I said, "before 'Dicie' cropped up in our family, so why should I try to trace it that far back?"

He just stood there grinning, looking down on me like somebody inspecting a Model A car. Every once in a while he and Wangero sent eye signals over my head.

"How do you pronounce this name?" I asked.

"You don't have to call me by it if you don't want to," said Wangero.

"Why shouldn't I?" I asked. "If that's what you want us to call you, we'll call you."

"I know it might sound awkward at first," said Wangero.

"I'll get used to it," I said. "Ream it out again."

Well, soon we got the name out of the way. Asalamalakim had a name twice as long and three times as hard. After I tripped over it two or three times he told me to just call him Hakim-a-barber. I wanted to ask him was he a barber, but I didn't really think he was, so I didn't ask.

"You must belong to those beef-cattle peoples down the road," I said. They said "Asalamalakim" when they met you, too, but they didn't shake hands. Always too busy: feeding the cattle, fixing the fences, putting up salt-lick shelters, throwing down hay. When the white folks poisoned some of the herd the men stayed up all night with rifles in their hands. I walked a mile and a half just to see the sight.

Hakim-a-barber said, "I accept some of their doctrines, but farming and raising cattle is not my style." (They didn't tell me, and I didn't ask, whether Wangero (Dee) had really gone and married him.)

We sat down to eat and right away he said he didn't eat collards and pork was unclean. Wangero, though, went on through the chitlins and corn bread, the greens and everything else. She talked a blue streak over the sweet potatoes. Everything delighted her. Even the fact that we still used the benches her daddy made for the table when we couldn't afford to buy chairs.

"Oh, Mama!" she cried. Then turned to Hakim-a-barber. "I never knew how lovely these benches are. You can feel the rump prints," she said, running her hands underneath her and along the bench. Then she gave a sigh and her hand closed over Grandma Dee's butter dish. "That's it!" she said. "I knew there was something I wanted to ask you if I could have." She jumped up from the table and went over in the corner where the churn stood, the milk in it clabber by now. She looked at the churn and looked at it.

"This churn top is what I need," she said. "Didn't Uncle Buddy whittle it out of a tree you all used to have?"

"Yes," I said.

"Uh huh," she said happily. "And I want the dasher, too."

"Uncle Buddy whittle that, too?" asked the barber.

Dee (Wangero) looked up at me.

"Aunt Dee's first husband whittled the dash," said Maggie so low you almost couldn't hear her. "His name was Henry, but they called him Stash."

"Maggie's brain is like an elephant's," Wangero said, laughing. "I can use the churn top as a centerpiece for the alcove table," she said, sliding a plate over the churn, "and I'll think of something artistic to do with the dasher."

When she finished wrapping the dasher the handle stuck out. I took it for a moment in my hands. You didn't even have to look close to see where hands pushing the dasher up and down to make butter had left a kind of sink in the wood. In fact, there were a lot of small sinks; you could see where thumbs and fingers had sunk into the wood. It was beautiful light yellow wood, from a tree that grew in the yard where Big Dee and Stash had lived.

After dinner Dee (Wangero) went to the trunk at the foot of my bed and started rifling through it. Maggie hung back in the kitchen over the dishpan. Out came Wangero with two quilts. They had been pieced by Grandma Dee and then Big Dee and me had hung them on the quilt frames on the front porch and quilted them. One was in the Lone Star pattern. The other was Walk Around the Mountain. In both of them were scraps of dresses Grandma Dee had worn fifty and more years ago. Bits and pieces of Grandpa Jarrell's Paisley shirts. And one teeny faded blue piece, about the size of a penny matchbox, that was from Great Grandpa Ezra's uniform that he wore in the Civil War.

"Mama," Wangero said sweet as a bird. "Can I have these old quilts?"

I heard something fall in the kitchen, and a minute later the kitchen door slammed.

"Why don't you take one or two of the others?" I asked. "These old things was just done by me and Big Dee from some tops your grandma pieced before she died."

"No," said Wangero. "I don't want those. They are stitched around the borders by machine."

"That'll make them last better," I said.

"That's not the point," said Wangero. "These are all pieces of dresses Grandma used to wear. She did all this stitching by hand. Imagine!" She held the quilts securely in her arms, stroking them.

"Some of the pieces, like those lavender ones, come from old clothes her mother handed down to her," I said, moving up to touch the quilts. Dee

(Wangero) moved back just enough so that I couldn't reach the quilts. They already belonged to her.

"Imagine!" she breathed again, clutching them closely to her bosom.

"The truth is," I said, "I promised to give them quilts to Maggie, for when she marries John Thomas."

She gasped like a bee had stung her.

"Maggie can't appreciate these quilts!" she said. "She'd probably be backward enough to put them to everyday use."

"I reckon she would," I said. "God knows I been saving 'em for long enough with nobody using 'em. I hope she will!" I didn't want to bring up how I had offered Dee (Wangero) a quilt when she went away to college. Then she had told me they were old-fashioned, out of style.

"But they're *priceless!*" she was saying now, furiously; for she has a temper. "Maggie would put them on the bed and in five years they'd be in rags. Less than that!"

"She can always make some more," I said. "Maggie knows how to quilt."

Dee (Wangero) looked at me with hatred. "You just will not understand. The point is these quilts, *these* quilts!"

"Well," I said, stumped. "What would *you* do with them?"

"Hang them," she said. As if that was the only thing you *could* do with quilts.

Maggie by now was standing in the door. I could almost hear the sound her feet made as they scraped over each other.

"She can have them, Mama," she said, like somebody used to never winning anything, or having anything reserved for her. "I can 'member Grandma Dee without the quilts."

I looked at her hard. She had filled her bottom lip with checkerberry snuff and it gave her face a kind of dopey, hangdog look. It was Grandma Dee and Big Dee who taught her how to quilt herself. She stood there with her scarred hands hidden in the folds of her skirt. She looked at her sister with something like fear but she wasn't mad at her. This was Maggie's portion. This was the way she knew God to work.

When I looked at her like that something hit me in the top of my head and ran down to the soles of my feet. Just like when I'm in church and the spirit of God touches me and I get happy and shout. I did something I never had done before: hugged Maggie to me, then dragged her on into the room, snatched the quilts out of Miss Wangero's hands and dumped them into Maggie's lap. Maggie just sat there on my bed with her mouth open.

"Take one or two of the others," I said to Dee.

But she turned without a word and went out to Hakim-a-barber.

"You just don't understand," she said, as Maggie and I came out to the car.

"What don't I understand?" I wanted to know.

"Your heritage," she said. And then she turned to Maggie, kissed her, and said, "You ought to try to make something of yourself, too, Maggie. It's really a new day for us. But from the way you and Mama still live you'd never know it."

She put on some sunglasses that hid everything above the tip of her nose and her chin.

Maggie smiled; maybe at the sunglasses. But a real smile, not scared. After we watched the car dust settle I asked Maggie to bring me a dip of snuff. And then the two of us sat there just enjoying, until it was time to go in the house and go to bed.

Who's Irish?

In China, people say mixed children are supposed to be smart, and definitely my granddaughter Sophie is smart. But Sophie is wild, Sophie is not like my daughter Natalie, or like me. I am work hard my whole life, and fierce besides. My husband always used to say he is afraid of me, and in our restaurant, busboys and cooks all afraid of me too. Even the gang members come for protection money, they try to talk to my husband. When I am there, they stay away. If they come by mistake, they pretend they are come to eat. They hide behind the menu, they order a lot of food. They talk about their mothers. Oh, my mother have some arthritis, need to take herbal medicine, they say. Oh, my mother getting old, her hair all white now.

I say, Your mother's hair used to be white, but since she dye it, it become black again. Why don't you go home once in a while and take a look? I tell them, Confucius say a filial son knows what color his mother's hair is.

My daughter is fierce too, she is vice president in the bank now. Her new house is big enough for everybody to have their own room, including me. But Sophie take after Natalie's husband's family, their name is Shea. Irish. I always thought Irish people are like Chinese people, work so hard on the railroad, but now I know why the Chinese beat the Irish. Of course, not all Irish are like the Shea family, of course not. My daughter tell me I should not say Irish this, Irish that.

How do you like it when people say the Chinese this, the Chinese that, she say.

You know, the British call the Irish heathen, just like they call the Chinese, she say.

You think the Opium War was bad, how would you like to live right next door to the British, she say.

And that is that. My daughter have a funny habit when she win an argument, she take a sip of something and look away, so the other person is not embarrassed. So I am not embarrassed. I do not call anybody anything either. I just happen to mention about the Shea family, an interesting fact: four brothers in the family, and not one of them work. The mother, Bess, have a job before she got sick, she was executive secretary in a big company. She is handle everything for a big shot, you would be surprised how complicated her job is, not just type this, type that. Now she is a nice woman with a clean house. But her boys, every one of them is on welfare, or so-called severance pay, or so-called disability pay. Something. They say they cannot find work, this is not the economy of the fifties, but I say, Even the black people doing better these days, some of

195

them live so fancy, you'd be surprised. Why the Shea family have so much trouble? They are white people, they speak English. When I come to this country, I have no money and do not speak English. But my husband and I own our restaurant before he die. Free and clear, no mortgage. Of course, I understand I am just lucky, come from a country where the food is popular all over the world. I understand it is not the Shea family's fault they come from a country where everything is boiled. Still, I say.

She's right, we should broaden our horizons, say one brother, Jim, at Thanksgiving. Forget about the car business. Think about egg rolls.

Pad thai, say another brother, Mike. I'm going to make my fortune in pad thai. It's going to be the new pizza.

I say, You people too picky about what you sell. Selling egg rolls not good enough for you, but at least my husband and I can say, We made it. What can you say? Tell me. What can you say?

Everybody chew their tough turkey.

I especially cannot understand my daughter's husband John, who has no job but cannot take care of Sophie either. Because he is a man, he say, and that's the end of the sentence.

Plain boiled food, plain boiled thinking. Even his name is plain boiled: John. Maybe because I grew up with black bean sauce and hoisin sauce and garlic sauce, I always feel something is missing when my son-in-law talk.

But, okay: so my son-in-law can be man, I am baby-sitter. Six hours a day, same as the old sitter, crazy Amy, who quit. This is not so easy, now that I am sixty-eight, Chinese age almost seventy. Still, I try. In China, daughter take care of mother. Here it is the other way around. Mother help daughter, mother ask, Anything else I can do? Otherwise daughter complain mother is not supportive. I tell daughter, We do not have this word in Chinese, *supportive*. But my daughter too busy to listen, she has to go to meeting, she has to write memo while her husband go to the gym to be a man. My daughter say otherwise he will be depressed. Seems like all his life he has this trouble, depression.

No one wants to hire someone who is depressed, she say. It is important for him to keep his spirits up.

Beautiful wife, beautiful daughter, beautiful house, oven can clean itself automatically. No money left over, because only one income, but lucky enough, got the baby-sitter for free. If John lived in China, he would be very happy. But he is not happy. Even at the gym things go wrong. One day, he pull a muscle. Another day, weight room too crowded. Always something.

Until finally, hooray, he has a job. Then he feel pressure.

I need to concentrate, he say. I need to focus.

He is going to work for insurance company. Salesman job. A paycheck, he say, and at least he will wear clothes instead of gym shorts. My daughter buy him some special candy bars from the health-food store. They say THINK! on them, and are supposed to help John think.

John is a good-looking boy, you have to say that, especially now that he shave so you can see his face.

I am an old man in a young man's game, say John.

I will need a new suit, say John.

This time I am not going to shoot myself in the foot, say John.

Good, I say.

She means to be supportive, my daughter say. Don't start the send her back to China thing, because we can't.

Sophie is three years old American age, but already I see her nice Chinese side swallowed up by her wild Shea side. She looks like mostly Chinese. Beautiful black hair, beautiful black eyes. Nose perfect size, not so flat looks like something fell down, not so large looks like some big deal got stuck in wrong face. Everything just right, only her skin is a brown surprise to John's family. So brown, they say. Even John say it. She never goes in the sun, still she is that color, he say. Brown. They say, Nothing the matter with brown. They are just surprised. So brown. Nattie is not that brown, they say. They say, It seems like Sophie should be a color in between Nattie and John. Seems funny, a girl named Sophie Shea be brown. But she is brown, maybe her name should be Sophie Brown. She never go in the sun, still she is that color, they say. Nothing the matter with brown. They are just surprised.

The Shea family talk is like this sometimes, going around and around like a Christmas-tree train.

Maybe John is not her father, I say one day, to stop the train. And sure enough, train wreck. None of the brothers ever say the word *brown* to me again.

Instead, John's mother, Bess, say, I hope you are not offended.

She say, I did my best on those boys. But raising four boys with no father is no picnic.

You have a beautiful family, I say.

I'm getting old, she say.

You deserve a rest, I say. Too many boys make you old.

I never had a daughter, she say. You have a daughter.

I have a daughter, I say. Chinese people don't think a daughter is so great, but you're right. I have a daughter.

I was never against the marriage, you know, she say. I never thought John was marrying down. I always thought Nattie was just as good as white.

I was never against the marriage either, I say. I just wonder if they look at the whole problem.

Of course you pointed out the problem, you are a mother, she say. And now we both have a granddaughter. A little brown granddaughter, she is so precious to me.

I laugh. A little brown granddaughter, I say. To tell you the truth, I don't know how she came out so brown.

We laugh some more. These days Bess need a walker to walk. She take so many pills, she need two glasses of water to get them all down. Her favorite TV show is about bloopers, and she love her bird feeder. All day long, she can watch that bird feeder, like a cat.

I can't wait for her to grow up, Bess say. I could use some female company.

Too many boys, I say.

Boys are fine, she say. But they do surround you after a while.

You should take a break, come live with us, I say. Lots of girls at our house.

Be careful what you offer, say Bess with a wink. Where I come from, people mean for you to move in when they say a thing like that.

Nothing the matter with Sophie's outside, that's the truth. It is inside that she is like not any Chinese girl I ever see. We go to the park, and this is what she does. She stand up in the stroller. She take off all her clothes and throw them in the fountain.

Sophie! I say. Stop!

But she just laugh like a crazy person. Before I take over as baby-sitter, Sophie has that crazy-person sitter, Amy the guitar player. My daughter thought this Amy very creative—another word we do not talk about in China. In China, we talk about whether we have difficulty or no difficulty. We talk about whether life is bitter or not bitter. In America, all day long, people talk about creative. Never mind that I cannot even look at this Amy, with her shirt so short that her belly button showing. This Amy think Sophie should love her body. So when Sophie take off her diaper, Amy laugh. When Sophie run around naked, Amy say she wouldn't want to wear a diaper either. When Sophie go *shu-shu* in her lap, Amy laugh and say there are no germs in pee. When Sophie take off her shoes, Amy say bare feet is best, even the pediatrician say so. That is why Sophie now walk around with no shoes like a beggar child. Also why Sophie love to take off her clothes.

Turn around! say the boys in the park. Let's see that ass!

Of course, Sophie does not understand. Sophie clap her hands, I am the only one to say, No! This is not a game.

It has nothing to do with John's family, my daughter say. Amy was too permissive, that's all.

But I think if Sophie was not wild inside, she would not take off her shoes and clothes to begin with.

You never take off your clothes when you were little, I say. All my Chinese friends had babies, I never saw one of them act wild like that.

Look, my daughter say. I have a big presentation tomorrow.

John and my daughter agree Sophie is a problem, but they don't know what to do.

You spank her, she'll stop, I say another day.

But they say, Oh no.

In America, parents not supposed to spank the child.

It gives them low self-esteem, my daughter say. And that leads to problems later, as I happen to know.

My daughter never have big presentation the next day when the subject of spanking come up.

I don't want you to touch Sophie, she say. No spanking, period.

Don't tell me what to do, I say.

I'm not telling you what to do, say my daughter. I'm telling you how I feel.

I am not your servant, I say. Don't you dare talk to me like that.

My daughter have another funny habit when she lose an argument. She spread out all her fingers and look at them, as if she like to make sure they are still there.

My daughter is fierce like me, but she and John think it is better to explain to Sophie that clothes are a good idea. This is not so hard in the cold weather. In the warm weather, it is very hard.

Use your words, my daughter say. That's what we tell Sophie. How about if you set a good example.

As if good example mean anything to Sophie. I am so fierce, the gang members who used to come to the restaurant all afraid of me, but Sophie is not afraid.

I say, Sophie, if you take off your clothes, no snack.

I say, Sophie, if you take off your clothes, no lunch.

I say, Sophie, if you take off your clothes, no park.

Pretty soon we are stay home all day, and by the end of six hours she still did not have one thing to eat. You never saw a child stubborn like that.

I'm hungry! she cry when my daughter come home.

What's the matter, doesn't your grandmother feed you? My daughter laugh.

No! Sophie say. She doesn't feed me anything!

My daughter laugh again. Here you go, she say.

She say to John, Sophie must be growing.

Growing like a weed, I say.

Still Sophie take off her clothes, until one day I spank her. Not too hard, but she cry and cry, and when I tell her if she doesn't put her clothes back on I'll spank her again, she put her clothes back on. Then I tell her she is good girl, and give her some food to eat. The next day we go to the park and, like a nice Chinese girl, she does not take off her clothes.

She stop taking off her clothes, I report. Finally!

How did you do it? my daughter ask.

After twenty-eight years experience with you, I guess I learn something, I say.

It must have been a phase, John say, and his voice is suddenly like an expert.

His voice is like an expert about everything these days, now that he carry a leather briefcase, and wear shiny shoes, and can go shopping for a new car.

On the company, he say. The company will pay for it, but he will be able to drive it whenever he want.

A free car, he say. How do you like that.

It's good to see you in the saddle again, my daughter say. Some of your family patterns are scary.

At least I don't drink, he say. He say, And I'm not the only one with scary family patterns.

That's for sure, say my daughter.

Everyone is happy. Even I am happy, because there is more trouble with Sophie, but now I think I can help her Chinese side fight against her wild side. I teach her to eat food with fork or spoon or chopsticks, she cannot just grab into the middle of a bowl of noodles. I teach her not to play with garbage cans. Sometimes I spank her, but not too often, and not too hard.

Still, there are problems. Sophie like to climb everything. If there is a railing, she is never next to it. Always she is on top of it. Also, Sophie like to hit the mommies of her friends. She learn this from her playground best friend, Sinbad, who is four. Sinbad wear army clothes every day and like to ambush his mommy. He is the one who dug a big hole under the play structure, a foxhole he call it, all by himself. Very hardworking. Now he wait in the foxhole with a shovel full of wet sand. When his mommy come, he throw it right at her.

Oh, it's all right, his mommy say. You can't get rid of war games, it's part of their imaginative play. All the boys go through it.

Also, he like to kick his mommy, and one day he tell Sophie to kick his mommy too.

I wish this story is not true.

Kick her, kick her! Sinbad say.

Sophie kick her. A little kick, as if she just so happened was swinging her little leg and didn't realize that big mommy leg was in the way. Still I spank Sophie and make Sophie say sorry, and what does the mommy say?

Really, it's all right, she say. It didn't hurt.

After that, Sophie learn she can attack mommies in the playground, and some will say, Stop, but others will say, Oh, she didn't mean it, especially if they realize Sophie will be punished.

This is how, one day, bigger trouble come. The bigger trouble start when Sophie hide in the foxhole with that shovel full of sand. She wait, and when I come look for her, she throw it at me. All over my nice clean clothes.

Did you ever see a Chinese girl act this way?

Sophie! I say. Come out of there, say you're sorry.

But she does not come out. Instead, she laugh. Naaah, naah-na, naaa-naaa, she say.

I am not exaggerate: millions of children in China, not one act like this.

Sophie! I say. Now! Come out now!

But she know she is in big trouble. She know if she come out, what will happen next. So she does not come out. I am sixty-eight, Chinese age almost seventy, how can I crawl under there to catch her? Impossible. So I yell, yell, yell, and what happen? Nothing. A Chinese mother would help, but American mothers, they look at you, they shake their head, they go home. And, of course, a Chinese child would give up, but not Sophie.

I hate you! she yell. I hate you, Meanie!

Meanie is my new name these days.

Long time this goes on, long long time. The foxhole is deep, you cannot see too much, you don't know where is the bottom. You cannot hear too much either. If she does not yell, you cannot even know she is still there or not. After a while, getting cold out, getting dark out. No one left in the playground, only us.

Sophie, I say. How did you become stubborn like this? I am go home without you now.

I try to use a stick, chase her out of there, and once or twice I hit her, but still she does not come out. So finally I leave. I go outside the gate.

Bye-bye! I say. I'm go home now.

But still she does not come out and does not come out. Now it is dinnertime, the sky is black. I think I should maybe go get help, but how can I leave a little girl by herself in the playground? A bad man could come. A rat could come. I go back in to see what is happen to Sophie. What if she have a shovel and is making a tunnel to escape?

Sophie! I say.

No answer.

Sophie!

I don't know if she is alive. I don't know if she is fall asleep down there. If she is crying, I cannot hear her.

So I take the stick and poke.

Sophie! I say. I promise I no hit you. If you come out, I give you a lollipop.

No answer. By now I worried. What to do, what to do, what to do? I poke some more, even harder, so that I am poking and poking when my daughter and John suddenly appear.

What are you doing? What is going on? say my daughter.

Put down that stick! say my daughter.

You are crazy! say my daughter.

John wiggle under the structure, into the foxhole, to rescue Sophie.

She fell asleep, say John the expert. She's okay. That is one big hole.

Now Sophie is crying and crying.

Sophia, my daughter say, hugging her. Are you okay, peanut? Are you okay?

She's just scared, say John.

Are you okay? I say too. I don't know what happen, I say.

She's okay, say John. He is not like my daughter, full of questions. He is full of answers until we get home and can see by the lamplight.

Will you look at her? he yell then. What the hell happened?

Bruises all over her brown skin, and a swollen-up eye.

You are crazy! say my daughter. Look at what you did! You are crazy!

I try very hard, I say.

How could you use a stick? I told you to use your words!

She is hard to handle, I say.

She's three years old! You cannot use a stick! say my daughter.

She is not like any Chinese girl I ever saw, I say.

I brush some sand off my clothes. Sophie's clothes are dirty too, but at least she has her clothes on.

Has she done this before? ask my daughter. Has she hit you before?

She hits me all the time, Sophie say, eating ice cream.

Your family, say John.

Believe me, say my daughter.

A daughter I have, a beautiful daughter. I took care of her when she could not hold her head up. I took care of her before she could argue with me, when she was a little girl with two pigtails, one of them always crooked. I took care of her when we have to escape from China, I took care of her when suddenly we live in a country with cars everywhere, if you are not careful your little girl get run over. When my husband die, I promise him I will keep the family together, even though it was just two of us, hardly a family at all.

But now my daughter take me around to look at apartments. After all, I can cook, I can clean, there's no reason I cannot live by myself, all I need is a telephone. Of course, she is sorry. Sometimes she cry, I am the one to say everything will be okay. She say she have no choice, she doesn't want to end up divorced. I say divorce is terrible, I don't know who invented this terrible idea. Instead of live with a telephone, though, surprise, I come to live with Bess.

Imagine that. Bess make an offer and, sure enough, where she come from, people mean for you to move in when they say things like that. A crazy idea, go to live with someone else's family, but she like to have some female company, not like my daughter, who does not believe in company. These days when my daughter visit, she does not bring Sophie. Bess say we should give Nattie time, we will see Sophie again soon. But seems like my daughter have more presentation than ever before, every time she come she have to leave.

I have a family to support, she say, and her voice is heavy, as if soaking wet. I have a young daughter and a depressed husband and no one to turn to.

When she say no one to turn to, she mean me.

These days my beautiful daughter is so tired she can just sit there in a chair and fall asleep. John lost his job again, already, but still they rather hire a baby-sitter than ask me to help, even they can't afford it. Of course, the new baby-sitter is much younger, can run around. I don't know if Sophie these days is wild or not wild. She call me Meanie, but she like to kiss me too, sometimes.

I remember that every time I see a child on TV. Sophie like to grab my hair, a fistful in each hand, and then kiss me smack on the nose. I never see any other child kiss that way.

The satellite TV has so many channels, more channels than I can count, including a Chinese channel from the Mainland and a Chinese channel from Taiwan, but most of the time I watch bloopers with Bess. Also, I watch the bird feeder—so many, many kinds of birds come. The Shea sons hang around all the time, asking when will I go home, but Bess tell them, Get lost.

She's a permanent resident, say Bess. She isn't going anywhere.

Then she wink at me, and switch the channel with the remote control.

Of course, I shouldn't say Irish this, Irish that, especially now I am become honorary Irish myself, according to Bess. Me! Who's Irish? I say, and she laugh. All the same, if I could mention one thing about some of the Irish, not all of them of course, I like to mention this: Their talk just stick. I don't know how Bess Shea learn to use her words, but sometimes I hear what she say a long time later. *Permanent resident. Not going anywhere.* Over and over I hear it, the voice of Bess.

VIRGIL SUÁREZ
A Perfect Hotspot

This idea of selling ice cream during the summer seems ridiculous, pointless. I'd much rather be close to water. The waves. Where I can hear them tumble in and then roll out, and see the tiny bubbles left behind on the sand pop one by one. Or feel the undercurrents warm this time of year. Swimming. Watching the girls in bikinis with sand stuck to the backs of their thighs walk up and down the boardwalk. At this time of the morning, the surfers are out riding the waves.

Instead I'm inside an ice cream truck with my father, selling, cruising the streets. The pumps suck oil out of the ground rapidly with the creaking sounds of iron biting iron in a fenced lot at the end of the street. They look like giant rocking horses. Father turns at the corner, then, suddenly, he points to another ice cream truck.

"There's the competition," he says. "If the economy doesn't improve soon, these streets'll be full of them."

He's smoking, and the smoke floats back my way and chokes me. I can't stand it. Some of the guys on the swim team smoke. I don't understand how they can smoke and do their best when it's time for competition. I wouldn't smoke. To do so would be like cheating myself out of winning.

All morning he's been instructing me on how to sell ice cream.

"Tonio," he says now, "come empty your pockets."

I walk to the front of the truck, stick my hands deep into my pockets and grab a handful of coins—what we've made in change all morning. The coins fall, overlap and multiply against the sides of the grease-smudged, change box. I turn my pockets inside-out until the last coin falls. He picks out the pieces of lint and paper from the coins.

When he begins to explain the truck's quirks, "the little problems," as he calls the water leaks, burning oil, and dirty carburetor, I return to the back of the truck and sit down on top of the wood counter next to the window.

"Be always on the lookout for babies," father says. "The ones in pampers. They pop out of nowhere. Check your mirrors all the time."

A CAUTION CHILDREN cardboard sign hangs from the rearview mirror. Running over children is a deep fear that seems to haunt him.

All I need, I keep reminding myself, is to pass the CPR course, get certified, and look for a job as a beach lifeguard.

"Stop!" a kid screams, slamming the screen door of his house open. He runs to the grassy part next to the sidewalk. Father stops the truck. The kid's hand comes up over the edge of the window with a dollar bill forked between his little fingers.

"What do you want?" I say.

"A Froze Toe," he says, jumping up and down, dirt rings visible on his neck. He wets the corners of his mouth with his cherry, Kool-aid-stained tongue. I reach inside the freezer and bring out a bar. On its wrapper is the picture of an orange foot with a blue bubble gum ball on the big toe.

"See what else he wants," father says. "Make sure they always leave the dollar."

The kid takes his ice cream, and he smiles.

"What else?" I ask him.

He shrugs his shoulders, shakes his head, and bites the wrapper off. The piece of paper falls on the grass. I give him his change; he walks back to his house.

"Should always make sure they leave all the money they bring," father says. "They get it to spend it. That's the only way you'll make a profit. Don't steal their money, but exchange it for merchandise." His ears stick out from underneath his L.A. Dodgers cap. The short hair on the back of his head stands out.

I grin up at the rearview mirror, but he isn't looking.

"Want to split a Pepsi, Tonio?" he says.

"I'm not thirsty."

"Get me some water then."

The cold mist inside the freezer crawls up my hand. After he drinks and returns the bottle, I place it back with the ice cream.

"Close the freezer," he says, "before all the cold gets out and they melt."

If the cold were out I'd be at the natatorium doing laps.

On another street, a group of kids jumps and skips around a short man. The smallest of the kids hangs from the man's thigh. The man signals my father to stop, then walks up to the window. The kids scream excitedly.

"Want this one, daddy," one of the girls says.

"This one!" a boy says.

The smallest kid jumps, pointing his finger at the display my father has made with all the toys and candies.

"No, Jose," the man says, taking the kid by the wrist. "No candy."

The kid turns to look up at his father, not fully understanding, and then looks at me. His little lips tremble.

"Give me six Popsicles," the man says.

"I don't want no Pop —"

"Popsicles or nothing. I don't have money to buy you what you want."

"A Blue Ghost. I want a Blue Ghost."

"No, I said."

The smallest kid cries.

"Be quiet, Jose, or I'm going to tell the man to go away."

I put the six Popsicles on the counter.

"How much?" the man asks. The skin around his eyes is a darker brown than that of his nose and cheeks.

"A dollar-fifty," I say.

He digs inside his pockets and produces two wrinkled green balls which he throws on the counter. The two dollar bills roll. I unfold the bills, smooth them, and give them to father, who returns the man his change through the front window.

The man gives each kid a Popsicle, then walks away with his hands in his pockets. Jose, still crying, grabs his as he follows his father back to their house.

"He doesn't want to spend his beer money," father says, driving away from the curb.

After that, we have no more customers for hours. Ever since he brought the truck home two years ago, father has changed. Ice creams have become his world. According to father, appearance and cleanliness isn't important as long as the truck passes the Health Department inspection in order to obtain the sales license. The inside of the truck is a mess: paint flakes off, rust hides between crevices, the freezer lids hold layer upon layer of dirt and melted ice cream. Here I'll have to spend the rest of my summer, I think, among the strewn Doritos, Munchos, and the rest of the merchandise.

The outside of the truck had been painted by father's friend, Gaspar, before mother died. I remember how Gaspar drank beer after beer while he painted the crown over the K in KING OF ICE CREAM and assured mother, who never missed one of my swim meets and who always encouraged me to become the best swimmer I could be, that I was going to make it all right in the end.

Father lives this way, I know, out of loneliness. He misses mother as much as I do.

I count the passing of time by how many ice creams I sell. It isn't anything like swimming laps. Doing laps involves the idea of setting and breaking new limits.

"How much do you think we have?" my father asks. The visor of his cap tilts upward.

"I don't know." I hate the metallic smell money leaves on my fingers.

"Any idea?"

"No."

"A couple of months on your own and you'll be able to guess approximately how much you make."

A couple of months, I think, and I'll be back in high school. Captain of the varsity swim team. A customer waits down the street.

"Make the kill fast," father says.

A barefooted woman holding a child to her breast comes to the window. She has dirty fingernails, short and uneven, as if she bites them all the time. Make the kill fast, I think.

Ice creams on the counter, I tell her, "Two dollars."

She removes the money out of her brassiere and hands it to me, then she walks away. She has yellow blisters on the back of each heel.

After that, he begins to tell me the story of the wild dog. When he was a kid, a wild bitch came down from the hills and started killing my grandfather's chickens. "Seeing the scattered feathers," father says, "made your grandfather so angry I thought his face would burst because it'd turned so red."

"Anyway," he continues, "the wild dog kept on killing chickens."

Not only my grandfather's, but other farmers' as well. The other farmers were scared because they thought the wild dog was a witch. One morning, my grandfather got my father out of bed early and took him up to the hills behind the house with a jar of poison. A farmer had found the bitch's litter. My grandfather left my father in charge of anointing the poison all over the puppies fur so that when the mother came back, if he hadn't shot it by then, she'd die the minute she licked her young. My father didn't want to do it, but my grandfather left him in command while he went after the wild dog to shoot it. The dog disappeared and the puppies licked each other to death.

When he finishes telling me the story, father looks at the rearview mirror and grins, then he drives on. He turns up the volume in the music box and now *Raindrops Keep Falling On My Head* blares out of the speakers. The old people'll complain, he says, because the loud music hurts their eardrums, but the louder the music, the more people'll hear it, and more ice creams'll get sold.

Farther ahead, another kid stops us. The kid has his tongue out. His eyes seem to be too small for his big face. Though he seems old, he still drools. He claps his small hands quickly.

"Does he have money?" father asks.

"Can't see."

The kid walks over to the truck and hangs from the edge of the window.

"Get him away from the truck," father says, then to the kid, "Hey, move away!"

"Come on," I tell the kid, "you might fall and hurt yourself."

"Wan icleam," the kid says.

"We'll be back in a little while," father tells him.

"Wan icleam!" He doesn't let go. "Wan icleam!"

"Move back!" father shouts. "Tonio, get him away from the truck."

I try to unstick the kid's pudgy fingers from the metal edge of the window, but he won't let go. His saliva falls on my hands.

"Wan icleam!"

I reach over to one of the shelves to get a penny candy for him so that I can bait him into letting go, but father catches me.

"Don't you dare," he says.

He opens the door and comes around the back to the kid, pulling him away from the truck to the sidewalk where he sets the kid down, and returns.

"Can't give your merchandise away," he says. "You can't make a profit that way, Tonio."

The kid runs after us shouting, waving his arms. I grab a handful of candies and throw them out the window to the sidewalk, where they fall on the grass and scatter.

The sun sets slowly, and, descending, it spreads Popsicle orange on the sky. Darkness creeps on the other side of the city.

If I don't get a job as a lifeguard, I think, then I'm going to travel southeast and visit the islands.

"How are the ice creams doing?" father asks. "Are they softening?"

I check by squeezing a bar and say, "I think we should call it a day."

"Tonio," he says. He turns off the music, makes a left turn to the main street, and heads home. "Why didn't you help me with that kid? You could have moved him. What will happen when you're here by yourself?"

"Couldn't do it."

"Here," he says, giving me the change box. "Take it inside when we get home."

"I'll get it when we get there."

He puts the blue box back down on top of the stand he built over the motor. Cars speed by. The air smells heavy with exhaust and chemical fumes. In the distance, columns of smoke rise from factory smokestacks.

He turns into the driveway, drives the truck all the way to the front of the garage, and parks underneath the long branches of the avocado tree.

"Take the box inside," he says, turning off the motor. He steps down from the truck and connects the freezer to the extension cord coming out of the kitchen window.

I want to tell him that I won't come out tomorrow.

"Come on, Tonio. Bring the box in."

"You do it," I say.

"What's the matter, son?"

"I'd rather you do it."

"Like you'd rather throw all my merchandise out of the window," he says, growing red in the face. "I saw you."

He walks toward me, and I sense another argument coming. Father stops in front of me and gives me a wry smile. "Dreamers like you," he says, "learn the hard way."

He turns around, picks up the change box, and says, "I'm putting the truck up for sale. From now on you're on your own, you hear. I'm not forcing you to do something you don't want to."

I don't like the expressionless look on his face when usually, whenever he got angry at me, his face would get red and sweaty.

He unlocks the kitchen door and enters the house.

I jump out of the truck, lock the door, and walk around our clapboard house to the patio. Any moment now, I think, father'll start slamming doors inside and throwing things around. He'll curse. I lean against the wall and feel the glass of the window behind me when it starts to tremble.

SHERMAN ALEXIE

This Is What It Means to Say
Phoenix, Arizona

Just after Victor lost his job at the BIA, he also found out that his father had died of a heart attack in Phoenix, Arizona. Victor hadn't seen his father in a few years, only talked to him on the telephone once or twice, but there still was a genetic pain, which was soon to be pain as real and immediate as a broken bone.

Victor didn't have any money. Who does have money on a reservation, except the cigarette and fireworks salespeople? His father had a savings account waiting to be claimed, but Victor needed to find a way to get to Phoenix. Victor's mother was just as poor as he was, and the rest of his family didn't have any use at all for him. So Victor called the Tribal Council.

"Listen," Victor said. "My father just died. I need some money to get to Phoenix to make arrangements."

"Now, Victor," the council said. "You know we're having a difficult time financially."

"But I thought the council had special funds set aside for stuff like this."

"Now, Victor, we do have some money available for the proper return of tribal members' bodies. But I don't think we have enough to bring your father all the way back from Phoenix."

"Well," Victor said. "It ain't going to cost all that much. He had to be cremated. Things were kind of ugly. He died of a heart attack in his trailer and nobody found him for a week. It was really hot, too. You get the picture."

"Now, Victor, we're sorry for your loss and the circumstances. But we can really only afford to give you one hundred dollars."

"That's not even enough for a plane ticket."

"Well, you might consider driving down to Phoenix."

"I don't have a car. Besides, I was going to drive my father's pickup back up here."

"Now, Victor," the council said. "We're sure there is somebody who could drive you to Phoenix. Or is there somebody who could lend you the rest of the money?"

"You know there ain't nobody around with that kind of money."

"Well, we're sorry, Victor, but that's the best we can do."

Victor accepted the Tribal Council's offer. What else could he do? So he signed the proper papers, picked up his check, and walked over to the Trading Post to cash it.

While Victor stood in line, he watched Thomas Builds-the-Fire standing near the magazine rack, talking to himself. Like he always did. Thomas was a storyteller that nobody wanted to listen to. That's like being a dentist in a town where everybody has false teeth.

Victor and Thomas Builds-the-Fire were the same age, had grown up and played in the dirt together. Ever since Victor could remember, it was Thomas who always had something to say.

Once, when they were seven years old, when Victor's father still lived with the family, Thomas closed his eyes and told Victor this story: "Your father's heart is weak. He is afraid of his own family. He is afraid of you. Late at night he sits in the dark. Watches the television until there's nothing but that white noise. Sometimes he feels like he wants to buy a motorcycle and ride away. He wants to run and hide. He doesn't want to be found."

Thomas Builds-the-Fire had known that Victor's father was going to leave, knew it before anyone. Now Victor stood in the Trading Post with a one-hundred-dollar check in his hand, wondering if Thomas knew that Victor's father was dead, if he knew what was going to happen next.

Just then Thomas looked at Victor, smiled, and walked over to him.

"Victor, I'm sorry about your father," Thomas said.

"How did you know about it?" Victor asked.

"I heard it on the wind. I heard it from the birds. I felt it in the sunlight. Also, your mother was just in here crying."

"Oh," Victor said and looked around the Trading Post. All the other Indians stared, surprised that Victor was even talking to Thomas. Nobody talked to Thomas anymore because he told the same damn stories over and over again. Victor was embarrassed, but he thought that Thomas might be able to help him. Victor felt a sudden need for tradition.

"I can lend you the money you need," Thomas said suddenly. "But you have to take me with you."

"I can't take your money," Victor said. "I mean, I haven't hardly talked to you in years. We're not really friends anymore."

"I didn't say we were friends. I said you had to take me with you."

"Let me think about it."

Victor went home with his one hundred dollars and sat at the kitchen table. He held his head in his hands and thought about Thomas Builds-the-Fire, remembered little details, tears and scars, the bicycle they shared for a summer, so many stories.

Thomas Builds-the-Fire sat on the bicycle, waited in Victor's yard. He was ten years old and skinny. His hair was dirty because it was the Fourth of July.

"Victor," Thomas yelled. "Hurry up. We're going to miss the fireworks."

After a few minutes, Victor ran out of his house, jumped the porch railing, and landed gracefully on the sidewalk.

"And the judges award him a 9.95, the highest score of the summer," Thomas said, clapped, laughed.

"That was perfect, cousin," Victor said. "And it's my turn to ride the bike."

Thomas gave up the bike and they headed for the fairgrounds. It was nearly dark and the fireworks were about to start.

"You know," Thomas said. "It's strange how us Indians celebrate the Fourth of July. It ain't like it was *our* independence everybody was fighting for."

"You think about things too much," Victor said. "It's just supposed to be fun. Maybe Junior will be there."

"Which Junior? Everybody on this reservation is named Junior."

And they both laughed.

The fireworks were small, hardly more than a few bottle rockets and a fountain. But it was enough for two Indian boys. Years later, they would need much more.

Afterwards, sitting in the dark, fighting off mosquitoes, Victor turned to Thomas Builds-the Fire.

"Hey," Victor said. "Tell me a story."

Thomas closed his eyes and told this story: "There were these two Indian boys who wanted to be warriors. But it was too late to be warriors in the old way. All the horses were gone. So the two Indian boys stole a car and drove to the city. They parked the stolen car in front of the police station and then hitchhiked back home to the reservation. When they got back, all their friends cheered and their parents' eyes shone with pride. *You were very brave,* everybody said to the two Indian boys. *Very brave.*"

"Ya-hey," Victor said. "That's a good one. I wish I could be a warrior."

"Me too," Thomas said.

They went home together in the dark, Thomas on the bike now, Victor on foot. They walked through shadows and light from streetlamps.

"We've come a long ways," Thomas said. "We have outdoor lighting."

"All I need is the stars," Victor said. "And besides, you still think about things too much."

They separated then, each headed for home, both laughing all the way.

Victor sat at his kitchen table. He counted his one hundred dollars again and again. He knew he needed more to make it to Phoenix and back. He knew he needed Thomas Builds-the-Fire. So he put his money in his wallet and opened the front door to find Thomas on the porch.

"Ya-hey, Victor," Thomas said. "I knew you'd call me."

Thomas walked into the living room and sat down on Victor's favorite chair.

"I've got some money saved up," Thomas said. "It's enough to get us down there, but you have to get us back."

"I've got this hundred dollars," Victor said. "And my dad had a savings account I'm going to claim."

"How much in your dad's account?"

"Enough. A few hundred."

"Sounds good. When we leaving?"

When they were fifteen and had long since stopped being friends, Victor and Thomas got into a fistfight. That is, Victor was really drunk and beat Thomas up for no reason at all. All the other Indian boys stood around and watched it happen. Junior was there and so were Lester, Seymour, and a lot of others. The beating might have gone on until Thomas was dead if Norma Many Horses hadn't come along and stopped it.

"Hey, you boys," Norma yelled and jumped out of her car. "Leave him alone."

If it had been someone else, even another man, the Indian boys would've just ignored the warnings. But Norma was a warrior. She was powerful. She could have picked up any two of the boys and smashed their skulls together. But worse than that, she would have dragged them all over to some tipi and made them listen to some elder tell a dusty old story.

The Indian boys scattered, and Norma walked over to Thomas and picked him up.

"Hey, little man, are you okay?" she asked.

Thomas gave her a thumbs up.

"Why they always picking on you?"

Thomas shook his head, closed his eyes, but no stories came to him, no words or music. He just wanted to go home, to lie in his bed and let his dreams tell his stories for him.

Thomas Builds-the-Fire and Victor sat next to each other in the airplane, coach section. A tiny white woman had the window seat. She was busy twisting her body into pretzels. She was flexible.

"I have to ask," Thomas said, and Victor closed his eyes in embarrassment.

"Don't," Victor said.

"Excuse me, miss," Thomas asked. "Are you a gymnast or something?"

"There's no something about it," she said. "I was first alternate on the 1980 Olympic team."

"Really?" Thomas asked.

"Really."

"I mean, you used to be a world-class athlete?" Thomas asked.

"My husband still thinks I am."

Thomas Builds-the-Fire smiled. She was a mental gymnast, too. She pulled her leg straight up against her body so that she could've kissed her kneecap.

"I wish I could do that," Thomas said.

Victor was ready to jump out of the plane. Thomas, that crazy Indian storyteller with ratty old braids and broken teeth, was flirting with a beautiful

Olympic gymnast. Nobody back home on the reservation would ever believe it.

"Well," the gymnast said. "It's easy. Try it."

Thomas grabbed at his leg and tried to pull it up into the same position as the gymnast. He couldn't even come close, which made Victor and the gymnast laugh.

"Hey," she asked. "You two are Indian, right?"

"Full-blood," Victor said.

"Not me," Thomas said. "I'm half magician on my mother's side and half clown on my father's."

They all laughed.

"What are your names?" she asked.

"Victor and Thomas."

"Mine is Cathy. Pleased to meet you all."

The three of them talked for the duration of the flight. Cathy the gymnast complained about the government, how they screwed the 1980 Olympic team by boycotting.

"Sounds like you all got a lot in common with Indians," Thomas said.

Nobody laughed.

After the plane landed in Phoenix and they had all found their way to the terminal, Cathy the gymnast smiled and waved good-bye.

"She was really nice," Thomas said.

"Yeah, but everybody talks to everybody on airplanes," Victor said. "It's too bad we can't always be that way."

"You always used to tell me I think too much," Thomas said. "Now it sounds like you do."

"Maybe I caught it from you."

"Yeah."

Thomas and Victor rode in a taxi to the trailer where Victor's father died.

"Listen," Victor said as they stopped in front of the trailer. "I never told you I was sorry for beating you up that time."

"Oh, it was nothing. We were just kids and you were drunk."

"Yeah, but I'm still sorry."

"That's all right."

Victor paid for the taxi and the two of them stood in the hot Phoenix summer. They could smell the trailer.

"This ain't going to be nice," Victor said. "You don't have to go in."

"You're going to need help."

Victor walked to the front door and opened it. The stink rolled out and made them both gag. Victor's father had lain in that trailer for a week in hundred-degree temperatures before anyone found him. And the only reason anyone found him was because of the smell. They needed dental records to identify him. That's exactly what the coroner said. They needed dental records.

"Oh, man," Victor said. "I don't know if I can do this."

"Well, then don't."

"But there might be something valuable in there."

"I thought his money was in the bank."

"It is. I was talking about pictures and letters and stuff like that."

"Oh," Thomas said as he held his breath and followed Victor into the trailer.

★   ★   ★

When Victor was twelve, he stepped into an underground wasp nest. His foot was caught in the hole, and no matter how hard he struggled, Victor couldn't pull free. He might have died there, stung a thousand times, if Thomas Builds-the-Fire had not come by.

"Run," Thomas yelled and pulled Victor's foot from the hole. They ran then, hard as they ever had, faster than Billy Mills, faster than Jim Thorpe, faster than the wasps could fly.

Victor and Thomas ran until they couldn't breathe, ran until it was cold and dark outside, ran until they were lost and it took hours to find their way home. All the way back, Victor counted his stings.

"Seven," Victor said. "My lucky number."

Victor didn't find much to keep in the trailer. Only a photo album and a stereo. Everything else had that smell stuck in it or was useless anyway.

"I guess this is all," Victor said. "It ain't much."

"Better than nothing," Thomas said.

"Yeah, and I do have the pickup."

"Yeah," Thomas said. "It's in good shape."

"Dad was good about that stuff."

"Yeah, I remember your dad."

"Really?" Victor asked. "What do you remember?"

Thomas Builds-the-Fire closed his eyes and told this story: "I remember when I had this dream that told me to go to Spokane, to stand by the Falls in the middle of the city and wait for a sign. I knew I had to go there but I didn't have a car. Didn't have a license. I was only thirteen. So I walked all the way, took me all day, and I finally made it to the Falls. I stood there for an hour waiting. Then your dad came walking up. *What the hell are you doing here?* he asked me. I said, *Waiting for a vision.* Then your father said, *All you're going to get here is mugged.* So he drove me over to Denny's, bought me dinner, and then drove me home to the reservation. For a long time I was mad because I thought my dreams had lied to me. But they didn't. Your dad was my vision. *Take care of each other* is what my dreams were saying. *Take care of each other.*"

Victor was quiet for a long time. He searched his mind for memories of his father, found the good ones, found a few bad ones, added it all up, and smiled.

"My father never told me about finding you in Spokane," Victor said.

"He said he wouldn't tell anybody. Didn't want me to get in trouble. But he said I had to watch out for you as part of the deal."

"Really?"

"Really. Your father said you would need the help. He was right."

"That's why you came down here with me, isn't it?" Victor asked.

"I came because of your father."

Victor and Thomas climbed into the pickup, drove over to the bank, and claimed the three hundred dollars in the savings account.

★ ★ ★

Thomas Builds-the-Fire could fly.

Once, he jumped off the roof of the tribal school and flapped his arms like a crazy eagle. And he flew. For a second, he hovered, suspended above all the other Indian boys who were too smart or too scared to jump.

"He's flying," Junior yelled, and Seymour was busy looking for the trick wires or mirrors. But it was real. As real as the dirt when Thomas lost altitude and crashed to the ground.

He broke his arm in two places.

"He broke his wing," Victor chanted, and the other Indian boys joined in, made it a tribal song.

"He broke his wing, he broke his wing, he broke his wing," all the Indian boys chanted as they ran off, flapping their wings, wishing they could fly, too. They hated Thomas for his courage, his brief moment as a bird. Everybody has dreams about flying. Thomas flew.

One of his dreams came true for just a second, just enough to make it real.

Victor's father, his ashes, fit in one wooden box with enough left over to fill a cardboard box.

"He always was a big man," Thomas said.

Victor carried part of his father and Thomas carried the rest out to the pickup. They set him down carefully behind the seats, put a cowboy hat on the wooden box and a Dodgers cap on the cardboard box. That's the way it was supposed to be.

"Ready to head back home," Victor asked.

"It's going to be a long drive."

"Yeah, take a couple days, maybe."

"We can take turns," Thomas said.

"Okay," Victor said, but they didn't take turns. Victor drove for sixteen hours straight north, made it halfway up Nevada toward home before he finally pulled over.

"Hey, Thomas," Victor said. "You got to drive for a while."

"Okay."

Thomas Builds-the Fire slid behind the wheel and started off down the road. All through Nevada, Thomas and Victor had been amazed at the lack of animal life, at the absence of water, of movement.

"Where is everything?" Victor had asked more than once.

Now when Thomas was finally driving they saw the first animal, maybe the only animal in Nevada. It was a long-eared jackrabbit.

"Look," Victor yelled. "It's alive."

Thomas and Victor were busy congratulating themselves on their discovery when the jackrabbit darted out into the road and under the wheels of the pickup.

"Stop the goddamn car," Victor yelled, and Thomas did stop, backed the pickup off the dead jackrabbit.

"Oh, man, he's dead," Victor said as he looked at the squashed animal. "Really dead."

"The only thing alive in this whole state and we just killed it."

"I don't know," Thomas said. "I think it was suicide."

Victor looked around the desert, sniffed the air, felt the emptiness and loneliness, and nodded his head.

"Yeah," Victor said. "It had to be suicide."

"I can't believe this," Thomas said. "You drive for a thousand miles and there ain't even any bugs smashed on the windshield. I drive for ten seconds and kill the only living thing in Nevada."

"Yeah," Victor said. "Maybe I should drive."

"Maybe you should."

Thomas Builds-the-Fire walked through the corridors of the tribal school by himself. Nobody wanted to be anywhere near him because of all those stories. Story after story.

Thomas closed his eyes and this story came to him: "We are all given one thing by which our lives are measured, one determination. Mine are the stories which can change or not change the world. It doesn't matter which as long as I continue to tell the stories. My father, he died on Okinawa in World War II, died fighting for this country, which had tried to kill him for years. My mother, she died giving birth to me, died while I was still inside her. She pushed me out into the world with her last breath. I have no brothers or sisters. I have only my stories which came to me before I even had the words to speak. I learned a thousand stories before I took my first thousand steps. They are all I have. It's all I can do."

Thomas Builds-the-Fire told his stories to all those who would stop and listen. He kept telling them long after people had stopped listening.

Victor and Thomas made it back to the reservation just as the sun was rising. It was the beginning of a new day on earth, but the same old shit on the reservation.

"Good morning," Thomas said.

"Good morning."

The tribe was waking up, ready for work, eating breakfast, reading the newspaper, just like everybody else does. Willene LeBret was out in her garden wearing a bathrobe. She waved when Thomas and Victor drove by.

"Crazy Indians made it," she said to herself and went back to her roses.

Victor stopped the pickup in front of Thomas Builds-the-Fire's HUD house. They both yawned, stretched a little, shook dust from their bodies.

"I'm tired," Victor said.

"Of everything," Thomas added.

They both searched for words to end the journey. Victor needed to thank Thomas for his help, for the money, and make the promise to pay it all back.

"Don't worry about the money," Thomas said. "It don't make any difference anyhow."

"Probably not, enit?"

"Nope."

Victor knew that Thomas would remain the crazy storyteller who talked to dogs and cars, who listened to the wind and pine trees. Victor knew that he couldn't really be friends with Thomas, even after all that had happened. It was cruel but it was real. As real as the ashes, as Victor's father, sitting behind the seats.

"I know how it is," Thomas said. "I know you ain't going to treat me any better than you did before. I know your friends would give you too much shit about it."

Victor was ashamed of himself. Whatever happened to the tribal ties, the sense of community? The only real thing he shared with anybody was a bottle and broken dreams. He owed Thomas something, anything.

"Listen," Victor said and handed Thomas the cardboard box which contained half of his father. "I want you to have this."

Thomas took the ashes and smiled, closed his eyes, and told this story: "I'm going to travel to Spokane Falls one last time and toss these ashes into the water. And your father will rise like a salmon, leap over the bridge, over me, and find his way home. It will be beautiful. His teeth will shine like silver, like a rainbow. He will rise, Victor, he will rise."

Victor smiled.

"I was planning on doing the same thing with my half," Victor said. "But I didn't imagine my father looking anything like a salmon. I thought it'd be like cleaning the attic or something. Like letting things go after they've stopped having any use."

"Nothing stops, cousin," Thomas said. "Nothing stops."

Thomas Builds-the Fire got out of the pickup and walked up his driveway. Victor started the pickup and began the drive home.

"Wait," Thomas yelled suddenly from his porch. "I just got to ask one favor."

Victor stopped the pickup, leaned out the window, and shouted back. "What do you want?"

"Just one time when I'm telling a story somewhere, why don't you stop and listen?" Thomas asked.

"Just once?"

"Just once."

Victor waved his arms to let Thomas know that the deal was good. It was a fair trade, and that was all Victor had ever wanted from his whole life. So Victor drove his father's pickup toward home while Thomas went into his house, closed the door behind him, and heard a new story come to him in the silence afterwards.

●
○

SANDRA CISNEROS
The House on Mango Street (Excerpt)

We didn't always live on Mango Street. Before that we lived on Loomis on the third floor, and before that we lived on Keeler. Before Keeler it was Paulina, and before that I can't remember. But what I remember most is moving a lot. Each time it seemed there'd be one more of us. By the time we got to Mango Street we were six — Mama, Papa, Carlos, Kiki, my sister Nenny and me.

The house on Mango Street is ours, and we don't have to pay rent to anybody, or share the yard with the people downstairs, or be careful not to make too much noise, and there isn't a landlord banging on the ceiling with a broom. But even so, it's not the house we'd thought we'd get.

We had to leave the flat on Loomis quick. The water pipes broke and the landlord wouldn't fix them because the house was too old. We had to leave fast. We were using the washroom next door and carrying water over in empty milk gallons. That's why Mama and Papa looked for a house, and that's why we moved into the house on Mango Street, far away, on the other side of town.

They always told us that one day we would move into a house, a real house that would be ours for always so we wouldn't have to move each year. And our house would have running water and pipes that worked. And inside it would have real stairs, not hallway stairs, but stairs inside like the houses on TV. And we'd have a basement and at least three washrooms so when we took a bath we wouldn't have to tell everybody. Our house would be white with trees around it, a great big yard and grass growing without a fence. This was the house Papa talked about when he held a lottery ticket and this was the house Mama dreamed up in the stories she told us before we went to bed.

But the house on Mango Street is not the way they told it at all. It's small and red with tight steps in front and windows so small you'd think they were holding their breath. Bricks are crumbling in places, and the front door is so swollen you have to push hard to get in. There is no front yard, only four little elms the city planted by the curb. Out back is a small garage for the car we don't own yet and a small yard that looks smaller between the two buildings on either side. There are stairs in our house, but they're ordinary hallway stairs, and the house has only one washroom. Everybody has to share a bedroom — Mama and Papa, Carlos and Kiki, me and Nenny.

Once when we were living on Loomis, a nun from my school passed by and saw me playing out front. The laundromat downstairs had been boarded up because it had been robbed two days before and the owner had painted on the wood YES WE'RE OPEN so as not to lose business.

Where do you live? she asked.

There, I said pointing up to the third floor.

You live *there?*

There. I had to look to where she pointed—the third floor, the paint peeling, wooden bars Papa had nailed on the windows so we wouldn't fall out. You live *there?* The way she said it made me feel like nothing. *There.* I lived *there.* I nodded.

I knew then I had to have a house. A real house. One I could point to. But this isn't it. The house on Mango Street isn't it. For the time being, Mama says. Temporary, says Papa. But I know how those things go.

JHUMPA LAHIRI
Interpreter of Maladies

At the tea stall Mr. and Mrs. Das bickered about who should take Tina to the toilet. Eventually Mrs. Das relented when Mr. Das pointed out that he had given the girl her bath the night before. In the rearview mirror Mr. Kapasi watched as Mrs. Das emerged slowly from his bulky white Ambassador, dragging her shaved, largely bare legs across the back seat. She did not hold the little girl's hand as they walked to the rest room.

They were on their way to see the Sun Temple at Konarak. It was a dry, bright Saturday, the mid-July heat tempered by a steady ocean breeze, ideal weather for sightseeing. Ordinarily Mr. Kapasi would not have stopped so soon along the way, but less than five minutes after he'd picked up the family that morning in front of Hotel Sandy Villa, the little girl had complained. The first thing Mr. Kapasi had noticed when he saw Mr. and Mrs. Das, standing with their children under the portico of the hotel, was that they were very young, perhaps not even thirty. In addition to Tina they had two boys, Ronny and Bobby, who appeared very close in age and had teeth covered in a network of flashing silver wires. The family looked Indian but dressed as foreigners did, the children in stiff, brightly colored clothing and caps with translucent visors. Mr. Kapasi was accustomed to foreign tourists; he was assigned to them regularly because he could speak English. Yesterday he had driven an elderly couple from Scotland, both with spotted faces and fluffy white hair so thin it exposed their sunburnt scalps. In comparison, the tanned, youthful faces of Mr. and Mrs. Das were all the more striking. When he'd introduced himself, Mr. Kapasi had pressed his palms together in greeting, but Mr. Das squeezed hands like an American so that Mr. Kapasi felt it in his elbow. Mrs. Das, for her part, had flexed one side of her mouth, smiling dutifully at Mr. Kapasi, without displaying any interest in him.

As they waited at the tea stall, Ronny, who looked like the older of the two boys, clambered suddenly out of the back seat, intrigued by a goat tied to a stake in the ground.

"Don't touch it," Mr. Das said. He glanced up from his paperback tour book, which said "INDIA" in yellow letters and looked as if it had been published abroad. His voice, somehow tentative and a little shrill, sounded as though it had not yet settled into maturity.

"I want to give it a piece of gum," the boy called back as he trotted ahead.

Mr. Das stepped out of the car and stretched his legs by squatting briefly to the ground. A clean-shaven man, he looked exactly like a magnified version of Ronny. He had a sapphire blue visor, and was dressed in shorts, sneakers, and a T-shirt. The camera slung around his neck, with an impressive telephoto lens and numerous buttons and markings, was the only complicated thing he wore. He frowned, watching as Ronny rushed toward the goat, but appeared to have no intention of intervening. "Bobby, make sure that your brother doesn't do anything stupid."

"I don't feel like it," Bobby said, not moving. He was sitting in the front seat beside Mr. Kapasi, studying a picture of the elephant god taped to the glove compartment.

"No need to worry," Mr. Kapasi said. "They are quite tame." Mr. Kapasi was forty-six years old, with receding hair that had gone completely silver, but his butterscotch complexion and his unlined brow, which he treated in spare moments to dabs of lotus-oil balm, made it easy to imagine what he must have looked like at an earlier age. He wore gray trousers and a matching jacket-style shirt, tapered at the waist, with short sleeves and a large pointed collar, made of a thin but durable synthetic material. He had specified both the cut and the fabric to his tailor—it was his preferred uniform for giving tours because it did not get crushed during his long hours behind the wheel. Through the windshield he watched as Ronny circled around the goat, touched it quickly on its side, then trotted back to the car.

"You left India as a child?" Mr. Kapasi asked when Mr. Das had settled once again into the passenger seat.

"Oh, Mina and I were both born in America," Mr. Das announced with an air of sudden confidence. "Born and raised. Our parents live here now, in Assansol. They retired. We visit them every couple years." He turned to watch as the little girl ran toward the car, the wide purple bows of her sundress flopping on her narrow brown shoulders. She was holding to her chest a doll with yellow hair that looked as if it had been chopped, as a punitive measure, with a pair of dull scissors. "This is Tina's first trip to India, isn't it, Tina?"

"I don't have to go to the bathroom anymore," Tina announced.

"Where's Mina?" Mr. Das asked.

Mr. Kapasi found it strange that Mr. Das should refer to his wife by her first name when speaking to the little girl. Tina pointed to where Mrs. Das was purchasing something from one of the shirtless men who worked at the tea stall. Mr. Kapasi heard one of the shirtless men sing a phrase from a popular Hindi love song as Mrs. Das walked back to the car, but she did not appear to understand the words of the song, for she did not express irritation, or embarrassment, or react in any other way to the man's declarations.

He observed her. She wore a red-and-white-checkered skirt that stopped above her knees, slip-on shoes with a square wooden heel, and a close-fitting blouse styled like a man's undershirt. The blouse was decorated at chest-level with a calico appliqué in the shape of a strawberry. She was a short woman, with small hands like paws, her frosty pink fingernails painted to match her lips, and was slightly plump in her figure. Her hair, shorn only a little longer than her husband's, was parted far to one side. She was wearing large dark brown sunglasses with a pinkish tint to them, and carried a big straw bag, almost as big as her torso, shaped like a bowl, with a water bottle poking out of it. She walked slowly, carrying some puffed rice tossed with peanuts and chili peppers in a large packet made from newspapers. Mr. Kapasi turned to Mr. Das.

"Where in America do you live?"

"New Brunswick, New Jersey."

"Next to New York?"

"Exactly. I teach middle school there."

"What subject?"

"Science. In fact, every year I take my students on a trip to the Museum of Natural History in New York City. In a way we have a lot in common, you could say, you and I. How long have you been a tour guide, Mr. Kapasi?"

"Five years."

Mrs. Das reached the car. "How long's the trip?" she asked, shutting the door.

"About two and a half hours," Mr. Kapasi replied.

At this Mrs. Das gave an impatient sigh, as if she had been traveling her whole life without pause. She fanned herself with a folded Bombay film magazine written in English.

"I thought that the Sun Temple is only eighteen miles north of Puri," Mr. Das said, tapping on the tour book.

"The roads to Konarak are poor. Actually it is a distance of fifty-two miles," Mr. Kapasi explained.

Mr. Das nodded, readjusting the camera strap where it had begun to chafe the back of his neck.

Before starting the ignition, Mr. Kapasi reached back to make sure the cranklike locks on the inside of each of the back doors were secured. As soon as the car began to move the little girl began to play with the lock on her side, clicking it with some effort forward and backward, but Mrs. Das said nothing to stop her. She sat a bit slouched at one end of the back seat, not offering her puffed rice to anyone. Ronny and Tina sat on either side of her, both snapping bright green gum.

"Look," Bobby said as the car began to gather speed. He pointed with his finger to the tall trees that lined the road. "Look."

"Monkeys!" Ronny shrieked. "Wow!"

They were seated in groups along the branches, with shining black faces, silver bodies, horizontal eyebrows, and crested heads. Their long gray tails dangled like a series of ropes among the leaves. A few scratched themselves with black leathery hands, or swung their feet, staring as the car passed.

"We call them the hanuman," Mr. Kapasi said. "They are quite common in the area."

As soon as he spoke, one of the monkeys leaped into the middle of the road, causing Mr. Kapasi to brake suddenly. Another bounced onto the hood of the car, then sprang away. Mr. Kapasi beeped his horn. The children began to get excited, sucking in their breath and covering their faces partly with their hands. They had never seen monkeys outside of a zoo, Mr. Das explained. He asked Mr. Kapasi to stop the car so that he could take a picture.

While Mr. Das adjusted his telephoto lens, Mrs. Das reached into her straw bag and pulled out a bottle of colorless nail polish, which she proceeded to stroke on the tip of her index finger.

The little girl stuck out a hand. "Mine too. Mommy, do mine too."

"Leave me alone," Mrs. Das said, blowing on her nail and turning her body slightly. "You're making me mess up."

The little girl occupied herself by buttoning and unbuttoning a pinafore on the doll's plastic body.

"All set," Mr. Das said, replacing the lens cap.

The car rattled considerably as it raced along the dusty road, causing them all to pop up from their seats every now and then, but Mrs. Das continued to polish her nails. Mr. Kapasi eased up on the accelerator, hoping to produce a smoother ride. When he reached for the gearshift the boy in front accommodated him by swinging his hairless knees out of the way. Mr. Kapasi noted that this boy was slightly paler than the other children. "Daddy, why is the driver sitting on the wrong side in this car, too?" the boy asked.

"They all do that here, dummy," Ronny said.

"Don't call your brother a dummy," Mr. Das said. He turned to Mr. Kapasi. "In America, you know . . . it confuses them."

"Oh yes, I am well aware," Mr. Kapasi said. As delicately as he could, he shifted gears again, accelerating as they approached a hill in the road. "I see it on *Dallas,* the steering wheels are on the left-hand side."

"What's *Dallas?*" Tina asked, banging her now naked doll on the seat behind Mr. Kapasi.

"It went off the air," Mr. Das explained. "It's a television show."

They were all like siblings, Mr. Kapasi thought as they passed a row of date trees. Mr. and Mrs. Das behaved like an older brother and sister, not parents. It seemed that they were in charge of the children only for the day; it was hard to believe they were regularly responsible for anything other than themselves. Mr. Das tapped on his lens cap, and his tour book, dragging his thumbnail occasionally across the pages so that they made a scraping sound. Mrs. Das continued to polish her nails. She had still not removed her sunglasses. Every now and then Tina renewed her plea that she wanted her nails done, too, and so at one point Mrs. Das flicked a drop of polish on the little girl's finger before depositing the bottle back inside her straw bag.

"Isn't this an air-conditioned car?" she asked, still blowing on her hand. The window on Tina's side was broken and could not be rolled down.

"Quit complaining," Mr. Das said. "It isn't so hot."

"I told you to get a car with air-conditioning," Mrs. Das continued. "Why do you do this, Raj, just to save a few stupid rupees. What are you saving us, fifty cents?"

Their accents sounded just like the ones Mr. Kapasi heard on American television programs, though not like the ones on *Dallas.*

"Doesn't it get tiresome, Mr. Kapasi, showing people the same thing every day?" Mr. Das asked, rolling down his own window all the way. "Hey, do you mind stopping the car. I just want to get a shot of this guy."

Mr. Kapasi pulled over to the side of the road as Mr. Das took a picture of a barefoot man, his head wrapped in a dirty turban, seated on top of a cart of grain sacks pulled by a pair of bullocks. Both the man and the bullocks were emaciated. In the back seat Mrs. Das gazed out another window, at the sky, where nearly transparent clouds passed quickly in front of one another.

"I look forward to it, actually," Mr. Kapasi said as they continued on their way. "The Sun Temple is one of my favorite places. In that way it is a reward for me. I give tours on Fridays and Saturdays only. I have another job during the week."

"Oh? Where?" Mr. Das asked.

"I work in a doctor's office."

"You're a doctor?"

"I am not a doctor. I work with one. As an interpreter."

"What does a doctor need an interpreter for?"

"He has a number of Gujarati patients. My father was Gujarati, but many people do not speak Gujarati in this area, including the doctor. And so the doctor asked me to work in his office, interpreting what the patients say."

"Interesting. I've never heard of anything like that," Mr. Das said.

Mr. Kapasi shrugged. "It is a job like any other."

"But so romantic," Mrs. Das said dreamily, breaking her extended silence. She lifted her pinkish brown sunglasses and arranged them on top of her head like a tiara. For the first time, her eyes met Mr. Kapasi's in the rearview mirror: pale, a bit small, their gaze fixed but drowsy.

Mr. Das craned to look at her. "What's so romantic about it?"

"I don't know. Something." She shrugged, knitting her brows together for an instant. "Would you like a piece of gum, Mr. Kapasi?" she asked brightly. She reached into her straw bag and handed him a small square wrapped in green-and-white-striped paper. As soon as Mr. Kapasi put the gum in his mouth a thick sweet liquid burst onto his tongue.

"Tell us more about your job, Mr. Kapasi," Mrs. Das said.

"What would you like to know, madame?"

"I don't know," she shrugged, munching on some puffed rice and licking the mustard oil from the corners of her mouth. "Tell us a typical situation." She settled back in her seat, her head tilted in a patch of sun, and closed her eyes. "I want to picture what happens."

"Very well. The other day a man came in with a pain in his throat."

"Did he smoke cigarettes?"

"No. It was very curious. He complained that he felt as if there were long pieces of straw stuck in his throat. When I told the doctor he was able to prescribe the proper medication."

"That's so neat."

"Yes," Mr. Kapasi agreed after some hesitation.

"So these patients are totally dependent on you," Mrs. Das said. She spoke slowly, as if she were thinking aloud. "In a way, more dependent on you than the doctor."

"How do you mean? How could it be?"

"Well, for example, you could tell the doctor that the pain felt like a burning, not straw. The patient would never know what you had told the doctor, and the doctor wouldn't know that you had told the wrong thing. It's a big responsibility."

"Yes, a big responsibility you have there, Mr. Kapasi," Mr. Das agreed.

Mr. Kapasi had never thought of his job in such complimentary terms. To him it was a thankless occupation. He found nothing noble in interpreting people's maladies, assiduously translating the symptoms of so many swollen bones, countless cramps of bellies and bowels, spots on people's palms that changed color, shape, or size. The doctor, nearly half his age, had an affinity for bell-bottom trousers and made humorless jokes about the Congress party. Together they worked in a stale little infirmary where Mr. Kapasi's smartly tailored clothes clung to him in the heat, in spite of the blackened blades of a ceiling fan churning over their heads.

The job was a sign of his failings. In his youth he'd been a devoted scholar of foreign languages, the owner of an impressive collection of dictionaries. He had dreamed of being an interpreter for diplomats and dignitaries, resolving conflicts between people and nations, settling disputes of which he alone could understand both sides. He was a self-educated man. In a series of notebooks, in the evenings before his parents settled his marriage, he had listed the common etymologies of words, and at one point in his life he was confident that he could converse, if given the opportunity, in English, French, Russian, Portuguese, and Italian, not to mention Hindi, Bengali, Orissi, and Gujarati. Now only a handful of European phrases remained in his memory, scattered words for things like saucers and chairs. English was the only non-Indian language he spoke fluently anymore. Mr. Kapasi knew it was not a remarkable talent. Sometimes he feared that his children knew better English than he did, just from watching television. Still, it came in handy for the tours.

He had taken the job as an interpreter after his first son, at the age of seven, contracted typhoid—that was how he had first made the acquaintance of the doctor. At the time Mr. Kapasi had been teaching English in a grammar school, and he bartered his skills as an interpreter to pay the increasingly exorbitant medical bills. In the end the boy had died one evening in his mother's arms, his limbs burning with fever, but then there was the funeral to pay for, and the other children who were born soon enough, and the newer, bigger house, and the good schools and tutors, and the fine shoes and the television, and the countless other ways he tried to console his wife and to keep her from crying in her sleep, and so when the doctor offered to pay him twice as much as he earned at the grammar school, he accepted. Mr. Kapasi knew that his wife had little regard for his career as an interpreter. He knew it reminded her of the son she'd lost, and that she resented the other lives he helped, in his own small way, to save. If ever she referred to his position, she used the phrase "doctor's assistant," as if the process of interpretation were equal to taking someone's temperature, or changing a bedpan. She never asked him about the patients who came to the doctor's office, or said that his job was a big responsibility.

For this reason it flattered Mr. Kapasi that Mrs. Das was so intrigued by his job. Unlike his wife, she had reminded him of its intellectual challenges. She had also used the word "romantic." She did not behave in a romantic way toward her husband, and yet she had used the word to describe him. He wondered if Mr. and Mrs. Das were a bad match, just as he and his wife were. Perhaps they, too, had little in common apart from three children and a decade of their lives. The signs he recognized from his own marriage were there—the bickering, the indifference, the protracted silences. Her sudden interest in him, an interest she did not express in either her husband or her children, was mildly intoxicating. When Mr. Kapasi thought once again about how she had said "romantic," the feeling of intoxication grew.

He began to check his reflection in the rearview mirror as he drove, feeling grateful that he had chosen the gray suit that morning and not the brown one, which tended to sag a little in the knees. From time to time he glanced through the mirror at Mrs. Das. In addition to glancing at her face he glanced at the strawberry between her breasts, and the golden brown hollow in her throat. He decided to tell Mrs. Das about another patient, and another: the young woman who had complained of a sensation of raindrops in her spine, the gentleman whose birthmark had begun to sprout hairs. Mrs. Das listened attentively, stroking her hair with a small plastic brush that resembled an oval bed of nails, asking more questions, for yet another example. The children were quiet, intent on spotting more monkeys in the trees, and Mr. Das was absorbed by his tour book, so it seemed like a private conversation between Mr. Kapasi and Mrs. Das. In this manner the next half hour passed, and when they stopped for lunch at a roadside restaurant that sold fritters and omelette sandwiches, usually something Mr. Kapasi looked forward to on his tours so that he could sit in peace and enjoy some hot tea, he was disappointed. As the Das family settled together under a magenta umbrella fringed with white and orange tassels, and placed their orders with one of the waiters who marched about in tricornered caps, Mr. Kapasi reluctantly headed toward a neighboring table.

"Mr. Kapasi, wait. There's room here," Mrs. Das called out. She gathered Tina onto her lap, insisting that he accompany them. And so, together, they had bottled mango juice and sandwiches and plates of onions and potatoes deep-fried in graham-flour batter. After finishing two omelette sandwiches Mr. Das took more pictures of the group as they ate.

"How much longer?" he asked Mr. Kapasi as he paused to load a new roll of film in the camera.

"About half an hour more."

By now the children had gotten up from the table to look at more monkeys perched in a nearby tree, so there was a considerable space between Mrs. Das and Mr. Kapasi. Mr. Das placed the camera to his face and squeezed one eye shut, his tongue exposed at one corner of his mouth. "This looks funny. Mina, you need to lean in closer to Mr. Kapasi."

She did. He could smell a scent on her skin, like a mixture of whiskey and rosewater. He worried suddenly that she could smell his perspiration, which he knew had collected beneath the synthetic material of his shirt. He polished off his mango juice in one gulp and smoothed his silver hair with his hands. A bit of the juice dripped onto his chin. He wondered if Mrs. Das had noticed.

She had not. "What's your address, Mr. Kapasi?" she inquired, fishing for something inside her straw bag.

"You would like my address?"

"So we can send you copies," she said. "Of the pictures." She handed him a scrap of paper which she had hastily ripped from a page of her film magazine. The blank portion was limited, for the narrow strip was crowded by lines of text and a tiny picture of a hero and heroine embracing under a eucalyptus tree.

The paper curled as Mr. Kapasi wrote his address in clear, careful letters. She would write to him, asking about his days interpreting at the doctor's office, and he would respond eloquently, choosing only the most entertaining anecdotes, ones that would make her laugh out loud as she read them in her house in New Jersey. In time she would reveal the disappointment of her marriage, and he his. In this way their friendship would grow, and flourish. He would possess a picture of the two of them, eating fried onions under a magenta umbrella, which he would keep, he decided, safely tucked between the pages of his Russian grammar. As his mind raced, Mr. Kapasi experienced a mild and pleasant shock. It was similar to a feeling he used to experience long ago when, after months of translating with the aid of a dictionary, he would finally read a passage from a French novel, or an Italian sonnet, and understand the words, one after another, unencumbered by his own efforts. In those moments Mr. Kapasi used to believe that all was right with the world, that all struggles were rewarded, that all of life's mistakes made sense in the end. The promise that he would hear from Mrs. Das now filled him with the same belief.

When he finished writing his address Mr. Kapasi handed her the paper, but as soon as he did so he worried that he had either misspelled his name, or accidentally reversed the numbers of his postal code. He dreaded the possibility of a lost letter, the photograph never reaching him, hovering somewhere in Orissa, close but ultimately unattainable. He thought of asking for the slip of paper again, just to make sure he had written his address accurately, but Mrs. Das had already dropped it into the jumble of her bag.

They reached Konarak at two-thirty. The temple, made of sandstone, was a massive pyramid-like structure in the shape of a chariot. It was dedicated to the great master of life, the sun, which struck three sides of the edifice as it made its journey each day across the sky. Twenty-four giant wheels were carved on the north and south sides of the plinth. The whole thing was drawn by a team of seven horses, speeding as if through the heavens. As they approached, Mr. Kapasi explained that the temple had been built between A.D. 1243 and 1255, with the efforts of twelve hundred artisans, by the great ruler of the Ganga dynasty, King Narasimhadeva the First, to commemorate his victory against the Muslim army.

"It says the temple occupies about a hundred and seventy acres of land," Mr. Das said, reading from his book.

"It's like a desert," Ronny said, his eyes wandering across the sand that stretched on all sides beyond the temple.

"The Chandrabhaga River once flowed one mile north of here. It is dry now," Mr. Kapasi said, turning off the engine.

They got out and walked toward the temple, posing first for pictures by the pair of lions that flanked the steps. Mr. Kapasi led them next to one of the wheels of the chariot, higher than any human being, nine feet in diameter.

"'The wheels are supposed to symbolize the wheel of life,'" Mr. Das read. "'They depict the cycle of creation, preservation, and achievement of re-alization.' Cool." He turned the page of his book. "'Each wheel is divided into eight thick and thin spokes, dividing the day into eight equal parts. The rims are carved with designs of birds and animals, whereas the medallions in the spokes are carved with women in luxurious poses, largely erotic in nature.'"

What he referred to were the countless friezes of entwined naked bodies, making love in various positions, women clinging to the necks of men, their knees wrapped eternally around their lovers' thighs. In addition to these were assorted scenes from daily life, of hunting and trading, of deer being killed with bows and arrows and marching warriors holding swords in their hands.

It was no longer possible to enter the temple, for it had filled with rubble years ago, but they admired the exterior, as did all the tourists Mr. Kapasi brought there, slowly strolling along each of its sides. Mr. Das trailed behind, taking pictures. The children ran ahead, pointing to figures of naked people, in-trigued in particular by the Nagamithunas, the half-human, half-serpentine couples who were said, Mr. Kapasi told them, to live in the deepest waters of the sea. Mr. Kapasi was pleased that they liked the temple, pleased especially that it appealed to Mrs. Das. She stopped every three or four paces, staring silently at the carved lovers, and the processions of elephants, and the topless fe-male musicians beating on two-sided drums.

Though Mr. Kapasi had been to the temple countless times, it occurred to him, as he, too, gazed at the topless women, that he had never seen his own wife fully naked. Even when they had made love she kept the panels of her blouse hooked together, the string of her petticoat knotted around her waist.

He had never admired the backs of his wife's legs the way he now admired those of Mrs. Das, walking as if for his benefit alone. He had, of course, seen plenty of bare limbs before, belonging to the American and European ladies who took his tours. But Mrs. Das was different. Unlike the other women, who had an interest only in the temple, and kept their noses buried in a guidebook, or their eyes behind the lens of a camera, Mrs. Das had taken an interest in him.

Mr. Kapasi was anxious to be alone with her, to continue their private conversation, yet he felt nervous to walk at her side. She was lost behind her sunglasses, ignoring her husband's requests that she pose for another picture, walking past her children as if they were strangers. Worried that he might disturb her, Mr. Kapasi walked ahead, to admire, as he always did, the three life-sized bronze avatars of Surya, the sun god, each emerging from its own niche on the temple facade to greet the sun at dawn, noon, and evening. They wore elaborate headdresses, their languid, elongated eyes closed, their bare chests draped with carved chains and amulets. Hibiscus petals, offerings from previous visitors, were strewn at their gray-green feet. The last statue, on the northern wall of the temple, was Mr. Kapasi's favorite. This Surya had a tired expression, weary after a hard day of work, sitting astride a horse with folded legs. Even his horse's eyes were drowsy. Around his body were smaller sculptures of women in pairs, their hips thrust to one side.

"Who's that?" Mrs. Das asked. He was startled to see that she was standing beside him.

"He is the Astachala-Surya," Mr. Kapasi said. "The setting sun."

"So in a couple of hours the sun will set right here?" She slipped a foot out of one of her square-heeled shoes, rubbed her toes on the back of her other leg.

"That is correct."

She raised her sunglasses for a moment, then put them back on again. "Neat."

Mr. Kapasi was not certain exactly what the word suggested, but he had a feeling it was a favorable response. He hoped that Mrs. Das had understood Surya's beauty, his power. Perhaps they would discuss it further in their letters. He would explain things to her, things about India, and she would explain things to him about America. In its own way this correspondence would fulfill his dream, of serving as an interpreter between nations. He looked at her straw bag, delighted that his address lay nestled among its contents. When he pictured her so many thousands of miles away he plummeted, so much so that he had an overwhelming urge to wrap his arms around her, to freeze with her, even for an instant, in an embrace witnessed by his favorite Surya. But Mrs. Das had already started walking.

"When do you return to America?" he asked, trying to sound placid.

"In ten days."

He calculated: A week to settle in, a week to develop the pictures, a few days to compose her letter, two weeks to get to India by air. According to his schedule, allowing room for delays, he would hear from Mrs. Das in approximately six weeks' time.

The family was silent as Mr. Kapasi drove them back, a little past four-thirty, to Hotel Sandy Villa. The children had bought miniature granite versions of the chariot's wheels at a souvenir stand, and they turned them round in their hands. Mr. Das continued to read his book. Mrs. Das untangled Tina's hair with her brush and divided it into two little ponytails.

Mr. Kapasi was beginning to dread the thought of dropping them off. He was not prepared to begin his six-week wait to hear from Mrs. Das. As he stole glances at her in the rearview mirror, wrapping elastic bands around Tina's hair, he wondered how he might make the tour last a little longer. Ordinarily he sped back to Puri using a shortcut, eager to return home, scrub his feet and hands with sandalwood soap, and enjoy the evening newspaper and a cup of tea that his wife would serve him in silence. The thought of that silence, something to which he'd long been resigned, now oppressed him. It was then that he suggested visiting the hills at Udayagiri and Khandagiri, where a number of monastic dwellings were hewn out of the ground, facing one another across a defile. It was some miles away, but well worth seeing, Mr. Kapasi told them.

"Oh yeah, there's something mentioned about it in this book," Mr. Das said. "Built by a Jain king or something."

"Shall we go then?" Mr. Kapasi asked. He paused at a turn in the road. "It's to the left."

Mr. Das turned to look at Mrs. Das. Both of them shrugged.

"Left, left," the children chanted.

Mr. Kapasi turned the wheel, almost delirious with relief. He did not know what he would do or say to Mrs. Das once they arrived at the hills. Perhaps he would tell her what a pleasing smile she had. Perhaps he would compliment her strawberry shirt, which he found irresistibly becoming. Perhaps, when Mr. Das was busy taking a picture, he would take her hand.

He did not have to worry. When they got to the hills, divided by a steep path thick with trees, Mrs. Das refused to get out of the car. All along the path, dozens of monkeys were seated on stones, as well as on the branches of the trees. Their hind legs were stretched out in front and raised to shoulder level, their arms resting on their knees.

"My legs are tired," she said, sinking low in her seat. "I'll stay here."

"Why did you have to wear those stupid shoes?" Mr. Das said. "You won't be in the pictures."

"Pretend I'm there."

"But we could use one of these pictures for our Christmas card this year. We didn't get one of all five of us at the Sun Temple. Mr. Kapasi could take it."

"I'm not coming. Anyway, those monkeys give me the creeps."

"But they're harmless," Mr. Das said. He turned to Mr. Kapasi. "Aren't they?"

"They are more hungry than dangerous," Mr. Kapasi said. "Do not provoke them with food, and they will not bother you."

Mr. Das headed up the defile with the children, the boys at his side, the little girl on his shoulders. Mr. Kapasi watched as they crossed paths with a Japanese man and woman, the only other tourists there, who paused for a final photograph, then stepped into a nearby car and drove away. As the car disappeared out of view some of the monkeys called out, emitting soft whooping sounds, and then walked on their flat black hands and feet up the path. At one point a group of them formed a little ring around Mr. Das and the children. Tina screamed in delight. Ronny ran in circles around his father. Bobby bent down and picked up a fat stick on the ground. When he extended it, one of the monkeys approached him and snatched it, then briefly beat the ground.

"I'll join them," Mr. Kapasi said, unlocking the door on his side. "There is much to explain about the caves."

"No. Stay a minute," Mrs. Das said. She got out of the back seat and slipped in beside Mr. Kapasi. "Raj has his dumb book anyway." Together, through the windshield, Mrs. Das and Mr. Kapasi watched as Bobby and the monkey passed the stick back and forth between them.

"A brave little boy," Mr. Kapasi commented.

"It's not so surprising," Mrs. Das said.

"No?"

"He's not his."

"I beg your pardon?"

"Raj's. He's not Raj's son."

Mr. Kapasi felt a prickle on his skin. He reached into his shirt pocket for the small tin of lotus-oil balm he carried with him at all times, and applied it to three spots on his forehead. He knew that Mrs. Das was watching him, but he did not turn to face her. Instead he watched as the figures of Mr. Das and the children grew smaller, climbing up the steep path, pausing every now and then for a picture, surrounded by a growing number of monkeys.

"Are you surprised?" The way she put it made him choose his words with care.

"It's not the type of thing one assumes," Mr. Kapasi replied slowly. He put the tin of lotus-oil balm back in his pocket.

"No, of course not. And no one knows, of course. No one at all. I've kept it a secret for eight whole years." She looked at Mr. Kapasi, tilting her chin as if to gain a fresh perspective. "But now I've told you."

Mr. Kapasi nodded. He felt suddenly parched, and his forehead was warm and slightly numb from the balm. He considered asking Mrs. Das for a sip of water, then decided against it.

"We met when we were very young," she said. She reached into her straw bag in search of something, then pulled out a packet of puffed rice. "Want some?"

"No, thank you."

She put a fistful in her mouth, sank into the seat a little, and looked away from Mr. Kapasi, out the window on her side of the car. "We married when we were still in college. We were in high school when he proposed. We went to the same college, of course. Back then we couldn't stand the thought of being separated, not for a day, not for a minute. Our parents were best friends who lived in the same town. My entire life I saw him every weekend, either at our house or theirs. We were sent upstairs to play together while our parents joked about our marriage. Imagine! They never caught us at anything, though in a way I think it was all more or less a setup. The things we did those Friday and Saturday nights, while our parents sat downstairs drinking tea . . . I could tell you stories, Mr. Kapasi."

As a result of spending all her time in college with Raj, she continued, she did not make many close friends. There was no one to confide in about him at the end of a difficult day, or to share a passing thought or a worry. Her parents now lived on the other side of the world, but she had never been very close to them, anyway. After marrying so young she was overwhelmed by it all, having a child so quickly, and nursing, and warming up bottles of milk and testing their temperature against her wrist while Raj was at work, dressed in sweaters and corduroy pants, teaching his students about rocks and dinosaurs. Raj never looked cross or harried, or plump as she had become after the first baby.

Always tired, she declined invitations from her one or two college girl-friends, to have lunch or shop in Manhattan. Eventually the friends stopped calling her, so that she was left at home all day with the baby, surrounded by toys that made her trip when she walked or wince when she sat, always cross and tired. Only occasionally did they go out after Ronny was born, and even more rarely did they entertain. Raj didn't mind; he looked forward to coming home from teaching and watching television and bouncing Ronny on his knee. She had been outraged when Raj told her that a Punjabi friend, someone whom she had once met but did not remember, would be staying with them for a week for some job interviews in the New Brunswick area.

Bobby was conceived in the afternoon, on a sofa littered with rubber teething toys, after the friend learned that a London pharmaceutical company had hired him, while Ronny cried to be freed from his playpen. She made no protest when the friend touched the small of her back as she was about to make a pot of coffee, then pulled her against his crisp navy suit. He made love to her swiftly, in silence, with an expertise she had never known, without the meaningful expressions and smiles Raj always insisted on afterward. The next day Raj drove the friend to JFK. He was married now, to a Punjabi girl, and they lived in London still, and every year they exchanged Christmas cards with Raj and Mina, each couple tucking photos of their families into the envelopes. He did not know that he was Bobby's father. He never would.

"I beg your pardon, Mrs. Das, but why have you told me this information?" Mr. Kapasi asked when she had finally finished speaking, and had turned to face him once again.

"For God's sake, stop calling me Mrs. Das. I'm twenty-eight. You probably have children my age."

"Not quite." It disturbed Mr. Kapasi to learn that she thought of him as a parent. The feeling he had had toward her, that had made him check his reflection in the rearview mirror as they drove, evaporated a little.

"I told you because of your talents." She put the packet of puffed rice back into her bag without folding over the top.

"I don't understand," Mr. Kapasi said.

"Don't you see? For eight years I haven't been able to express this to anybody, not to friends, certainly not to Raj. He doesn't even suspect it. He thinks I'm still in love with him. Well, don't you have anything to say?"

"About what?"

"About what I've just told you. About my secret, and about how terrible it makes me feel. I feel terrible looking at my children, and at Raj, always terrible. I have terrible urges, Mr. Kapasi, to throw things away. One day I had the urge to throw everything I own out the window, the television, the children, everything. Don't you think it's unhealthy?"

He was silent.

"Mr. Kapasi, don't you have anything to say? I thought that was your job."

"My job is to give tours, Mrs. Das."

"Not that. Your other job. As an interpreter."

"But we do not face a language barrier. What need is there for an interpreter?"

"That's not what I mean. I would never have told you otherwise. Don't you realize what it means for me to tell you?"

"What does it mean?"

"It means that I'm tired of feeling so terrible all the time. Eight years, Mr. Kapasi, I've been in pain eight years. I was hoping you could help me feel better, say the right thing. Suggest some kind of remedy."

He looked at her, in her red plaid skirt and strawberry T-shirt, a woman not yet thirty, who loved neither her husband nor her children, who had already fallen out of love with life. Her confession depressed him, depressed him all the more when he thought of Mr. Das at the top of the path, Tina clinging to his shoulders, taking pictures of ancient monastic cells cut into the hills to show his students in America, unsuspecting and unaware that one of his sons was not his own. Mr. Kapasi felt insulted that Mrs. Das should ask him to interpret her common, trivial little secret. She did not resemble the patients in the doctor's office, those who came glassy-eyed and desperate, unable to sleep or breathe or urinate with ease, unable, above all, to give words to their pains. Still, Mr. Kapasi believed it was his duty to assist Mrs. Das. Perhaps he ought to tell her to confess the truth to Mr. Das. He would explain that honesty was the best policy. Honesty, surely, would help her feel better, as she'd put it. Perhaps he would offer to preside over the discussion, as a mediator. He decided to begin with the most obvious question, to get to the heart of the matter, and so he asked, "Is it really pain you feel, Mrs. Das, or is it guilt?"

She turned to him and glared, mustard oil thick on her frosty pink lips. She opened her mouth to say something, but as she glared at Mr. Kapasi some certain knowledge seemed to pass before her eyes, and she stopped. It crushed him; he knew at that moment that he was not even important enough to be properly insulted. She opened the car door and began walking up the path, wobbling a little on her square wooden heels, reaching into her straw bag to eat handfuls of puffed rice. It fell through her fingers, leaving a zigzagging trail, causing a monkey to leap down from a tree and devour the little white grains. In search of more, the monkey began to follow Mrs. Das. Others joined him, so that she was soon being followed by about half a dozen of them, their velvety tails dragging behind.

Mr. Kapasi stepped out of the car. He wanted to holler, to alert her in some way, but he worried that if she knew they were behind her, she would grow nervous. Perhaps she would lose her balance. Perhaps they would pull at her bag or her hair. He began to jog up the path, taking a fallen branch in his hand to scare away the monkeys. Mrs. Das continued walking, oblivious, trailing grains of puffed rice. Near the top of the incline, before a group of cells fronted by a row of squat stone pillars, Mr. Das was kneeling on the ground, focusing the lens of his camera. The children stood under the arcade, now hiding, now emerging from view.

"Wait for me," Mrs. Das called out. "I'm coming."

Tina jumped up and down. "Here comes Mommy!"

"Great," Mr. Das said without looking up. "Just in time. We'll get Mr. Kapasi to take a picture of the five of us."

Mr. Kapasi quickened his pace, waving his branch so that the monkeys scampered away, distracted, in another direction.

"Where's Bobby?" Mrs. Das asked when she stopped.

Mr. Das looked up from the camera. "I don't know. Ronny, where's Bobby?"

Ronny shrugged. "I thought he was right here."

"Where is he?" Mrs. Das repeated sharply. "What's wrong with all of you?"

They began calling his name, wandering up and down the path a bit. Because they were calling, they did not initially hear the boy's screams. When they found him, a little farther down the path under a tree, he was surrounded by a group of monkeys, over a dozen of them, pulling at his T-shirt with their long black fingers. The puffed rice Mrs. Das had spilled was scattered at his feet, raked over by the monkeys' hands. The boy was silent, his body frozen, swift tears running down his startled face. His bare legs were dusty and red with welts from where one of the monkeys struck him repeatedly with the stick he had given to it earlier.

"Daddy, the monkey's hurting Bobby," Tina said.

Mr. Das wiped his palms on the front of his shorts. In his nervousness he accidentally pressed the shutter on his camera; the whirring noise of the advancing film excited the monkeys, and the one with the stick began to beat Bobby more intently. "What are we supposed to do? What if they start attacking?"

"Mr. Kapasi," Mrs. Das shrieked, noticing him standing to one side. "Do something, for God's sake, do something!"

Mr. Kapasi took his branch and shooed them away, hissing at the ones that remained, stomping his feet to scare them. The animals retreated slowly, with a measured gait, obedient but unintimidated. Mr. Kapasi gathered Bobby in his arms and brought him back to where his parents and siblings were standing. As he carried him he was tempted to whisper a secret into the boy's ear. But Bobby was stunned, and shivering with fright, his legs bleeding slightly where the stick had broken the skin. When Mr. Kapasi delivered him to his parents, Mr. Das brushed some dirt off the boy's T-shirt and put the visor on him the right way. Mrs. Das reached into her straw bag to find a bandage which she taped over the cut on his knee. Ronny offered his brother a fresh piece of gum. "He's fine. Just a little scared, right, Bobby?" Mr. Das said, patting the top of his head.

"God, let's get out of here," Mrs. Das said. She folded her arms across the strawberry on her chest. "This place gives me the creeps."

"Yeah. Back to the hotel, definitely," Mr. Das agreed.

"Poor Bobby," Mrs. Das said. "Come here a second. Let Mommy fix your hair." Again she reached into her straw bag, this time for her hairbrush, and began to run it around the edges of the translucent visor. When she whipped out the hairbrush, the slip of paper with Mr. Kapasi's address on it fluttered away in the wind. No one but Mr. Kapasi noticed. He watched as it rose, carried higher and higher by the breeze, into the trees where the monkeys now sat, solemnly observing the scene below. Mr. Kapasi observed it too, knowing that this was the picture of the Das family he would preserve forever in his mind.

GUY DE MAUPASSANT
The Necklace

She was one of those pretty and charming girls who are sometimes, as if by a mistake of destiny, born in a family of clerks. She had no dowry, no expectations, no means of being known, understood, loved, wedded by any rich and distinguished man; and she let herself be married to a little clerk at the Ministry of Public Instructions.

She dressed plainly because she could not dress well, but she was as unhappy as though she had really fallen from her proper station, since with women there is neither caste nor rank: and beauty, grace, and charm act instead of family and birth. Natural fineness, instinct for what is elegant, suppleness of wit, are the sole hierarchy, and make from women of the people the equals of the very greatest ladies.

She suffered ceaselessly, feeling herself born for all the delicacies and all the luxuries. She suffered from the poverty of her dwelling, from the wretched look of the walls, from the worn-out chairs, from the ugliness of the curtains. All those things, of which another woman of her rank would never even have been conscious, tortured her and made her angry. The sight of the little Breton peasant, who did her humble housework aroused in her regrets which were despairing, and distracted dreams. She thought of the silent antechambers hung with Oriental tapestry, lit by tall bronze candelabra, and of the two great footmen in knee breeches who sleep in the big armchairs, made drowsy by the heavy warmth of the hot-air stove. She thought of the long *salons* fitted up with ancient silk, of the delicate furniture carrying priceless curiosities, and of the coquettish perfumed boudoirs made for talks at five o'clock with intimate friends, with men famous and sought after, whom all women envy and whose attention they all desire.

When she sat down to dinner, before the round table covered with a tablecloth three days old, opposite her husband, who uncovered the soup tureen and declared with an enchanted air, "Ah, the good *pot-au-feu*! I don't know anything better than that," she thought of dainty dinners, of shining silverware, of tapestry which peopled the walls with ancient personages and with strange birds flying in the midst of a fairy forest; and she thought of delicious dishes served on marvelous plates, and of the whispered gallantries which you listen to with a sphinx-like smile, while you are eating the pink flesh of a trout or the wings of a quail.

She had no dresses, no jewels, nothing. And she loved nothing but that; she felt made for that. She would so have liked to please, to be envied, to be charming, to be sought after.

_____

Translated by Marjorie Laurie, 1934.

She had a friend, a former schoolmate at the convent, who was rich, and whom she did not like to go and see any more, because she suffered so much when she came back.

But one evening, her husband returned home with a triumphant air, and holding a large envelope in his hand.

"There," said he. "Here is something for you."

She tore the paper sharply, and drew out a printed card which bore these words:

"The Minister of Public Instruction and Mme. Georges Ramponneau request the honor of M. and Mme. Loisel's company at the palace of the Ministry on Monday evening, January eighteenth."

Instead of being delighted, as her husband hoped, she threw the invitation on the table with disdain, murmuring:

"What do you want me to do with that?"

"But, my dear, I thought you would be glad. You never go out, and this is such a fine opportunity. I had awful trouble to get it. Everyone wants to go; it is very select, and they are not giving many invitations to clerks. The whole official world will be there."

She looked at him with an irritated glance, and said, impatiently:

"And what do you want me to put on my back?"

He had not thought of that; he stammered:

"Why, the dress you go to the theater in. It looks very well, to me."

He stopped, distracted, seeing his wife was crying. Two great tears descended slowly from the corners of her eyes toward the corners of her mouth. He stuttered:

"What's the matter? What's the matter?"

But, by violent effort, she had conquered her grief, and she replied, with a calm voice, while she wiped her wet cheeks:

"Nothing. Only I have no dress and therefore I can't go to this ball. Give your card to some colleague whose wife is better equipped than I."

He was in despair. He resumed:

"Come, let us see, Mathilde. How much would it cost, a suitable dress, which you could use on other occasions. Something very simple?"

She reflected several seconds, making her calculations and wondering also what sum she could ask without drawing on herself an immediate refusal and a frightened exclamation from the economical clerk.

Finally, she replied, hesitatingly:

"I don't know exactly, but I think I could manage it with four hundred francs."

He had grown a little pale, because he was laying aside just that amount to buy a gun and treat himself to a little shooting next summer on the plain of Nanterre, with several friends who went to shoot larks down there, of a Sunday.

But he said:

"All right. I will give you four hundred francs. And try to have a pretty dress."

The day of the ball drew near, and Mme. Loisel seemed sad, uneasy, anxious. Her dress was ready, however. Her husband said to her one evening:

"What is the matter? Come, you've been so queer these last three days."

And she answered:

"It annoys me not to have a single jewel, not a single stone, nothing to put on. I shall look like distress. I should almost rather not go at all."

He resumed:

"You might wear natural flowers. It's very stylish at this time of the year. For ten francs you can get two or three magnificent roses."

She was not convinced.

"No; there's nothing more humiliating than to look poor among other women who are rich."

But her husband cried:

"How stupid you are! Go look up your friend Mme. Forestier, and ask her to lend you some jewels. You're quite thick enough with her to do that."

She uttered a cry of joy:

"It's true. I never thought of it."

The next day she went to her friend and told of her distress.

Mme. Forestier went to a wardrobe with a glass door, took out a large jewelbox, brought it back, opened it, and said to Mme. Loisel:

"Choose, choose, my dear."

She saw first of all some bracelets, then a pearl necklace, then a Venetian cross, gold and precious stones of admirable workmanship. She tried on the ornaments before the glass, hesitated, could not make up her mind to part with them, to give them back. She kept asking:

"Haven't you any more?"

"Why, yes. Look. I don't know what you like."

All of a sudden she discovered, in a black satin box, a superb necklace of diamonds, and her heart began to beat with an immoderate desire. Her hands trembled as she took it. She fastened it around her throat, outside her high necked dress, and remained lost in ecstasy at the sight of herself.

Then she asked, hesitating, filled with anguish:

"Can you lend me that, only that?"

"Why, yes, certainly."

She sprang upon the neck of her friend, kissed her passionately, then fled with her treasure.

The day of the ball arrived. Mme. Loisel made a great success. She was prettier than them all, elegant, gracious, smiling, and crazy with joy. All the men looked at her, asked her name, endeavored to be introduced. All the attachés of the Cabinet wanted to waltz with her. She was remarked by the minister himself.

She danced with intoxication, with passion, made drunk by pleasure, forgetting all, in the triumph of her beauty, in the glory of her success, in a sort of cloud of happiness composed of all this homage, of all this admiration, of all these awakened desires, and of that sense of complete victory which is so sweet to a woman's heart.

She went away about four o'clock in the morning. Her husband had been sleeping since midnight, in a little deserted anteroom, with three other gentlemen whose wives were having a good time. He threw over her shoulders the wraps which he had brought, modest wraps of common life, whose poverty contrasted with the elegance of the ball dress. She felt this, and wanted to escape so as not to be remarked by the other women, who were enveloping themselves in costly furs.

Loisel held her back.

"Wait a bit. You will catch cold outside. I will go and call a cab."

But she did not listen to him, and rapidly descended the stairs. When they were in the street they did not find a carriage; and they began to look for one, shouting after the cabmen whom they saw passing by at a distance.

They went down toward the Seine, in despair, shivering with cold. At last they found on the quay one of those ancient noctambulant coupés° which, exactly as if they were ashamed to show their misery during the day, are never seen round Paris until after nightfall.

It took them to their door in the Rue des Martyrs, and once more, sadly, they climbed up homeward. All was ended, for her. And as to him, he reflected that he must be at the Ministry at ten o'clock.

She removed the wraps which covered her shoulders before the glass, so as once more to see herself in all her glory. But suddenly she uttered a cry. She no longer had the necklace around her neck!

Her husband, already half undressed, demanded:

"What is the matter with you?"

She turned madly toward him:

"I have—I have—I've lost Mme. Forestier's necklace."

He stood up, distracted.

"What!—how?—impossible!"

And they looked in the folds of her dress, in the folds of her cloak, in her pockets, everywhere. They did not find it.

He asked:

"You're sure you had it on when you left the ball?"

"Yes, I felt it in the vestibule of the palace."

"But if you had lost it in the street we should have heard it fall. It must be in the cab."

"Yes. Probably. Did you take his number?"

"No. And you, didn't you notice it?"

---

coupé: An enclosed carriage.

"No."

They looked, thunderstruck, at one another. At last Loisel put on his clothes.

"I shall go back on foot," said he, "over the whole route which we have taken to see if I can find it."

And he went out. She sat waiting on a chair in her ball dress, without strength to go to bed, overwhelmed, without fire, without a thought.

Her husband came back about seven o'clock. He had found nothing.

He went to Police Headquarters, to the newspaper offices, to offer a reward; he went to the cab companies—everywhere, in fact, whither he was urged by the least suspicion of hope.

She waited all day, in the same condition of mad fear before this terrible calamity.

Loisel returned at night with a hollow, pale face; he had discovered nothing.

"You must write to your friend," said he, "that you have broken the clasp of her necklace and that you are having it mended. That will give us time to turn round."

She wrote at his dictation.

At the end of a week they had lost all hope.

And Loisel, who had aged five years, declared:

"We must consider how to replace that ornament."

The next day they took the box which had contained it, and they went to the jeweler whose name was found within. He consulted his books.

"It was not I, madame, who sold that necklace; I must simply have furnished the case."

Then they went from jeweler to jeweler, searching for a necklace like the other, consulting their memories, sick both of them with chagrin and anguish.

They found, in a shop at the Palais Royal, a string of diamonds which seemed to them exactly like the one they looked for. It was worth forty thousand francs. They could have it for thirty-six.

So they begged the jeweler not to sell it for three days yet. And they made a bargain that he should buy it back for thirty-four thousand francs, in case they found the other one before the end of February.

Loisel possessed eighteen thousand francs which his father had left him. He would borrow the rest.

He did borrow, asking a thousand francs of one, five hundred of another, five louis here, three louis there. He gave notes, took up ruinous obligations, dealt with usurers and all the race of lenders. He compromised all the rest of his life, risked his signature without even knowing if he could meet it; and, frightened by the pains yet to come, by the black misery which was about to fall upon him, by the prospect of all the physical privation and of all the moral tortures which he was to suffer, he went to get the new necklace, putting down upon the merchant's counter thirty-six thousand francs.

When Mme. Loisel took back the necklace, Mme. Forestier said to her, with a chilly manner:

"You should have returned it sooner; I might have needed it."

She did not open the case, as her friend had so much feared. If she had detected the substitution, what would she have thought, what would she have said? Would she not have taken Mme. Loisel for a thief?

Mme. Loisel now knew the horrible existence of the needy. She took her part, moreover, all of a sudden, with heroism. That dreadful debt must be paid. She would pay it. They dismissed their servant; they changed their lodgings; they rented a garret under the roof.

She came to know what heavy housework meant and the odious cares of the kitchen. She washed the dishes, using her rosy nails on the greasy pots and pans. She washed the dirty linen, the shirts, and the dishcloths, which she dried upon a line; she carried the slops down to the street every morning, and carried up the water, stopping for breath at every landing. And, dressed like a woman of the people, she went to the fruiterer, the grocer, the butcher, her basket on her arm, bargaining, insulted, defending her miserable money sou by sou.

Each month they had to meet some notes, renew others, obtain more time.

Her husband worked in the evening making a fair copy of some tradesman's accounts, and late at night he often copied manuscript for five sous a page.

And this life lasted for ten years.

At the end of ten years, they had paid everything, everything, with the rates of usury, and the accumulations of the compound interest.

Mme. Loisel looked old now. She had become the woman of impoverished households—strong and hard and rough. With frowsy hair, skirts askew, and red hands, she talked loud while washing the floor with great swishes of water. But sometimes, when her husband was at the office, she sat down near the window, and she thought of that gay evening of long ago, of that ball where she had been so beautiful and so fêted.

What would have happened if she had not lost that necklace? Who knows? Who knows? How life is strange and changeful! How little a thing is needed for us to be lost or to be saved!

But, one Sunday, having gone to take a walk in the Champs Elysées to refresh herself from the labor of the week, she suddenly perceived a woman who was leading a child. It was Mme. Forestier, still young, still beautiful, still charming.

Mme. Loisel felt moved. Was she going to speak to her? Yes, certainly. And now that she had paid, she was going to tell her all about it. Why not?

She went up.

"Good-day, Jeanne."

The other, astonished to be familiarly addressed by this plain goodwife, did not recognize her at all, and stammered.

"But—madam!—I do not know—you must be mistaken."

"No. I am Mathilde Loisel."

Her friend uttered a cry.

"Oh, my poor Mathilde! How you are changed!"

"Yes, I have had days hard enough, since I have seen you, days wretched enough—and that because of you!"

"Of me! How so?"

"Do you remember that diamond necklace which you lent me to wear at the ministerial ball?"

"Yes. Well?"

"Well, I lost it."

"What do you mean? You brought it back."

"I brought you back another just like it. And for this we have been ten years paying. You can understand that it was not easy for us, who had nothing. At last it is ended, and I am very glad."

Mme. Forestier had stopped.

"You say that you bought a necklace of diamonds to replace mine?"

"Yes. You never noticed it, then! They were very like."

And she smiled with a joy which was proud and naïve at once.

Mme. Forestier, strongly moved, took her two hands.

"Oh, my poor Mathilde! Why, my necklace was paste. It was worth at most five hundred francs!"

[1884]

SHIRLEY JACKSON
The Lottery

The morning of June 27th was clear and sunny, with the fresh warmth of a full-summer day; the flowers were blossoming profusely and the grass was richly green. The people of the village began to gather in the square, between the post office and the bank, around ten o'clock; in some towns there were so many people that the lottery took two days and had to be started on June 26th, but in this village, where there were only about three hundred people, the whole lottery took less than two hours, so it could begin at ten o'clock in the morning and still be through in time to allow the villagers to get home for noon dinner.

The children assembled first, of course. School was recently over for the summer, and the feeling of liberty sat uneasily on most of them; they tended to gather together quietly for a while before they broke into boisterous play, and their talk was still of the classroom and teacher, of books and reprimands. Bobby Martin had already stuffed his pockets full of stones, and the other boys soon followed his example, selecting the smoothest and roundest stones; Bobby and Harry Jones and Dickie Delacroix — the villagers pronounced this name "Dellacroy" — eventually made a great pile of stones in one corner of the square and guarded it against the raids of the other boys. The girls stood aside, talking among themselves, looking over their shoulders at the boys, and the very small children rolled in the dust or clung to the hands of their older brothers or sisters.

Soon the men began to gather, surveying their own children, speaking of planting and rain, tractors and taxes. They stood together, away from the pile of stones in the corner, and their jokes were quiet and they smiled rather than laughed. The women, wearing faded house dresses and sweaters, came shortly after their menfolk. They greeted one another and exchanged bits of gossip as they went to join their husbands. Soon the women, standing by their husbands, began to call to their children, and the children came reluctantly, having to be called four or five times. Bobby Martin ducked under his mother's grasping hand and ran, laughing, back to the pile of stones. His father spoke up sharply, and Bobby came quickly and took his place between his father and his oldest brother.

The lottery was conducted — as were the square dances, the teen-age club, the Halloween program — by Mr. Summers, who had time and energy to devote to civic activities. He was a round-faced, jovial man and he ran the coal business, and people were sorry for him, because he had no children and his wife was a scold. When he arrived in the square, carrying the black wooden

245

box, there was a murmur of conversation among the villagers, and he waved and called, "Little late today, folks." The postmaster, Mr. Graves, followed him, carrying a three-legged stool, and the stool was put in the center of the square and Mr. Summers set the black box down on it. The villagers kept their distance, leaving a space between themselves and the stool, and when Mr. Summers said, "Some of you fellows want to give me a hand?" there was a hesitation before two men, Mr. Martin and his oldest son, Baxter, came forward to hold the box steady on the stool while Mr. Summers stirred up the papers inside it.

The original paraphernalia for the lottery had been lost long ago, and the black box now resting on the stool had been put into use even before Old Man Warner, the oldest man in town, was born. Mr. Summers spoke frequently to the villagers about making a new box, but no one liked to upset even as much tradition as was represented by the black box. There was a story that the present box had been made with some pieces of the box that had preceded it, the one that had been constructed when the first people settled down to make a village here. Every year, after the lottery, Mr. Summers began talking again about a new box, but every year the subject was allowed to fade off without anything's being done. The black box grew shabbier each year; by now it was no longer completely black but splintered badly along one side to show the original wood color, and in some places faded or stained.

Mr. Martin and his oldest son, Baxter, held the black box securely on the stool until Mr. Summers had stirred the papers thoroughly with his hand. Because so much of the ritual had been forgotten or discarded, Mr. Summers had been successful in having slips of paper substituted for the chips of wood that had been used for generations. Chips of wood, Mr. Summers had argued, had been all very well when the village was tiny, but now that the population was more than three hundred and likely to keep on growing, it was necessary to use something that would fit more easily into the black box. The night before the lottery, Mr. Summers and Mr. Graves made up the slips of paper and put them in the box, and it was then taken to the safe of Mr. Summers's coal company and locked up until Mr. Summers was ready to take it to the square next morning. The rest of the year, the box was put away, sometimes one place, sometimes another; it had spent one year in Mr. Graves's barn and another year underfoot in the post office, and sometimes it was set on a shelf in the Martin grocery and left there.

There was a great deal of fussing to be done before Mr. Summers declared the lottery open. There were the lists to make up — of heads of families, heads of households in each family, members of each household in each family. There was the proper swearing-in of Mr. Summers by the postmaster, as the official of the lottery; at one time, some people remembered, there had been a recital of some sort, performed by the official of the lottery, a perfunctory, tuneless chant that had been rattled off duly each year; some people believed that the official of the lottery used to stand just so when he said or sang it, others believed that he was supposed to walk among the people, but years and years ago this part of the ritual had been allowed to lapse. There had been, also, a ritual salute, which the official of the lottery had had to use in addressing each person who came up to draw from the box, but this also had changed with time, until now it was felt necessary only for the official to speak to each person approaching. Mr. Summers was very good at all this; in his clean white shirt and blue jeans, with one hand resting carelessly on the black box, he seemed very proper and important as he talked interminably to Mr. Graves and the Martins.

Just as Mr. Summers finally left off talking and turned to the assembled villagers, Mrs. Hutchinson came hurriedly along the path to the square, her sweater thrown over her shoulders, and slid into place in the back of the crowd. "Clean forgot what day it was," she said to Mrs. Delacroix, who stood next to her, and they both laughed softly. "Thought my old man was out back stacking wood," Mrs. Hutchinson went on, "and then I looked out the window and the kids was gone, and then I remembered it was the twenty-seventh and came a-running." She dried her hands on her apron, and Mrs. Delacroix said, "You're in time, though. They're still talking away up there."

Mrs. Hutchinson craned her neck to see through the crowd and found her husband and children standing near the front. She tapped Mrs. Delacroix on the arm as a farewell and began to make her way through the crowd. The people separated good-humoredly to let her through; two or three people said, in voices just loud enough to be heard across the crowd, "Here comes your Missus, Hutchinson," and "Bill, she made it after all." Mrs. Hutchinson reached her husband, and Mr. Summers, who had been waiting, said cheerfully, "Thought we were going to have to get on without you, Tessie." Mrs. Hutchinson said, grinning, "Wouldn't have me leave m'dishes in the sink, now, would you, Joe?" and soft laughter ran through the crowd as the people stirred back into position after Mrs. Hutchinson's arrival.

"Well, now," Mr. Summers said soberly, "guess we better get started, get this over with, so's we can go back to work. Anybody ain't here?"

"Dunbar," several people said. "Dunbar, Dunbar."

Mr. Summers consulted his list. "Clyde Dunbar," he said. "That's right. He's broke his leg, hasn't he? Who's drawing for him?"

"Me, I guess," a woman said, and Mr. Summers turned to look at her. "Wife draws for her husband," Mr. Summers said. "Don't you have a grown boy to do it for you, Janey?" Although Mr. Summers and everyone else in the village knew the answer perfectly well, it was the business of the official of the lottery to ask such questions formally. Mr. Summers waited with an expression of polite interest while Mrs. Dunbar answered.

"Horace's not but sixteen yet," Mrs. Dunbar said regretfully. "Guess I gotta fill in for the old man this year."

"Right," Mr. Summers said. He made a note on the list he was holding. Then he asked, "Watson boy drawing this year?"

A tall boy in the crowd raised his hand. "Here," he said. "I'm drawing for m'mother and me." He blinked his eyes nervously and ducked his head as several voices in the crowd said things like "Good fellow, Jack," and "Glad to see your mother's got a man to do it."

"Well," Mr. Summers said, "guess that's everyone. Old Man Warner make it?"

"Here," a voice said, and Mr. Summers nodded.

A sudden hush fell on the crowd as Mr. Summers cleared his throat and looked at the list. "All ready?" he called. "Now, I'll read the names—heads of families first—and the men come up and take a paper out of the box. Keep the paper folded in your hand without looking at it until everyone has had a turn. Everything clear?"

The people had done it so many times that they only half listened to the directions; most of them were quiet, wetting their lips, not looking around. Then Mr. Summers raised one hand high and said, "Adams." A man disengaged himself from the crowd and came forward. "Hi, Steve," Mr. Summers said, and Mr. Adams said, "Hi, Joe." They grinned at one another humorlessly and nervously. Then Mr. Adams reached into the black box and took out a folded paper. He held it firmly by one corner as he turned and went hastily back to his place in the crowd, where he stood a little apart from his family, not looking down at his hand.

"Allen," Mr. Summers said, "Anderson. . . . Bentham."

"Seems like there's no time at all between lotteries any more," Mrs. Delacroix said to Mrs. Graves in the back row. "Seems like we got through with the last one only last week."

"Time sure goes fast," Mrs. Graves said.

"Clark. . . . Delacroix."

"There goes my old man," Mrs. Delacroix said. She held her breath while her husband went forward.

"Dunbar," Mr. Summers said, and Mrs. Dunbar went steadily to the box while one of the women said, "Go on, Janey," and another said, "There she goes."

"We're next," Mrs. Graves said. She watched while Mr. Graves came around from the side of the box, greeted Mr. Summers gravely, and selected a slip of paper from the box. By now, all through the crowd there were men holding the small folded papers in their large hands, turning them over and over nervously. Mrs. Dunbar and her two sons stood together, Mrs. Dunbar holding the slip of paper.

"Harburt. . . . Hutchinson."

"Get up there, Bill," Mrs. Hutchinson said, and the people near her laughed.

"Jones."

"They do say," Mr. Adams said to Old Man Warner, who stood next to him, "that over in the north village they're talking of giving up the lottery."

Old Man Warner snorted. "Pack of crazy fools," he said. "Listening to the young folks, nothing's good enough for *them*. Next thing you know, they'll be wanting to go back to living in caves, nobody work any more, live *that* way for a while. Used to be a saying about 'Lottery in June, corn be heavy soon.' First thing you know, we'd all be eating stewed chickweed and acorns. There's *always* been a lottery," he added petulantly. "Bad enough to see young Joe Summers up there joking with everybody."

"Some places have already quit lotteries," Mrs. Adams said.

"Nothing but trouble in *that*," Old Man Warner said stoutly. "Pack of young fools."

"Martin." And Bobby Martin watched his father go forward. "Overdyke. . . . Percy."

"I wish they'd hurry," Mrs. Dunbar said to her older son. "I wish they'd hurry."

"They're almost through," her son said.

"You get ready to run tell Dad," Mrs. Dunbar said.

Mr. Summers called his own name and then stepped forward precisely and selected a slip from the box. Then he called, "Warner."

"Seventy-seventh year I been in the lottery," Old Man Warner said as he went through the crowd. "Seventy-seventh time."

"Watson." The tall boy came awkwardly through the crowd. Someone said, "Don't be nervous, Jack," and Mr. Summers said, "Take your time, son."

"Zanini."

After that, there was a long pause, a breathless pause, until Mr. Summers, holding his slip of paper in the air, said, "All right, fellows." For a minute, no one moved, and then all the slips of paper were opened. Suddenly, all the women began to speak at once, saying, "Who is it?" "Who's got it?" "Is it the Dunbars?" "Is it the Watsons?" Then the voices began to say, "It's Hutchinson. It's Bill," "Bill Hutchinson's got it."

"Go tell your father," Mrs. Dunbar said to her older son.

People began to look around to see the Hutchinsons. Bill Hutchinson was standing quiet, staring down at the paper in his hand. Suddenly, Tessie Hutchinson shouted to Mr. Summers, "You didn't give him time enough to take any paper he wanted. I saw you. It wasn't fair!"

"Be a good sport, Tessie," Mrs. Delacroix called, and Mrs. Graves said, "All of us took the same chance."

"Shut up, Tessie," Bill Hutchinson said.

"Well, everyone," Mr. Summers said, "that was done pretty fast, and now we've got to be hurrying a little more to get done in time." He consulted his next list. "Bill," he said, "you draw for the Hutchinson family. You got any other households in the Hutchinsons?"

"There's Don and Eva," Mrs. Hutchinson yelled. "Make *them* take their chance!"

"Daughters drew with their husbands' families, Tessie," Mr. Summers said gently. "You know that as well as anyone else."

"It wasn't *fair,*" Tessie said.

"I guess not, Joe," Bill Hutchinson said regretfully. "My daughter draws with her husband's family, that's only fair. And I've got no other family except the kids."

"Then, as far as drawing for families is concerned, it's you," Mr. Summers said in explanation, "and as far as drawing for households is concerned, that's you, too. Right?"

"Right," Bill Hutchinson said.

"How many kids, Bill?" Mr. Summers asked formally.

"Three," Bill Hutchinson said. "There's Bill, Jr., and Nancy, and little Dave. And Tessie and me."

"All right, then," Mr. Summers said. "Harry, you got their tickets back?"

Mr. Graves nodded and held up the slips of paper. "Put them in the box, then," Mr. Summers directed. "Take Bill's and put it in."

"I think we ought to start over," Mrs. Hutchinson said, as quietly as she could. "I tell you it wasn't *fair.* You didn't give him time enough to choose. *Every*body saw that."

Mr. Graves had selected the five slips and put them in the box, and he dropped all the papers but those onto the ground, where the breeze caught them and lifted them off.

"Listen, everybody," Mrs. Hutchinson was saying to the people around her.

"Ready, Bill?" Mr. Summers asked, and Bill Hutchinson, with one quick glance around at his wife and children, nodded.

"Remember," Mr. Summers said, "take the slips and keep them folded until each person has taken one. Harry, you help little Dave." Mr. Graves took the hand of the little boy, who came willingly with him up to the box. "Take a paper out of the box, Davy," Mr. Summers said. Davy put his hand into the box and laughed. "Take just *one* paper," Mr. Summers said. "Harry, you hold it for him." Mr. Graves took the child's hand and removed the folded paper from the tight fist and held it while little Dave stood next to him and looked up at him wonderingly.

"Nancy next," Mr. Summers said. Nancy was twelve, and her school friends breathed heavily as she went forward, switching her skirt, and took a slip daintily from the box. "Bill, Jr.," Mr. Summers said, and Billy, his face red and his feet overlarge, nearly knocked the box over as he got a paper out. "Tessie," Mr. Summers said. She hesitated for a minute, looking around defiantly, and then set her lips and went up to the box. She snatched a paper out and held it behind her.

"Bill," Mr. Summers said, and Bill Hutchinson reached into the box and felt around, bringing his hand out at last with the slip of paper in it.

The crowd was quiet. A girl whispered, "I hope it's not Nancy," and the sound of the whisper reached the edges of the crowd.

"It's not the way it used to be," Old Man Warner said clearly. "People ain't the way they used to be."

"All right," Mr. Summers said. "Open the papers. Harry, you open little Dave's."

Mr. Graves opened the slip of paper and there was a general sigh through the crowd as he held it up and everyone could see that it was blank. Nancy and Bill, Jr., opened theirs at the same time, and both beamed and laughed, turning around to the crowd and holding their slips of paper above their heads.

"Tessie," Mr. Summers said. There was a pause, and then Mr. Summers looked at Bill Hutchinson, and Bill unfolded his paper and showed it. It was blank.

"It's Tessie," Mr. Summers said, and his voice was hushed. "Show us her paper, Bill."

Bill Hutchinson went over to his wife and forced the slip of paper out of her hand. It had a black spot on it, the black spot Mr. Summers had made the night before with the heavy pencil in the coal-company office. Bill Hutchinson held it up and there was a stir in the crowd.

"All right, folks," Mr. Summers said. "Let's finish quickly."

Although the villagers had forgotten the ritual and lost the original black box, they still remembered to use stones. The pile of stones the boys had made earlier was ready; there were stones on the ground with the blowing scraps of paper that had come out of the box. Mrs. Delacroix selected a stone so large she had to pick it up with both hands and turned to Mrs. Dunbar. "Come on," she said. "Hurry up."

Mrs. Dunbar had small stones in both hands, and she said, gasping for breath, "I can't run at all. You'll have to go ahead and I'll catch up with you."

The children had stones already, and someone gave little Davy Hutchinson a few pebbles.

Tessie Hutchinson was in the center of a cleared space by now, and she held her hands out desperately as the villagers moved in on her. "It isn't fair," she said. A stone hit her on the side of the head.

Old Man Warner was saying, "Come on, come on, everyone." Steve Adams was in the front of the crowd of villagers, with Mrs. Graves beside him.

"It isn't fair, it isn't right," Mrs. Hutchinson screamed and then they were upon her.

[1948]

JAMAICA KINCAID
Girl

Wash the white clothes on Monday and put them on the stone heap; wash the color clothes on Tuesday and put them on the clothesline to dry; don't walk barehead in the hot sun; cook pumpkin fritters in very hot sweet oil; soak your little cloths right after you take them off; when buying cotton to make yourself a nice blouse, be sure that it doesn't have gum on it, because that way it won't hold up well after a wash; soak salt fish overnight before you cook it; is it true that you sing benna° in Sunday school?; always eat your food in such a way that it won't turn someone else's stomach; on Sundays try to walk like a lady and not like the slut you are so bent on becoming; don't sing benna in Sunday school; you mustn't speak to wharf-rat boys, not even to give directions; don't eat fruits on the street—flies will follow you; *but I don't sing benna on Sundays at all and never in Sunday school;* this is how to sew on a button; this is how to make a button-hole for the button you have just sewed on; this is how to hem a dress when you see the hem coming down and so to prevent yourself from looking like the slut I know you are so bent on becoming; this is how you iron your father's khaki shirt so that it doesn't have a crease; this is how you iron your father's khaki pants so that they don't have a crease; this is how you grow okra—far from the house, because okra tree harbors red ants; when you are growing dasheen, make sure it gets plenty of water or else it makes your throat itch when you are eating it; this is how you sweep a corner; this is how you sweep a whole house; this is how you sweep a yard; this is how you smile to someone you don't like too much; this is how you smile to someone you don't like at all; this is how you smile to someone you like completely; this is how you set a table for tea; this is how you set a table for dinner; this is how you set a table for dinner with an important guest; this is how you set a table for lunch; this is how you set a table for breakfast; this is how to behave in the presence of men who don't know you very well, and this way they won't recognize immediately the slut I have warned you against becoming; be sure to wash every day, even if it is with your own spit; don't squat down to play marbles—you are not a boy, you know; don't pick people's flowers—you might catch something; don't throw stones at blackbirds, because it might not be a blackbird at all; this is how to make a bread pudding; this is how to make doukona;° this is how to make pepper pot; this is how to make a good medicine for a cold; this is how to make a good medicine to throw away a child before it even becomes a child;

---

benna: Calypso music.
doukona: A spicy plantain pudding.

this is how to catch a fish; this is how to throw back a fish you don't like, and that way something bad won't fall on you; this is how to bully a man; this is how a man bullies you; this is how to love a man, and if this doesn't work there are other ways, and if they don't work don't feel too bad about giving up; this is how to spit up in the air if you feel like it, and this is how to move quick so that it doesn't fall on you; this is how to make ends meet; always squeeze bread to make sure it's fresh; *but what if the baker won't let me feel the bread?;* you mean to say that after all you are really going to be the kind of woman who the baker won't let near the bread?

[1978]

Poetry

●

○

AUDRE LORDE
Hanging Fire

I am fourteen
and my skin has betrayed me
the boy I cannot live without
still sucks his thumb
in secret
how come my knees are
always so ashy
what if I die
before morning
and momma's in the bedroom
with the door closed.

I have to learn how to dance
in time for the next party
my room is too small for me
suppose I die before graduation
they will sing sad melodies
but finally
tell the truth about me
There is nothing I want to do
and too much
that has to be done
and momma's in the bedroom
with the door closed.

★   ★   ★

Nobody even stops to think
about my side of it
I should have been on Math Team
my marks were better than his
why do I have to be
the one
wearing braces
I have nothing to wear tomorrow
will I live long enough
to grow up
and momma's in the bedroom
with the door closed.

A. K. RAMANUJAN
Self-Portrait

I resemble everyone
but myself, and sometimes see
in shop-windows,
    despite the well-known laws
    of optics,
the portrait of a stranger,
date unknown,
often signed in a corner
by my father.

ROBERT FROST
The Road Not Taken

Two roads diverged in a yellow wood,
And sorry I could not travel both
And be one traveler, long I stood
And looked down one as far as I could
To where it bent in the undergrowth;

Then took the other, as just as fair,
And having perhaps the better claim,
Because it was grassy and wanted wear;
Though as for that, the passing there
Had worn them really about the same,

★   ★   ★

And both that morning equally lay
In leaves no step had trodden black.
Oh, I kept the first for another day!
Yet knowing how way leads on to way,
I doubted if I should ever come back.

I shall be telling this with a sigh
Somewhere ages and ages hence:
Two roads diverged in a wood, and I—
I took the one less traveled by,
And that has made all the difference.

ROSARIO MORALES
AND AURORA LEVINS MORALES
Ending Poem

I am what I am.
A child of the Americas.
A light-skinned mestiza of the Caribbean.
A child of many diaspora, born into this continent at a crossroads.
I am Puerto Rican. I am U.S. American.

I am New York Manhattan and the Bronx
A mountain-born, country-bred, homegrown jibara child,
up from the shtetl, a California Puerto Rican Jew
A product of the New York ghettos I have never known.
I am an immigrant
And the daughter and granddaughter of immigrants.
We didn't know our forbears' names with a certainty.
They aren't written anywhere.
First names only or mija, negra, ne, honey, sugar, dear

I come from the dirt where the cane was grown.
My people didn't go to dinner parties. They weren't invited.
I am caribeña, island grown.
Spanish is my flesh, ripples from my tongue, lodges in my hips,
the language of garlic and mangoes.
Boricua. As Boricuas come from the isle of Manhattan.
I am of latinoamerica, rooted in the history of my continent.
I speak from that body. Just brown and pink and full of drums inside.

I am not African.
Africa waters the roots of my tree, but I cannot return.

I am not Taína.
I am a late leaf of that ancient tree,
and my roots reach into the soil of two Americas.
Taíno is in me, but there is no way back.

I am not European, though I have dreamt of those cities.
Each plate is different.
wood, clay, papier maché, metals, basketry, a leaf, a coconut shell.
Europe lives in me but I have no home there.

The table has a cloth woven by one, dyed by another,
embroidered by another still.
I am a child of many mothers.
They have kept it all going
All the civilizations erected on their backs.
All the dinner parties given with their labor.

We are new.
They gave us life, kept us going,
brought us to where we are.
Born at a crossroads.
Come, lay that dishcloth down. Eat, dear, eat.

History made us.
We will not eat ourselves up inside anymore.

And we are whole.

ALLISON JOSEPH

On Being Told I Don't Speak
Like a Black Person

Emphasize the "h," you hignorant ass,
was what my mother was told
when colonial-minded teachers
slapped her open palm with a ruler
in that Jamaican schoolroom.
Trained in England, they tried
to force their pupils to speak
like Eliza Doolittle° after
her transformation, fancying themselves
British as Henry Higgins,°
despite dark, sun-ripened skin.
Mother never lost her accent,
though, the music of her voice
charming everyone, an infectious lilt
I can imitate, not duplicate.
No one in the States told her
to eliminate the accent,
my high school friends adoring
the way her voice would lift
when she called me to the phone —
A-ll-i-son, it's friend Cathy.
Why don't you sound like her,
they'd ask. I didn't sound
like anyone or anything,
no grating New Yorker nasality,
no fastidious British mannerisms
like the ones my father affected
when he wanted to sell someone
something. And I didn't sound
like a Black American,
college acquaintances observed,

Eliza Doolittle . . . Henry Higgins: Flower-girl with a strong Cockney (working class)
accent in George Bernard Shaw's play *Pygmalion* and the musical based on it, *My Fair Lady.*
Henry Higgins, a linguistics professor, takes on the challenge of teaching her how to speak (and
act and dress) like a proper British lady.

261

sure they knew what a black person
was supposed to sound like.
Was I supposed to sound lazy,
dropping syllables here and there
not finishing words but
slurring their final letters
so each sentence joined
the next, sliding past the listener?
Were certain words off limits,
too erudite for someone whose skin
came with a natural tan?
I asked them what they meant
and they stuttered, blushed,
said *you know, Black English,*
applying a term from that
semester's text. *Does everyone
in your family speak alike,*
I'd ask, and they'd say *don't
take this the wrong way,
nothing personal.*

Now I realize there's nothing
more personal than speech,
that I don't have to defend
how I speak, how any person,
black, white, chooses to speak.
Let us speak. Let us talk
with the sounds of our mothers
and fathers still reverberating
in our minds, wherever our mothers
or fathers come from:
Arkansas, Belize, Alabama,
Brazil, Aruba, Arizona.
Let us simply speak
to one another,
listen and prize the inflections,
never assuming how any person will sound
until his mouth opens, until her
mouth opens, greetings welcome
in any language.

EDWIN ARLINGTON ROBINSON
Richard Cory

Whenever Richard Cory went down town,
We people on the pavement looked at him:
He was a gentleman from sole to crown,
Clean favored, and imperially slim.

And he was always quietly arrayed,
And he was always human when he talked;
But still he fluttered pulses when he said,
"Good-morning," and he glittered when he walked.

And he was rich—yes, richer than a king—
And admirably schooled in every grace:
In fine, we thought that he was everything
To make us wish that we were in his place.

So on we worked, and waited for the light,
And went without the meat, and cursed the bread;
And Richard Cory, one calm summer night,
Went home and put a bullet through his head.

EMILY DICKINSON
I'm Nobody! Who are you?

I'm Nobody! Who are you?
Are you - Nobody - Too?
Then there's a pair of us?
Don't tell! they'd advertise - you know!

How dreary - to be - Somebody!
How public - like a Frog -
To tell one's name - the livelong June -
To an admiring Bog!

MARGE PIERCY
Barbie Doll

This girlchild was born as usual
and presented dolls that did pee-pee
and miniature GE stoves and irons
and wee lipsticks the color of cherry candy.
Then in the magic of puberty, a classmate said:
You have a great big nose and fat legs.

She was healthy, tested intelligent,
possessed strong arms and back,
abundant sexual drive and manual dexterity.
She went to and fro apologizing.
Everyone saw a fat nose on thick legs.

She was advised to play coy,
exhorted to come on hearty,
exercise, diet, smile and wheedle.
Her good nature wore out
like a fan belt.
So she cut off her nose and her legs
and offered them up.

In the casket displayed on satin she lay
with the undertaker's cosmetics painted on,
a turned-up putty nose,
dressed in a pink and white nightie.
Doesn't she look pretty? everyone said.
Consummation at last.
To every woman a happy ending.

ROBERT HAYDEN

Those Winter Sundays

Sundays too my father got up early
and put his clothes on in the blueblack cold,
then with cracked hands that ached
from labor in the weekday weather made
banked fires blaze. No one ever thanked him.

I'd wake and hear the cold splintering, breaking.
When the rooms were warm, he'd call,
and slowly I would rise and dress,
fearing the chronic angers of that house,

Speaking indifferently to him,
who had driven out the cold
and polished my good shoes as well.
What did I know, what did I know
of love's austere and lonely offices?

NIKKI GIOVANNI

Nikka-Rosa

childhood rememberances are always a drag
if you're Black
you always remember things like living in Woodlawn°
with no inside toilet
and if you become famous or something
they never talk about how happy you were to have your mother
all to yourself and
how good the water felt when you got your bath from one of those
big tubs that folk in chicago barbecue in
and somehow when you talk about home
it never gets across how much you
understood their feelings
as the whole family attended meetings about Hollydale°
and even though you remember
your biographers never understand
your father's pain as he sells his stock
and another dream goes
and though you're poor it isn't poverty that
concerns you
and though they fought a lot
it isn't your father's drinking that makes any difference
but only that everybody is together and you
and your sister have happy birthdays and very good christmasses
and I really hope no white person ever has cause to write about me
because they never understand Black love is Black wealth and they'll
probably talk about my hard childhood and never understand that
all the while I was quite happy

Woodlawn: A suburb of Cincinnati.
Hollydale: An all-black housing development in which Giovanni's father invested money.

DENNIS BRUTUS
Nightsong: City

Sleep well, my love, sleep well:
the harbour lights glaze over restless docks,
police cars cockroach through the tunnel streets;

from the shanties creaking iron-sheets
violence like a bug-infested rag is tossed
and fear is immanent as sound in the wind-swung bell;

the long day's anger pants from sand and rocks;
but for this breathing night at least,
my land, my love, sleep well.

CORNELIUS EADY
My Mother, If She Had Won Free Dance Lessons

Would she have been a person
With a completely different outlook on life?
There are times when I visit
And find her settled on a chair
In our dilapidated house,
The neighborhood crazy lady
Doing what the neighborhood crazy lady is supposed to do,
Which is absolutely nothing

And I wonder as we talk our sympathetic talk,
Abandoned in easy dialogue,
I, the son of the crazy lady,
Who crosses easily into her point of view
As if yawning
Or taking off an overcoat.
Each time I visit
I walk back into our lives

And I wonder, like any child who wakes up one day to find themself
Abandoned in a world larger than their
      Bad dreams,
I wonder as I see my mother sitting there,
Landed to the right-hand window in the living room,
Pausing from time to time in the endless loop of our dialogue
To peek for rascals through the
Venetian blinds,

I wonder a small thought.
I walk back into our lives.
Given the opportunity,
How would she have danced?
Would it have been as easily

As we talk to each other now,
The crazy lady
And the crazy lady's son,
As if we were old friends from opposite coasts
Picking up the thread of a long conversation,

Or two ballroom dancers
Who only know
One step?

What would have changed
If the phone had rung like a suitor,
If the invitation had arrived in the mail
Like Jesus, extending a hand?

RAY GONZÁLEZ

Praise the Tortilla, Praise the Menudo, Praise the Chorizo

I praise the tortilla in honor of El Panzón,
who hit me in school every day and made me see
how the bruises on my arms looked like
the brown clouds on my mother's tortillas.
I praise the tortilla because I know
they can fly into our hands like
eager flesh of the one we love,
those soft yearnings we delight in biting
as we tear the tortilla and wipe the plate clean.

★ ★ ★

I praise the menudo° as visionary food that it is,
the tripas y posole° tight flashes of color
we see as the red caldo° smears across our notebooks
like a vision we have not had in years,
our lives going down like the empty bowl
of menudo exploding in our stomachs
with the chili piquin° of our poetic dreams.

I praise the chorizo° and smear it
across my face and hands,
the dayglow brown of it painting me
with the desire to find out
what happened to la familia,
why the chorizo sizzled in the pan
and covered the house with a smell
of childhood we will never have again,
the chorizo burrito hot in our hands,

---

menudo: Mexican soup made with hominy and tripe; said to have special powers.
tripas y posole: Tripe and hominy.
caldo: Soup.
chili piquin: Type of pepper, added to menudo or other soups.
chorizo: Mexican sausage.

as we ran out to play and show the vatos°
it's time to cut the chorizo,
tell it like it is before la manteca° runs down
our chins and drips away.

---

vatos: Guys.
la manteca: Lard or grease.

DWIGHT OKITA

In Response to Executive Order 9066:
All Americans of Japanese Descent
Must Report to Relocation Centers

Dear Sirs:
Of course I'll come. I've packed my galoshes
and three packets of tomato seeds. Denise calls them
love apples. My father says where we're going
they won't grow.

I am a fourteen-year-old girl with bad spelling
and a messy room. If it helps any, I will tell you
I have always felt funny using chopsticks
and my favorite food is hot dogs.
My best friend is a white girl named Denise—
we look at boys together. She sat in front of me
all through grade school because of our names:
O'Connor, Ozawa. I know the back of Denise's head very well.

I tell her she's going bald. She tells me I copy on tests.
We're best friends.

I saw Denise today in Geography class.
She was sitting on the other side of the room.
"You're trying to start a war," she said, "giving secrets
away to the Enemy, Why can't you keep your big
mouth shut?"

I didn't know what to say.
I gave her a packet of tomato seeds
and asked her to plant them for me, told her
when the first tomato ripened
she'd miss me.

WILLIAM SHAKESPEARE
Sonnets 18, 73, and 130

Sonnet 18

Shall I compare thee to a summer's day?
Thou art more lovely and more temperate:
Rough winds do shake the darling buds of May,
And summer's lease° hath all too short a date;°   *allotted time/duration*
Sometimes too hot the eye of heaven shines,
And often is his gold complexion dimmed;
And every fair° from fair° sometimes declines,   *beautiful thing/beauty*
By chance or nature's changing course untrimmed;°   *stripped of its beauty*
But thy eternal summer shall not fade,
Nor lose possession of that fair thou ow'st;°   *beauty you own*
Nor shall death brag thou wand'rest in his shade,
When in eternal lines° to time thou grow'st:°
    So long as men can breathe, or eyes can see,
    So long lives this,° and this gives life to thee.   *this sonnet*
                                      [1609]

---

lines: (Of poetry);
grow'st: You are grafted to time.

Sonnet 73

That time of year thou mayst in me behold
When yellow leaves, or none, or few, do hang
Upon those boughs which shake against the cold,
Bare ruined choirs,° where late° the sweet birds sang.   *choirstalls/lately*
In me thou seest the twilight of such day
As after sunset fadeth in the west,
Which by and by black night doth take away,
Death's second self, that seals up all in rest.
In me thou seest the glowing of such fire

That on the ashes of his youth doth lie,
As the deathbed whereon it must expire,
Consumed with that which it was nourished by.
    This thou perceiv'st, which makes thy love more strong,
    To love that well which thou must leave ere long.

[1609]

SONNET 130

My mistress' eyes are nothing like the sun;
Coral is far more red than her lips' red;
If snow be white, why then her breasts are dun;°   *dull grayish brown*
If hairs be wires, black wires grow on her head.
I have seen roses damasked,° red and white,   *variegated*
But no such roses see I in her cheeks;
And in some perfumes is there more delight
Than in the breath that from my mistress reeks.
I love to hear her speak, yet well I know
That music hath a far more pleasing sound.
I grant I never saw a goddess go;°   *walk*
My mistress, when she walks, treads on the ground.
    And yet, by heaven, I think my love as rare
    As any she° belied° with false compare.   *woman / misrepresented*

[1609]

COUNTEE CULLEN
Incident

for Eric Walrond

Once riding in old Baltimore,
    Heart-filled, head-filled with glee,
I saw a Baltimorean
    Keep looking straight at me.

Now I was eight and very small,
    And he was no whit bigger,
And so I smiled, but he poked out
    His tongue, and called me, "Nigger."

I saw the whole of Baltimore
    From May until December;
Of all the things that happened there
    That's all that I remember.

[1925]

GWENDOLYN BROOKS
We Real Cool

The Pool Players.
Seven at the Golden Shovel.

We real cool. We
Left school. We

Lurk late. We
Strike straight. We

Sing sin. We
Thin gin. We

Jazz June.° We   *sexual intercourse*
Die soon.

[1960]

ANITA ENDREZZE
The Girl Who Loved the Sky

Outside the second grade room,
the jacaranda tree blossomed
into purple lanterns, the papery petals
drifted, darkening the windows.
Inside, the room smelled like glue.
The desks were made of yellowed wood,
the tops littered with eraser rubbings,
rulers, and big fat pencils.
Colored chalk meant special days.
The walls were covered with precise
bright tulips and charts with shiny stars
by certain names. There, I learned
how to make butter by shaking a jar
until the pale cream clotted
into one sweet mass. There, I learned
that numbers were fractious beasts
with dens like dim zeros. And there,
I met a blind girl who thought the sky
tasted like cold metal when it rained
and whose eyes were always covered
with the bruised petals of her lids.

She loved the formless sky, defined
only by sounds, or the cool umbrellas
of clouds. On hot, still days
we listened to the sky falling
like chalk dust. We heard the noon
whistle of the pig-mash factory,
smelled the sourness of home-bound men.
I had no father; she had no eyes;
we were best friends. The other girls
drew shaky hop-scotch squares
on the dusty asphalt, talked about
pajama parties, weekend cook-outs,
and parents who bought sleek-finned cars.
Alone, we sat in the canvas swings,

our shoes digging into the sand, then pushing,
until we flew high over their heads,
our hands streaked with red rust
from the chains that kept us safe.

I was born blind, she said, an act of nature.
Sure, I thought, like birds born
without wings, trees without roots.
I didn't understand. The day she moved
I saw the world clearly; the sky
backed away from me like a departing father.
I sat under the jacaranda, catching
the petals in my palm, enclosing them
until my fist was another lantern
hiding a small and bitter flame.

[1988]

Andrew Nelson, "Wilma Mankiller." This article first appeared in *Salon.com*, www.salon.com, November 20, 2001. An online version remains in the Salon archives. Reprinted with permission of Salon.com.

Dwight Okita, "In Response to Executive Order 9066" from *Crossing with the Light* (Tia Chucha Press). Copyright by Dwight Okita. Reprinted by permission of the author.

Marge Piercy, "Barbie Doll" from *Circles on the Water.* Copyright © 1982 by Marge Piercy. Used by permission of Alfred A. Knopf, a division of Random House, Inc.

Jennifer L. Pozner, "Triumph of the Shill" from *Bitch* Magazine, Spring 2004, pp. 55–61, 93. Copyright 2004. Reprinted with the permission of the author, founder, and Executive Director of Women in Media & News (WIMN), a media analysis, training, and advocacy group. She can be reached via www.wimnonline.org

A. K. Ramanujan, "Self-Portrait" from *The Striders: Poems.* Reproduced by permission of Oxford University Press India, New Delhi.

Read Mercer Schuchardt, "Swoosh!" from *Re:Generation Quarterly,* Summer 1997. Copyright © 1997 by Read Mercer Schuchardt. Reprinted with permission of Read Mercer Schuchardt.

Adam Sternbergh, "Britney Spears: The Pop Tart in Winter." First published on *Slate.com,* October 28, 2004. Copyright © 2004 by Adam Sternbergh. Reprinted by permission of the author.

David Sterritt, "Face of an Angel." First published in the *Christian Science Monitor,* July 11, 2003 (www.csmonitor.com). Copyright © 2003 The Christian Science Monitor. Reproduced by permission of The Christian Science Monitor. All rights reserved.

Jon Stewart, "Commencement Address." Reprinted by permission of William and Mary College.

Virgil Suárez, "A Perfect Hotspot" has been reprinted with permission from the publisher of *Welcome to the Oasis and Other Stories* (Houston: Arte Publico Press, University of Houston, 1992).

Deborah Tannen. "There Is No Unmarked Woman." "Wears Jump Suit. Sensible Shoes. Uses Husband's Last Name." from the *New York Times Magazine,* June 20, 1993. Copyright © 1993 by Deborah Tannen, distributed by the New York Times Special Features. Reprinted by permission of the author. This article was originally titled "Marked Women, Unmarked Men" by the author.

Mim Udovitch, "A Secret Society of the Starving." Originally published in the *New York Times Magazine,* September 8, 2002. Copyright © 2002 by The New York Times Company. Reprinted by permission of the author.

Alice Walker, "Beauty: When the Other Dancer Is the Self" from *In Search of Our Mothers' Gardens: Womanist Prose.* Copyright © 1983 by Alice Walker. Reprinted by permission of Harcourt, Inc. "Everyday Use" from *In Love and Trouble: Stories of Black Women.* Copyright © 1973 by Alice Walker. Reprinted by permission of Harcourt, Inc.

Emily White, "High School's Secret Life" from *Fast Girls: Teenage Tribes and the Myth of the Slut.* Copyright © 2002 by Emily White. Reprinted with permission of Scribner, an imprint of Simon & Schuster Adult Publishing Group.

Kathy Wilson, "Dude Looks Like a Lady" from *Your Negro Tour Guide* by Kathy Wilson. Copyright © 2004 Kathy Y. Wilson. Reprinted by permission of Emmis Books.